The
New Feminism in
Twentieth-Century
America

PROBLEMS IN
AMERICAN CIVILIZATION

Under the editorial direction of
Edwin C. Rozwenc

The New Feminism in Twentieth-Century America

Edited and with an Introduction by

June Sochen
Northeastern Illinois State College

D. C. HEATH AND COMPANY
Lexington, Massachusetts   Toronto   London

Contents

INTRODUCTION   vii
CONFLICT OF OPINION   xiv

I THE SUFFRAGE MOVEMENT

Susan B. Anthony and Ida Husted Harper
THE STRUGGLE FOR WOMAN'S SUFFRAGE   1

Martha Gruening
TWO SUFFRAGE MOVEMENTS   10

W. E. B. Du Bois
SUFFERING SUFFRAGETTES   14

Winnifred Harper Cooley
THE YOUNGER SUFFRAGISTS   17

II FEMINISM IN THE 1910's

The General Attack on the Subordination of Women

Florence Guy Seabury
STEREOTYPES   27

Floyd Dell
THE NATURE OF WOMAN   33

Charlotte Perkins Gilman
THE WASTE OF PRIVATE HOUSEKEEPING   36

Women and Birth Control

Margaret Sanger
THE CASE FOR BIRTH CONTROL   42

Max Eastman
REVOLUTIONARY BIRTH CONTROL   45

Radical Feminism

George MacAdam
HENRIETTA RODMAN: AN INTERVIEW WITH A FEMINIST   47

Survey Report
WOMEN'S PEACE PARTY ORGANIZED   60

Crystal Eastman
NOW WE CAN BEGIN   64

III FEMINISM IN THE 1960's

The Revival of Feminism

Brigid Brophy
WOMEN ARE PRISONERS OF THEIR SEX   73

Paula Stern
THE WOMANLY IMAGE   79

Alice S. Rossi
EQUALITY BETWEEN THE SEXES: AN IMMODEST PROPOSAL   87

The Old and the New Ideas in the New Feminism

Pat Mainardi
THE POLITICS OF HOUSEWORK   113

Midge Decter
THE PEACE LADIES   120

Naomi Weisstein
WOMAN AS NIGGER   133

Anne Koedt
THE MYTH OF THE VAGINAL ORGASM   140

Jo Freeman
THE REVOLUTION IS HAPPENING IN OUR MINDS   149

Martha Weinman Lear
THE SECOND FEMINIST WAVE   161

Strategies of the New Feminism

Lisa Hammel
NOW ORGANIZED   173

Aileen Hernandez
EDITORIAL FROM NOW'S PRESIDENT   176

Roxanne Dunbar
FEMALE LIBERATION AS THE BASIS FOR SOCIAL
REVOLUTION   179

Margaret Benston
THE POLITICAL ECONOMY OF WOMEN'S LIBERATION   192

Alice S. Rossi
VISIONS FOR THE FUTURE   203

SUGGESTIONS FOR ADDITIONAL READING   206

INTRODUCTION

Abigail Adams asked her husband John why women were not mentioned in the Declaration of Independence. Ever since, American women, a small number of them at least, have questioned their role in American life. In this country of freedom, opportunity, and openness, the limited nature of the woman's role has seemed to be contradictory at best. In the land of upward mobility, how come women were, and still are, confined to the home? How does the role and status of American women harmonize with democratic ideals? What has been the relationship of women to reform movements in our history? How have women been treated generally in the history books? These questions have been vocalized frequently and persistently in the nineteenth and twentieth centuries. Since the Industrial Revolution, the chores of the home have been considerably reduced; middle- and upper-class American women have been practicing birth control; and the roles of wife and mother have come under serious scrutiny as being insufficiently demanding of the time and energy of modern women. And yet the value system that governs America is still decidedly traditional. The words of Ida Tarbell, for example, written in 1912 still describe the primary tasks of women according to the views of most people.

> To bear and to rear, to feel the dependence of man and child—the necessity for this—to know that upon them depend the health, the character, the happiness, the future of certain human beings—to see themselves laying and preserving the foundations of so imposing a thing as a family —to build so that this family shall become a strong stone in the state— to feel themselves through this family perpetuating and perfecting church, society, republic—this is their destiny—this is worthwhile.[1]

[1] Ida M. Tarbell, *The Business of Being a Woman* (New York: Macmillan Company, 1912), p. 19.

Miss Tarbell may have been a muckraker who ruthlessly exposed the evils of Standard Oil, but her views regarding women were very conventional indeed. How can we explain the fact that Progressive crusader Ida Tarbell held traditional ideas about women? The Progressive Era, in fact, coined the term "new woman" to describe the young woman who was questioning the typical cultural definition of her role in society. The new woman was better educated than her mother, more interested in experimenting with life, and ready for a career outside the home. More women were going to college in the 1910's than ever before; further, from the point of view of percentages, more women obtained degrees, especially the Ph.D. in 1920 than ever before or since.[2] Six percent of all the doctors in our country were women in 1910—the same percentage as now. What went wrong? Why did not women continue to increase their share in the professions?

While everyone is aware of the articulate concern for redefining the role of women in the late 1960's and 1970's, we are less knowledgeable about the fact that the 1910's was a decade that had much feminist activity and agitation. Clearly, the number of new women involved in feminist organizations was small but their impact was great. The majority of "organization" women, of course, were in the suffrage movement during that period. Most suffragists were not feminists; that is, they focused solely upon the vote and did not deal with the larger issue of the role of women in society. The suffragists argued that once women had the vote, equality would naturally follow. They interpreted political power as being the panacea for all the other inequities that prevailed against women. After all, during the first ten years of this century, women still could not sue for divorce, own property in their own right, obtain birth-control information, or generally control their own destinies.

Greenwich Village was the setting for much feminist thinking, talking, and writing in the 1910's. Male and female Bohemians naturally accepted the latest ideas of Freud, Edward Carpenter, and Havelock Ellis. They believed in sexual freedom, individual determination regardless of sex, equal educational opportunities for women, and treating women as human beings and not sex objects. Floyd

---

[2] Fifteen percent of all Ph.D.'s granted in 1920 were given to women.

Dell and Max Eastman, the coeditors of the radical magazine *The Masses,* frequently wrote about the modern woman and the validity of her struggle for freedom. Crystal Eastman, Max's sister, and Henrietta Rodman typified the new woman. Both were college graduates; in fact, Miss Eastman was a trained social worker and attorney while Miss Rodman was a high school English teacher. Both lived the lives of feminists; they retained their maiden names after marriage and led numerous fights for feminist equality. For example, they propagandized against the professional schools discriminating against women; they marched with Margaret Sanger for the free distribution of birth-control information; they advocated child-care centers; they worked to change the restrictive New York educational policy which prevented married teachers, once they had become pregnant, from returning to the school system; and finally, in 1914, they worked for peace and tried to keep America out of the war.

The small group of feminists in the 1910's anticipated many of the themes and causes of the current crop of feminists. They recognized that industrialization had radically altered the functions of modern women and they hoped that society's value system would also change to reflect the different life-style of the twentieth century. Further, many of these women were Socialists and advocated collective living arrangements. They wanted the home to be more efficient (see Charlotte Perkins Gilman selection) and they wanted boys and girls to be raised according to human, rather than sexual values. Anthropology was a relatively new member of the social sciences but its findings had already convinced these women that most roles in society were culturally, not biologically, determined. Thus, there was no reason, argued Henrietta Rodman, for boys to be taught not to cry when they were hurt and girls to be told that it was perfectly proper for them to display emotion.

The feminists envisioned an open society where each human being, in this land of infinite opportunity, could develop his or her potential to its fullest. Women who enjoyed housecleaning and homemaking could do so; women who wanted a husband, a family, and a profession could do so. Women who wanted a career, with or without marriage, could also do so. The society would rearrange its institutions to provide for this. Collective nurseries, flexible residence requirements for graduate studies, and husbands that accepted equal responsibility in the home would enable the feminist dream to become a reality. In the early 1910's, especially before the war, this dream seemed to be near fulfillment.

Why did not the suffragists in league with the feminists create the desired social revolution? In what ways does the feminism of the current generation differ from that of their sisters of the 1910's? When women received the vote in 1920, they helped the men elect handsome Warren G. Harding to the Presidency. Woman's power, a goal of the current feminist movement, was not to be fulfilled in the 1920's. Rather, young women viewed themselves as emancipated already and found the existing women's organizations old-fashioned and out of touch with reality. How did this happen? Is the flapper image a feminist or anti-feminist one? More women have been a part of the labor force since 1920 but they have viewed work as a temporary necessity or as a supplement to their husbands' earnings. Why is this so? Is there a male conspiracy at work to prevent women from advancing in the business world? Are women intellectually inferior to men? Who, or what, is to blame for this situation?

It was not until the 1960's that an articulate and organized outcry again came from women. The feminists of this generation share many views with their sisters of the 1910's. Generally, they share an interest in changing America's values so that people are judged according to human standards and not sexually defined ones. They want women to have all of the opportunities and experiences open to a man. Why, they ask, don't we talk about a career boy? While the women's liberation groups of the sixties and seventies talk about liberal abortion laws and the right of every woman to control her own body, the feminists of the 1910's advocated birth control and the free distribution of birth-control pamphlets to all women. In less colorful language, perhaps, they argued for the same essential goal. Thus, whether we discuss sexual freedom, educational opportunities, or rearranging the traditional home, the two groups of women reformers share the same fundamental world view. Just as many feminists today blame capitalism for the biased treatment of women, so did their ancestors. Most of the feminists of the 1910 generation as well as the 1960's generation have been upper-middle-class women, well educated, and relatively free by the standards of their day. It is often through their experience in college and the professions that women have come to recognize the ways in which our society has stereotyped them.

But the contemporary feminists also have some unique features. First of all, there are more of them. Given the huge number of young women in college today, probably over three million, even if an infinitesimal fraction of that number are feminists or feminist sympathizers, it represents a large constituency. Further, with instant publicity characterizing any new point of view today, the feminist voice is heard in a disproportionate amount to her strength. Everyone has seen a talk show with at least one woman's liberation member on it; everyone has read the popular news magazines' coverage of the subject.

Both the feminists of the 1910's and the 1960's experienced a war and had to come to terms with it. What was each generation's relationship to its respective war? What were the feminists' assumptions about women's nature and war? What are other similarities and differences between the two generations? How historically conscious is the current crop of feminists? Who were the feminists in each generation? What kinds of women find feminism appealing? What has been, and still is, the relationship between the civil rights movement and feminism?

The feminists of the 1960's and 1970's display a candor and concern for sexual matters that their sisters of the 1910's did not possess. Given the culture of the Edwardian era, sex was not a subject discussed freely in public. Neither was it explored in private as fully as it is now. Thus, when the feminists of 1910 advocated birth-control methods, they were considered shockingly radical and avant-garde. Feminists have always considered the sexual arena the basic place where women have been used and abused by men. To earlier groups of feminists, this problem would be solved by providing birth-control methods to all women so that they could enjoy sexual relations within marriage without the fear of pregnancy; this solution, in turn, would eliminate the necessity for prostitution and the double standard. If a woman did not love her husband, educational and occupational equality and opportunity would allow the woman to divorce easily and become economically independent. To the feminists of the 1910's, economic and sexual dependency were interrelated. Freeing the woman economically would also free her sexually.

Our contemporary feminists, on the other hand, not only discuss birth-control methods and the right to abortions quite openly, but they have carried the analysis of male exploitation of the female sex to many interesting and various conclusions. First of all, many theoreticians of the current feminist movement see sexual exploitation as the central problem of American society. All other forms of repression and oppression are based upon this one. Thus, they have devoted much of their writing to this topic. (See the selection "Myth of the Vaginal Orgasm," for example.) Some feminists' solution to this problem is to recommend that women abstain from sexual relations with men and therefore remain free from male aggressiveness and enslavement. Other feminists advocate equal relations in sexual matters and argue that fidelity is not a female trait; still others suggest that healthy, respectful sexuality, in which both partners exhibit concern for each other, is the desired and achievable goal. Some feminists argue that men cannot be a part of their movement while others are willing to include sympathetic males. Still others advocate auto-eroticism and/or homosexuality. The answers to the sexual question are numerous. However, the exploration of this topic, in new and bold ways, is a unique feature of the current movement.

These are some of the concerns with which this volume will try to deal. The book is organized around three major time periods; Part I provides some background information on the suffrage movement, the important precursor to feminism. Part II deals with the feminist ideas and activities during the 1910's, and Part III treats the feminist movement of the sixties. Comparisons and contrasts between the two major periods in this century of feminist interest are crucial in order to understand how and why American women, with a little male support, are dealing with the problem of the woman in our society.

It is important for readers to appreciate that feminism did not arise suddenly and full-born in the last few years but that a small number of American women throughout our history wondered why democratic rhetoric never applied to them and asked: How do you create an attitudinal revolution? How do you change sacred institutions such as the family and the private home? How do you convince men and women that urban industrial society demands role changes for women? What are the significant differences between the sexes? How should a humane society deal with these differences? And finally, how can or will American society meet the feminist challenge during the remaining years of this century?

Conflict of Opinion

It is modern science which, by giving us a new view of the body, its functions, its needs, its claim upon the world, has laid the basis for a successful feminist movement.

FLOYD DELL, 1913

She [woman] can understand only something that she can touch or see, and from these things that she can touch or see she cannot abstract their qualities.

[Feminism is] the product of hysteria, sincere but cockleshell enthusiasm, a badly deranged sense of proportion, and general mental indigestion.

JAMES HENLE, 1915

O God, we pray thee for our sisters who are leaving the ancient shelter of the home to earn their wage in the store and shop amid the press of modern life. Grant them strength of body to bear the strain of unremitting toil, and may no present pressure unfit them for the holy duties of home and motherhood which the future may lay upon them. Give them grace to cherish under the new surroundings the old sweetness and gentleness of womanhood, and in the rough mingling of life to keep the purity of their hearts and lives untarnished.

WALTER RAUSCHENBUSCH, 1910

Remember that by nature you are not capable. If you have any masculine capabilities, you have acquired them unnaturally. God did not create woman for the strenuous masculine responsibilities.

HELEN B. ANDELIN, 1963

But in reality women in the Western, industrialized world today are like the animals in a modern zoo. There are no bars. . . . Yet in practice women are still kept in their place just as firmly as the animals are kept in their enclosures. The barriers which keep them in now are invisible.

BRIGID BROPHY, 1963

Women are an oppressed class. Our oppression is total affecting every facet of our lives. We are exploited as sex objects, breeders, domestic servants, and cheap labor. We are considered inferior beings, whose only purpose is to enhance men's lives. Our humanity is denied.

REDSTOCKINGS MANIFESTO, 1968

I THE SUFFRAGE MOVEMENT

During the 1910's, the decade of the final struggle for suffrage, two women's suffrage organizations existed. One, the National American Woman's Suffrage Association, was the oldest, largest, and most prestigious organization, boasting a membership of two million women. The other group in contrast was made up of younger women and was led by a fiery militant Quaker named Alice Paul; it began in the middle years of the decade as a committee of NAWSA and then took on an independent status. First called the Congressional Union, Miss Paul's group set out to convince Congress to pass a national suffrage amendment. The slow, costly, laborious, and mildly successful state-by-state campaigns of NAWSA frustrated the impatient Miss Paul. She wanted to see suffrage now. After all, women's suffrage had been a debatable issue for over sixty years and action had to be taken.

When America entered World War I, NAWSA pledged its wholehearted support and set about the task of showing President Wilson how patriotic American women were. The Fifth Avenue parades of a few years before in which women sang "I Didn't Raise My Son to Be a Soldier" were forgotten. Alice Paul's group, however, did not follow the lead of NAWSA. Neither did they take up the anti-war cause of some feminist-pacifists. They doggedly accelerated their campaign for the vote. In fact, from January 1917 until around July 1918 they picketed every day in Washington to remind Congress of their demands. They held suffrage meetings, protested America's inhuman treatment of women, were arrested, fasted in jail, and generally caused consternation to the authorities who were not used to radical women. Historians differ as to Miss Paul's contribution to the suffrage effort, but shortly after the war's end, in 1920, suffrage was won and the tired, middle-age suffragists basked in their glory while younger women searched for new causes.

Susan B. Anthony and Ida Husted Harper

THE STRUGGLE FOR WOMAN'S SUFFRAGE

*after the Civil War women and blacks were
Sure they would be granted equal rights*

*In the pre-Civil War period, the women's rights and abolitionist movements
were very much interwoven. Reformers often reasoned that equality would
be granted to both groups. However, after the Civil War, when the amendments to provide equal opportunity to black Americans did not include
provisions for women, a separate woman's suffrage organization arose. By
1900, the achievements of the National American Woman's Suffrage Association were modest. The following selection, taken from the introduction to
volume four of* The History of Woman Suffrage, *discusses some of the reasons for the slow progress. What were the reasons given by Miss Anthony
for the failure of woman's suffrage? What were the implicit American values
she held? What is the tone and mood of this piece?*

It has been frequently said that the first three volumes of *The History
of Woman Suffrage,* which bring the record to twenty years ago,
represent the seed-sowing time of the movement. They do far more
than this, for seeds sown in the early days which they describe
would have fallen upon ground so stony that if they had sprung up
they would soon have withered away. The pioneers in the work for
the redemption of women found an unbroken field, not fallow from
lying idle, but arid and barren, filled with the unyielding rocks of
prejudice and choked with the thorns of conservatism. It required
many years of labor as hard as that endured by the forefathers in
wresting their lands from undisturbed nature, before the ground was
even broken to receive the seed. Then followed the long period of
persistent tilling and sowing which brought no reaping until the last
quarter of the century, when the scanty harvest began to be gathered. The yield has seemed small indeed at the end of each twelve-
month and it is only when viewed in the aggregate that its size can
be appreciated. The condition of woman today compared with that
of last year seems unchanged, but contrasted with that of fifty years
ago it presents as great a revolution as the world has ever witnessed
in this length of time.

If the first organized demand for the rights of woman—made at

From *The History of Woman Suffrage,* edited by Susan B. Anthony and Ida Husted
Harper, Vol. 4, 1883–1900 (Indianapolis, Ind.: Hollenback Press, 1902).

the memorable convention of Seneca Falls, N.Y., in 1848*—had omitted the one for the franchise, those who made it would have lived to see all granted. It asked for woman the right to have personal freedom, to acquire an education, to earn a living, to claim her wages, to own property, to make contracts, to bring suit, to testify in court, to obtain a divorce for just cause, to possess her children, to claim a fair share of the accumulations during marriage. . . . In many of the States all these privileges are now accorded, and in not one are all refused, but when this declaration was framed all were denied by every State. For the past half century there has been a steady advance in the direction of equal rights for women. In many instances these have been granted in response to the direct efforts of women themselves; in others without exertion on their part but through the example of neighboring States and as a result of the general trend toward a long-delayed justice. Enough has been accomplished in all of the above lines to make it absolutely certain that within a few years women everywhere in the United States will enjoy entire equality of legal, civil and social rights.

Behind all of these has been the persistent demand for political rights, and the question naturally arises, "Why do these continue to be denied? Educated, property-owning, self-reliant and public-spirited, why are women still refused a voice in the Government? Citizens in the fullest sense of the word, why are they deprived of the suffrage in a country whose institutions rest upon individual representation?"

There are many reasons, but the first and by far the most important is the fact that this right, and this alone of all that have had to be gained for woman, can be secured only through Constitutional Law. All others have rested upon statute law, or upon the will of a board of trustees, or of a few individuals, or have needed no official or formal sanction. The suffrage alone must be had through a change of the constitution of the State and this can be obtained only by consent of the majority of the voters. Therefore this most valuable of all rights—the one which if possessed by women at the beginning would have brought all the others without a struggle—is placed absolutely in the hands of men to be granted or withheld at

* *Editor's note:* Elizabeth Cady Stanton and Lucretia Mott organized the first woman's rights convention there and issued a Declaration of Principles, modeled after the Declaration of Independence.

will from women. It is an unjust condition which does not exist even in a monarchy of the Old World, and it makes of the United States instead of a true republic an oligarchy in which one-half of the citizens have entire control of the other half. There is not another country having an elected representative body, where this body itself may not extend the suffrage. While the writing of this volume has been in progress the Parliament of Australia by a single Act has fully enfranchised the 800,000 women of that commonwealth. The Parliament of Great Britain has conferred on women every form of suffrage except that for its own members, and there is a favorable prospect of this being granted long before the women of the United States have a similar privilege.

Not another nation is hampered by a written Federal Constitution which it is almost impossible to change, and by forty-five written State constitutions none of which can be altered in the smallest particular except by consent of the majority of the voters. Every one of these constitutions was framed by a convention which no woman had a voice in selecting and of which no woman was a member. With the sole exception of Wyoming, not one woman in the forty-five States was permitted a vote on the constitution, and every one except Wyoming and Utah confined its elective franchise strictly to "male" citizens.

Thus, wherever woman turns in this boasted republic, from ocean to ocean, from lakes to gulf, seeking the citizen's right of self-representation, she is met by a dead wall of constitutional prohibition. It has been held in some of the States that this applies only to State and county suffrage and that the Legislature has power to grant the Municipal Franchise to women. Kansas is the only one, however, which has given such a vote. A bill for this purpose passed the Legislature of Michigan, after years of effort on the part of women, and was at once declared unconstitutional by its Supreme Court. Similar bills have been defeated in many Legislatures on the ground of unconstitutionality. It is claimed generally that they may bestow School Suffrage and this has been granted in over half the States, but frequently it is vetoed by the Governor as unconstitutional, as has been done several times in California. In New York, after four Acts of the Legislature attempting to give School Suffrage to all women, three decisions of the highest courts confined it simply to those of villages and country districts where questions are decided at "school meetings." Eminent lawyers hold that even this is "unconstitutional." . . . The Legislature and courts of Wisconsin have been trying since 1885 to give complete School Suffrage to women and yet they are enabled to exercise it this year (1902) for the first time. . . . Some State constitutions provide, as in Rhode Island, that no form even of School Suffrage can be conferred on women until it has been submitted as an amendment and sanctioned by a majority of the voters.

The constitutions of a number of States declare that it shall not be sufficient to carry an amendment for it to receive a majority of the votes cast upon it, but it must have a majority of the largest vote cast at the election. Not one State where this is the case ever has been able to secure an amendment for any purpose whatever. Minnesota submitted this question itself to the electors in 1898 in the form of an amendment and it was carried, receiving a total of 102,641, yet the largest number of votes cast at that election was 251,250, so if its own provisions had been required it would have been lost. Nebraska is about to make an effort to get rid of such a provision, but, as this can be done only by another amendment to the constitution, the dilemma is presented of the improbability of securing a vote for it which shall be equal to the majority of the highest number cast at the general election. Since it is impossible to get such a vote even on questions to which there is no special objection, it is clearly evident that an amendment enfranchising women, to which there is a large and strong opposition, would have no chance whatever in States making the above requirement.

It then remains to consider the situation in those States where only a majority of the votes cast upon the amendment itself is required. One or two instances will show the stubborn objection which exists among the masses of men to the very idea of woman suffrage. In 1887 the Legislature of New Jersey passed a law granting School Suffrage to women in villages and country districts. After they had exercised it until 1894 the Supreme Court declared it to be unconstitutional, as "the Legislature cannot enlarge or diminish the class of voters." The women decided it was worthwhile to preserve even this scrap of suffrage, so they made a vigorous effort to secure from the Legislature the submission of an amendment which should give it to them constitutionally. The resolution for this had to pass two successive Legislatures, and it happened in this case that by a technicality three were necessary, but with hard work and a petition signed by 7,000 the amendment was finally submitted in 1897. The unvarying testimony of the school authorities was that the women had used their vote wisely and to the great advantage of the schools during the seven years; there was no organized opposition from the class who might object to the Full Suffrage for women lest their business should be injured, or that other class who might fear their personal liberty would be curtailed; yet the proposition to restore to women in the villages and country districts the right simply to vote for school trustees was defeated by 75,170 noes, 65,029 ayes—over 10,000 majority.

South Dakota as a Territory permitted women to vote for all school officers. It entered the Union in 1889 with a clause in its constitution authorizing them to vote "at any election held solely for school purposes." They soon found that this did not include State and county superintendents, who are voted for at general elections, and that in order to get back their Territorial rights an amendment would have to be submitted to the electors. This was done by the Legislature of 1893. There had not been the slightest criticism of the way in which they had used their school suffrage during the past fourteen years, no class was antagonized, and yet this amendment was voted down by 22,682 noes, 17,010 ayes, an opposing majority of 5,672.

*   *   *

In probably no State is the general sentiment so strongly in favor of woman suffrage as in Iowa, and yet for the past thirty years the women have tried in vain to secure from the Legislature the submission of an amendment—simply an opportunity to carry their case to the electors. . . . The politics of that State is practically controlled by the great brewing interests and the balance of power rests in the German vote. It is believed that woman suffrage would be detrimental to their interests and they will not allow it. Here, as in many States, a resolution for an amendment must be acted upon by two successive Legislatures. If a majority of either party should pass this resolution, the enemy would be able to defeat its nominees for the next Legislature before the women could get the chance to vote for them. In other words, all the forces hostile to woman suffrage are already enfranchised and are experienced, active and influential in politics, while the women themselves can give no assistance, and the men in every community who favor it are very largely those who have not an aggressive political influence. This very refusal of certain Legislatures to let the voters pass upon the question is the strongest possible indication that they fear the result. If women could be enfranchised simply by an Act of Congress they would have an opportunity to vote for their benefactors at the same time as the enemies would vote against them, and thus the former would not, as at present, run the risk of personal defeat and the overthrow of their party by espousing the cause of woman suffrage.

If, however, Legislatures were willing to submit the question it is doubtful whether, under present conditions, it could be carried in any large number of States, as the same elements which influence legislators act also upon the voters through the party "machines." Amendments to strike the word "male" from the suffrage clause of the Constitution have been submitted by ten States, and by five of these twice—Kansas, 1867–94; Michigan, 1874; Colorado, 1877–93; Nebraska, 1882; Oregon, 1884–1900; Rhode Island, 1886; Washington, 1889–98; South Dakota, 1890–98; California, 1896; Idaho, 1896. Out of the fifteen trials the amendment has been adopted but twice —in Colorado and Idaho. In these two cases it was indorsed by all the political parties and carried with their permission. Wyoming and Utah placed equal suffrage in the constitution under which they entered Statehood. In both, as Territories, women had had the full franchise—in Wyoming twenty-one and in Utah seventeen years— and public sentiment was strongly in favor. In the States where the question was defeated it had practically no party support.

Aside from all political hostility, however, woman suffrage has to face a tremendous opposition from other sources. The attitude of a remonstrant is the natural one of the vast majority of people. Their first cry on coming into the world, if translated, would be, "I object." They are opposed on principle to every innovation, and the greatest of these is the enfranchisement of women. To grant woman an equality with man in the affairs of life is contrary to every tradition, every precedent, every inheritance, every instinct and every teaching. The acceptance of this idea is possible only to those of especially progressive tendencies and a strong sense of justice, and it is yet too soon to expect these from the majority. If it had been necessary to have the consent of the majority of the men in every State for women to enter the universities, to control their own property, to engage in the various professions and occupations, to speak from the public platform and to form great organizations, in not one would they be enjoying these privileges today. It is very probable that this would be equally true if they had depended upon the permission of a majority of women themselves. They are more conservative even than men, because of the narrowness and isolation of their lives, the subjection in which they always have been held, the severe punishment inflicted by society on those who dare step outside the prescribed sphere, and, stronger than all, perhaps, their religious tendencies through which it has been impressed upon them that their subordinate position was assigned by the Divine will and that to rebel against it is to defy the Creator. In all the generations, Church, State and society have combined to retard the development of women, with the inevitable result that those of every class are narrower, more bigoted and less progressive than the men of that class.

While the girls are crowding the colleges now until they threaten to exceed the number of boys, the demand for the higher education was made by the merest handful of women and granted by an equally small number of men, who, on the boards of trustees, were able to do so, but it would have been deferred for decades if it had depended on a popular vote of either men or women.

*   *   *

The consistent tendency since the right to individual representation was established by the Revolutionary War has been to extend this right, until now every man in the United States is enfranchised. While a few, usually those who are too exclusive to vote themselves, insist that this is detrimental to the electorate, the vast majority hold that in numbers there is the safety of its being more difficult to purchase or mislead; that even the ignorant may vote more honestly than the educated; that more knowledge and judgment can be added through ten million electors than through five; and also that by this universal male suffrage it is made impossible for one class of men to legislate against another class, and thus all excuse for anarchy or a resort to force is removed. Added to these advantages is the developing influence of the ballot upon the individual himself, which renders him more intelligent and gives him a broader conception of justice and liberty. All of these conditions must lead eventually to the enfranchising of the only remaining part of the citizenship without this means of protection and development.

The gradual movement in this direction in the United States is seen in the partial extension of the franchise which has taken place during the past thirty-three years, or within one generation. During this time over one-half of them have conferred School Suffrage on women; one has granted Municipal Suffrage; four a vote on questions of taxation; three have recognized them in local matters, and a number of cities have given such privileges as were possible by charter. Since 1890 four States, by a majority vote of the electors, have enfranchised 200,000 women by incorporating the complete suffrage in their constitutions, from which it never can be removed except by a vote of women themselves. During all these years there have been but two retrogressive steps—the disfranchising of the women of Washington Territory in 1888 by an unconstitutional decision of the Supreme Court, dictated by the disreputable elements then in control; and the taking away of the School Suffrage from all women of the second-class cities in Kentucky by its Legislature of 1902 for the purpose of eliminating the vote of colored women. In every other Legislature a bill to repeal any limited franchise which has been extended has been overwhelmingly voted down.

*   *   *

The struggle of the Nineteenth Century was the transference of power from one man or one class of men to all men, it has been said, and while but one country in 1800 had a constitutional government, in 1900 fifty had some form of constitution and some degree of male sovereignty. Must the Twentieth Century be consumed in securing for woman that which man spent a hundred years in obtaining for himself? The determination of those engaged in this righteous contest was thus expressed by the president of the National Suffrage Association in her address at the annual convention of 1902:

Before the attainment of equal rights for men and women there will be years of struggle and disappointment. We of a younger generation have taken up the work where our noble and consecrated pioneers left it. We, in turn, are enlisted for life, and generations yet unborn will take up the work where we lay it down. So, through centuries if need be, the education will continue, until a regenerated race of men and women who are equal before man and God shall control the destinies of the earth.

But have we not reason to hope, in this era of rapid fulfilment—when in all material things electricity is accomplishing in a day what required months under the old regime—that moral progress will keep pace? And that as much stronger as the electric power has shown itself than the coarse and heavy forces of the stone and iron periods, so much superior will prove the *noblesse oblige* of the men and women of the present, achieving in a generation what was not possible to the narrow selfishness and ignorant prejudice of all the past ages?

A part of the magnificent plan to beautify Washington, the capital of the nation, is a colossal statue to American Womanhood. The design embodies a great arch of marble standing on a base in the form of an oval and broken by sweeps of steps. On either side are large bronze panels, bearing groups of figures. One of these will be a symbolic design showing the spirit of the people descending to lay offerings on woman's altar. Lofty pillars crowned by figures representing Victory are to be placed at the approaches. Surmounting the arch will be the chief group of the composition, symbolizing Woman Glorified. She is rising from her throne to greet War and Peace, Literature and Art, Science and Industry, who approach to lay homage at her feet. Inside the arch is a memorial hall for recording the achievements of women.

How soon this symbol shall become reality and woman stand forth in all the glory of freedom to reach her highest stature, depends upon the use she makes of the opportunities already hers and the fraternal assistance she receives from man. Fearless of criticism, courageous in faith, let each take for a guide these inspiring words which it has been said the Puritan of old would utter if he could speak: "I was a radical in my day; be thou the same in thine! I turned my back upon the old tyrannies and heresies and struck for the new liberties and beliefs; my liberty and my belief are doubtless already tyranny and heresy to thine age; strike thou for the new!"

Martha Gruening

TWO SUFFRAGE MOVEMENTS

The close link between the abolitionist and the woman's rights movement is effectively described in the following article. Martha Gruening provides the historical background to the twentieth-century struggle for woman's suffrage. What are the similarities between the plight of the blacks and the woman's struggle? Are there any significant differences to note? How do the goals of the suffrage movement in the twentieth century compare with the pre-Civil War woman's rights movement?

The woman suffrage movement in England and America really dates from the beginning of the anti-slavery struggle. It was not only contemporaneous with it, but it owes its existence in a large measure to this phase of the struggle for human rights. For it was in the abolitionist ranks that the early suffragists received their training, both as thinkers and propagandists. It was impossible for them to agitate continually for the freedom of the Negro without desiring freedom for themselves, or realizing the parallel between his situation and their own. For if the Negro was a slave the married woman of that day was no less a chattel. She was no longer openly bought and sold, but she had no more than he, a separate legal existence. If the Negro slave belonged to his master, she belonged no less, absolutely, to her husband as did her property, her earnings, and even her children. Both were disfranchised. Both were deprived of education and subject to economic disabilities which they shared with no other class. Even the constitutional right of free speech was not extended to woman when it meant public speech, as she found when she wished to join in the protest against slavery; and even among the abolitionists her presence on platforms and committees caused serious dissensions.

The most striking instance of this was offered at the World's Anti-slavery Convention held in London in 1840, when the credentials of the American women delegates were refused for no other reason than that they were women. They were, indeed, allowed to be present, but not to have any part in the proceedings. With this they

From *The Crisis*, Vol. 4 (September 1912), pp. 245–247.

had to be content, as their fellow delegates apparently were, the only exceptions being William Lloyd Garrison and Nathaniel Rogers, the editor of the *Herald of Freedom*. Of all the men present these two alone seemed to realize that a principle was at stake, and rather than compromise on a point they felt to be vital they resigned their seats in the convention, remaining merely as spectators in the gallery.

This was one of many bitter experiences that taught women the lesson of their own impotence. To many of those rejected delegates, among them Lucretia Mott and Elizabeth Cady Stanton, it brought an overwhelming realization that they were still something less than human in the minds of most men and a conviction that their first duty was to free themselves from the artificial restraints imposed on them because of their sex; that then and then only they could work with men as equals. In these two women, at least, the action of the convention kindled a profound resolve to work toward this end, resulting in an agitation which culminated in the women's rights convention of 1848 and its now famous "declaration of rights." This convention held at Seneca Falls, N.Y., and attended by about 100 men and women, was denounced by the press of that date as "the most unnatural and shocking incident in the history of humanity," while the declaration excited almost universal derision. This document stated the belief of its framers in the equality of men and women and demanded for women education, the liberty of entering all trades and professions, the right to appear in public, the right to "work with men in any good cause," reminiscent of the anti-slavery convention, and, finally, the ballot.

It is significant that of all the resolutions offered at this convention this one alone was not unanimously adopted. It was finally carried by a small majority, but throughout the discussion only two of those present, Elizabeth Cady Stanton and Frederick Douglass, warmly favored it. They alone at this stage seem to have grasped the fact that all rights and privileges go back to this most fundamental right. Throughout the storm of ridicule and abuse which broke out after the convention Douglass maintained his position and brilliantly defended the convention in his paper, *The North Star*.

The early history of the suffrage movement abounds with like incidents showing the help given to the cause by colored people.

Perhaps none is more striking than the story of Sojourner Truth at the Akron convention, quoted from the "Reminiscences of Mrs. Frances D. Gage":

The second day the work waxed warm. Methodist, Baptist, Episcopal, Presbyterian and Universalist ministers came in to hear and discuss the resolutions presented. One claimed superior rights and privileges for man, on the ground of "superior intellect"; another because of the "manhood of Christ"; another gave us a theological view of the "sin of our first mother." Through all these sessions Sojourner Truth, quiet and reticent, sat crouched against the wall, on the corner of the pulpit stairs, her elbows on her knees, her chin resting on her broad, hard palms. Again and again, timorous and trembling ones came to me and said with earnestness: "Don't let her speak, Mrs. Gage, it will ruin us."

There were very few in those days who dared "speak in meeting," and the august teachers of the people were seemingly getting the better of us, while the boys in the gallery and the sneerers in the pews were hugely enjoying the discomfiture as they supposed of the "strong minded." Some of the tender-skinned friends were on the point of losing dignity and the atmosphere betokened a storm, when slowly from her seat in the corner rose Sojourner Truth. "Don't let her speak," gasped half a dozen in my ear. She moved slowly and solemnly to the front and turned her great speaking eyes to me. There was a hissing sound of disapprobation, both above and below, as I announced "Sojourner Truth" and begged the audience to keep silence for a few minutes. At her first words there was a profound hush. She spoke in deep tones, not loud, but which reached every ear in the house, and away through the throng at the doors and windows.

"Wall, chilern, whar dar is so much racket dar must be somethin' out o' kilter. I reckon dat 'twixt de Niggers in de Souf and de women in de Norf, de white men will be in a fix pretty soon. But what's all dis here talkin' about?

"Dat man ober dar says dat women needs to be helped into carriages, and lifted ober ditches, and to hab de best place everywhar. Nobody eber helps me into carriages or ober mud puddles, or gibs me de best place! And ain't I a woman? Look at me! Look at my arm" (and she bared her tremendous arm showing her great muscular power). "I have ploughed, I have planted and gathered into barns and noone could head me—and ain't I a woman? I could work as much and eat as much as a man— when I could get it—and bear de lash as well, and ain't I a woman? I have borne thirteen chilern and seen most of dem sold off into slavery, and when I cried out in my mother's grief, none but Jesus heard me; and ain't I a woman?

"Den dey talks 'bout dis ting in de head. What dey call it?" ("Intellect," someone whispered.) "Dat's it, honey. What's dat got to do with Nigger's

rights or women's rights? If my cup won't hold but a pint and yours holds a quart, wouldn't you be mean not to let me have my little half measure full?" (And she sent a keen glance at the minister who made the argument. The cheering was long and loud.)

"Den dat man ober dar, he say women can't have as much right as men 'cause Christ wan't a woman! Whar did your Christ come from?" (Rolling thunder couldn't have stilled the crowd as did those deep wonderful tones as she stood with outstretched arms and eyes of fire.) "Whar did your Christ come from? From God and a woman. Man had nothin' to do with him!" What a rebuke that was to the little man!

Lastly she took up the defense of Mother Eve, eliciting almost deafening applause at every word, and finally returned to her corner, leaving many of us with streaming eyes and hearts beating with gratitude. She had taken us up in her strong arms and carried us safely over the slough of difficulty, turning the whole tide in our favor. I have never seen anything like the magical influence which turned the sneers and jeers of an excited crowd into notes of respect and admiration.

If such incidents have been less frequent in recent years it is not because the profound and close connection between the Negro and women movements no longer exists. The parallel between their respective situations is as clear to-day as it was in 1848, but it is too frequently ignored by the reformers on both sides. Both have made some progress toward complete emancipation, the gains of women in the direction of enfranchisement being seemingly the more lasting. Both, however, are still very largely disfranchised, and subject to those peculiar educational, legal and economic discriminations that are the natural results of disfranchisement. And finally, both are being brought with every onward step nearer to the identical temptation—to sacrifice the principle of true democracy to the winning of a single skirmish. So when one sees a national body of suffragists refusing to pass a universal suffrage resolution, one is compelled to wonder at the logic of those who, knowing so well what disfranchisement means, would allow it to be inflicted on others. "Let us not confuse the issue," these suffragists plead, some in good faith. Yet the confusion, if any, exists only in their minds. Here are not two distinct issues at stake, but merely the vital principle of democracy. Others insist that the granting of the ballot to women must precede all other reforms because "women have waited long enough" and recall the fact that women were forced to stand aside and see Negro men enfranchised at the close of the Civil War. This is undoubtedly true and was quite justly a source of bitter disappointment to the suffrage leaders of that day— a disappointment we should not underestimate—but merely to reverse the principles in an unjust occurrence is not to work justice. It is strange to see so many suffragists who point with pride to the action of Garrison in withdrawing from the anti-slavery convention, blind to the larger significance of that action. Stranger still to see them following, not Garrison's lead, but that of the convention in their attitude toward colored people, and forgetting that no cause is great to the exclusion of every other. This Robert Purvis, a noted colored leader, understood, as is shown by his noble reply to the suffragists' appeal: "I cannot agree that this or any hour is specially the Negro's. I am an anti-slavery man. With what grace could I ask the women of this country to labor for my enfranchisement and at the same time be unwilling to put forth a hand to remove the tyranny in some respects greater to which they are exposed?" This is what all suffragists must understand, whatever their sex or color —that all the disfranchised of the earth have a common cause.

W. E. B. Du Bois

SUFFERING SUFFRAGETTES

The Crisis, *the magazine of the National Association for the Advancement of Colored People, under the editorship of W. E. B. Du Bois, was very interested in securing complete human rights for all black Americans. Thus, they followed the activities of the woman's suffrage movement with care. Three million black women received the vote in 1920 but three quarters of them lived in the South where black men and women were disfranchised. The following editorial deals with evidence of discrimination by the National American Woman's Suffrage Association against black women. Du Bois presents the point of view of Anna Shaw, the president of NAWSA, as well as his own commentary. How convincing is Mrs. Shaw's defense of NAWSA policy? What were her objections to Miss Gruening's resolution? What is Du Bois' reply?*

From The Crisis, Vol. 4 (June 1912), pp. 76–77.

The woman suffragists are wincing a bit under the plain speaking of *The Crisis.* President Anna Shaw writes us:

> *There is not in the National Association any discrimination against colored people. If they do not belong to us it is merely because they have not organized and have not made application for membership. Many times we have had colored women on our program and as delegates, and I, personally, would be only too glad to welcome them as long as I am president of the National Association.*
>
> *At the State convention in Ithaca a few days ago, when I was conducting the question box, I was asked what I did in Louisville in regard to admitting women of Negro blood to the convention and my reply was: "I did nothing in regard to admitting women of Negro blood to the convention. Our association does not recognize either Negro blood or white blood; what we stand for is the demand for equal political rights for women with men, and we know no distinction of race." Our whole contention is for justice to women, white and colored, and I do not think it will be possible ever to change the platform of the National Association in this respect.*

The corresponding secretary has heard vague rumors in Ohio and says:

> *A somewhat indefinite report has reached me that there is being circulated a statement to the effect that the committee on resolutions of the National American Woman Suffrage Association, at the last annual convention held in Louisville, Ky., "snowed under" a resolution condemning disfranchisement of colored people in the South. As I remember the circumstance that probably gave rise to this misleading report it was as follows: In the hurry of the last meeting of the resolutions committee, which was composed of one member from each State, only a part of the committee being present, several resolutions on various subjects were presented, one being about as the above recites. I do not recall that it read "colored people," though it may have been meant to apply to them. No one objected in any way to its provisions, but one or two mentioned conditions in other parts of the United States which were against the free use of the ballot and said that the resolution was not broad enough. There was not time to discuss it fully, so this one and some other resolutions were not acted upon at all. Those who proposed any of the resolutions not acted upon by our committee had the opportunity and full liberty to present them from the floor, so that our committee did not feel that it was "snowing under" that resolution, or any other, which it had not had time to revise to make comprehensive enough to include all similar abridgments of rights guaranteed by the Constitution of the United States.*

> The ballotless women, I can assure you, who attended that convention are working for, and urging with all their ability, strength and talents, the guarantee of civil and political rights for all citizens of the United States entitled to them.

All this is pleasant and encouraging, but does it present the facts in the case exactly? Early in August Miss Martha Gruening sought a chance to have a colored delegate introduce the following resolution at the Louisville convention and speak on the floor:

> Resolved, that the women who are trying to lift themselves out of the class of the disfranchised, the class of the insane and criminal, express their sympathy with the black men and women who are fighting the same battle and recognize that it is as unjust and as undemocratic to disfranchise human beings on the ground of color as on the ground of sex.

President Anna Shaw refused absolutely to invite the colored lady suggested and said over her signature several weeks before the convention:

> I must oppose the presentation of that resolution at our national convention. I do not feel that we should go into a Southern State to hold our national convention and then introduce any subject which we know beforehand will do nothing but create discord and inharmony in the convention. The resolution which you proposed to introduce would do more to harm the success of our convention in Louisville than all the other things that we do would do good. I am in favor of colored people voting, but white women have no enemy in the world who does more to defeat our amendments, when submitted, than colored men, and until women are recognized and permitted to vote, I am opposed to introducing into our women suffrage convention a resolution in behalf of men who, if our resolution were carried, would go straight to the polls and defeat us every time.

We have already shown that the statement that colored men oppose woman suffrage is false, and we have only to add that every effort was made to keep this resolution from being presented; and when it finally appeared it was incontinently sidetracked in committee. We are not surprised that under the circumstances the information of the corresponding secretary is "somewhat indefinite."

Winnifred Harper Cooley

THE YOUNGER SUFFRAGISTS

To critics of women's rights, feminism and suffragism were one and the same evil thing. Anti-suffrage men and women assumed that the vote would lead inevitably to the downfall of Western civilization. Winnifred Harper Cooley, in the following essay, written for the popular Harper's Weekly *magazine, carefully distinguishes between the goals of feminism and the goals of suffrage. What are the major differences? In what ways would feminism implicitly criticize suffrage? Mrs. Cooley defines feminism as radical. Do you agree or disagree with this judgment? What is her measuring stick (as well as yours) by which you decide?*

Middle-aged reformers are tremendously excited over the radical utterances of some of the younger generation. Woman suffragists of a past decade, seeing the cherished goal of emancipation in sight, tremble lest the work of the pioneers be undone by revolutionary utterances of a few "hot-headed young women."

To these I would commend the following truth: *The radicalism of today becomes the conservatism of tomorrow.* Even in the memory of the youngest of us, the public once considered a woman suffragist a female outlaw, and the press pictured her invariably with short hair and trousers. Within a decade the entire attitude of the public has changed, until it is allowed that suffragists may be beautiful and fashionable, and only in rare instances is a little good-natured fun poked at them. I myself have witnessed the evolution of woman suffrage from a revolutionary measure to a conservative one!

The article signed by Mrs. Belmont in a contemporary magazine, which so passionately denies that the women leaders of the suffrage movement demand anything other than the vote, has a grain of truth, in that many of these women are of a past generation, and, while once radical, are now conservative. They have not kept ahead of the times. To them the vote is a fetish—a magician's wand to conjure with. Having once obtained it, all human problems are to be solved easily and expeditiously. Many of them, in fact, scarcely think ahead toward the solving of problems at all, but merely want the vote to prove their equality with man, and to demonstrate democracy.

From *Harper's Weekly*, Vol. 58 (September 27, 1913), pp. 7–8.

The younger generation has no quarrel with this attitude, for it is absolutely necessary for any democracy to enfranchise all of its adult population; but there are within the fold of modern franchise-seekers a number of women who consider the vote the merest tool, a means to an end—that end being a complete social revolution.

Any reformer is apt to be frightened for the success of his cause when others seek to couple with it still more unpopular measures. We have a deep sympathy with those older women who have borne the brunt and ignominy of the jeers and social ostracism of past public opinion. They are in terror lest the old unjust terms of oppro-brium—"free love," "destruction of the family," and such—will drag the vigorous present cause back a few paces.

The younger feminists, however, do not look with any alarm upon temporary setbacks that might conceivably be given to woman's enfranchisement. So certain are they that evolution is necessitating changes in social and economic conditions, which may on the sur-face appear revolutionary, that they smile contentedly, knowing that no human agency can stem the tide.

What, then, are the demands of the younger radicals who are so agitating the elders within the fold?

1. *The abolition of all arbitrary handicaps calculated to prevent woman's economic independence*   This applies to spiritual as well as to material stumbling-blocks, for public opinion forms quite as impassable a barrier as rules and regulations. The woman of the future—married or single—must be absolutely free to earn her live-lihood, and must receive equal pay for equal service. The younger feminists consider that the day is rapidly approaching when to be supported by a man in return for sexual privileges, or mere general housekeeping, or to be paid for motherhood, will be morally revolt-ing to every self-respecting wife. They claim that as soon as men and women elevate their standards to the conception of a free womanhood, choosing its mate from deliberate affection, rather than in a wild scramble to be "taken care of" in idleness, they will look with horror on the old days when women "married to get a home."

2. *The opportunity for women to serve in all civic capacities*— on municipal, educational, institutional, and reform boards, on juries, and in every function by which they can be of service to their own

sex and to children. This is coming about gradually, through women probation officers, attendants at Juvenile Courts, police matrons, "policewomen," physicians in insane asylums, in children's institutions, etc. It is only surprising that there yet is a violent struggle every time a woman runs for membership on a local school board.

3. *A demand for a single standard of morality* This is not to be interpreted arbitrarily as meaning either a strictly puritanical standard or an objectionably loose standard. It merely means that there shall be no unjust and persecuting *discrimination* against the woman offender, when both man and woman offend.

There is a violent altercation going on continually, within the ranks of feminists in all countries, regarding this question. Every woman in her right senses bitterly resents the injustices of the man-made world, which has for centuries branded the scarlet letter on the woman's breast, and let the man go scot-free. But the conservative women reformers think the solution is in hauling men up to the standard of virginal purity that has always been set for women. The other branch, claiming to have a broader knowledge of human nature, asserts that it is impossible and perhaps undesirable to expect asceticism from all men and women. Naturally, the former group of women are horrified that the latter are willing to face facts as they are, and constantly say to them: "In advocating a single standard of morality, instead of elevating men to the plane of women, you are dragging women down to the plane of man!"

Now, this is not a moral treatise. I am quite willing to let the future citizens work out their own salvation, with a fair certainty that they will attain considerably more fairness, and a generally higher standard, than ever before in any century. The all-important contention is that men and women as human beings, frail or strong as the case may be, must be judged from the broad human standpoint, and, legally and socially, receive fair play. The old-line suffragist who seeks the vote in order to gain laws by which the mother has an equal guardianship with the father of her children, an equal ownership of property, etc., and yet who condones the ostracism of a woman and the adulation of a man, when both have broken a law of conventionality, is absurdly inconsistent.

4. *The abolition of white slavery and prostitution* This is only one form of the age-long insistence of man's ownership of woman.

Its manifestations are quite as real in the harem, and in some phases of marriage, as in the poor creature who is sequestered, an absolute prisoner, in "houses" in our cities. The radical feminists consider it the highest moral duty of educated woman to instruct the young so that they may accomplish their own protection; and we resent the insinuation of the writer of the aforesaid article that women who wish to investigate and abolish the social evil are "morbid and discontented" and "discuss the subject from the housetops, dragging young women and children into it." White slavery is due very largely to the ignorance of young girls—in many cases regarded as highly desirable on the part of their parents. The trend of many modern dramas has been to awaken woman's responsibility for her sisters, and to impress upon her the actual criminality of ignorance.

The play "Hindle Wakes" certainly never was witnessed by the author of the article, who misstates the problem thus: "The play approves of a young man and a young woman slipping away for a weekend together to please the fancy of a moment." The entire point of the drama is missed. Any one who has seen the play knows that, sordid as it is, the effort is not to glorify a temporary liaison, but to claim that the girl was no more to be ostracized than the boy; nor could she be "made an honest woman" by marrying a youth whom she held in contempt. Her clearness of vision was brought out in her assertion of independence. Although an ignorant factory girl, she rose above the suggestion of jumping into matrimony with the rich mill-owner's son merely to shield her reputation. "As long as there are eight mills in Hindle, I shall not lack for work," she said coolly. "So why marry a man I do not love or respect?" Any suffragist who fails to see the high moral ground of the girl who will not marry to protect herself simply stamps herself as one of the old-time conservatives.

5. *The right to activity of expression and of creating social ideals, quite unhampered by old superstitions*   For centuries women, like cows, have been over-sexed. No wonder that they are often self-conscious and hysterical. They are regarded as "*the* sex," and are seldom allowed self-expression as individuals. Thus it is that, in discussing all questions of divorce, of marriage, of the home, of children, people eternally drivel and become effusive regarding women. They are never referred to except in their relation to men. It is always "the wife and mother," "the sweetheart and sister," not

simply "the woman." As a matter of fact, public opinion in the future will regard men as quite as essential to the home as are women; and women as quite as essential to the world as are men.

If the above claims of certain advanced feminine thinkers in all countries seem revolutionary and shocking, let me hasten to assert that they are not the claims of suffragists, *in toto.* All feminists are suffragists, but all suffragists are not feminists. As I suggested in the beginning, the suffragists who only a decade ago were regarded as wild radicals are now considered quite conservative. They claim the vote as "wives and mothers," as "home-makers," as "help-meets." They urge the rights of the child—the fact that pure food and milk and gas and water are municipal problems as well as housekeeping ones as reasons for women entering municipal house-keeping. The public and press, now educated up to this point, applaud this attitude which seems to them agreeably housewifely.

It is a well-established fact that woman suffrage in itself does not bring about a revolution. Wyoming, which has had women citizens for forty-three years, has a remarkable record for few divorces. Colorado and the other States where women are enfranchised show a praiseworthy list of laws relating to women and children, factory inspection, protection and reform, introduced as bills by women legislators. The feminists applaud all these things, but go much further in their demands. They are glad that suffrage has not disrupted homes; but they are quite willing to inquire frankly into monogamy, studying it with open mind, not churchly terror, and to see homes disrupted which rest on an immoral foundation, believing that divorce is far preferable to "legal prostitution."

They regard as somewhat absurd the statement of the writer previously alluded to, that the record of women's political rights "shows beyond all controversy that the effect of equal suffrage has been to raise the standards of domestic life, to make wives happier, to increase the number of marriages; and it is a literal fact that there is far less of the abnormal discussion of the sex question where women have the suffrage!" Just why wives should be happier, *as wives,* because they vote, is difficult to see. I am a born suffragist, dyed in the wool; but I certainly base my happiness as a wife on the excellent traits of my husband, not on the fact that I have gone to the polls several times in my lifetime.

Again, one can scarcely see how the most ardent suffragist can claim that the ballot increases the number of marriages! Does the dropping of the coveted little paper in the ballot-box really increase a girl's romance and desire for matrimony? If so, men should be very eager to enfranchise all the eligible young women. Again, how did the writer obtain statistics as to the amount of "abnormal discussion of the sex question" in States where women vote and in States where they do not? Just what is "abnormal discussion," anyway?

Woman suffrage today rests on a "safe," conservative basis. It does not abolish monogamy. Now, the younger generation are quite curious to see the experiment of monogamy tried in some country! The majority of women have always been constrained to a monogamous existence; but no sane person would assert that monogamy actually exists anywhere, except in rare cases. If it does, how can we account for the curious fact—claimed by investigating sociologists—that the great majority of the patrons of houses of prostitution are married men?

These may be "indirect utterances of young women who deny the necessity of a proper regard for the conventionalities, and claim for themselves a liberty of speech and an independence of action that are wholly indifferent to the effect on a critical public." And it may be true that "it is most unfortunate for any reform to be championed by this class of enthusiasts." However, it is not my belief that any reform ever really prospered through moral cowardice. However persecuted the pioneers who express what they believe to be the truth, the world has a way of justifying them in the end. A terror of public opinion is not a part of the mental equipment of the world's great leaders.

If the kind public will but exercise a little thinking power, and try to realize the mental concepts of those who present a new viewpoint, they frequently will find it to be *intensely moral.* Invariably, the feminists of the world, in seeking woman's social freedom, her economic independence, and her responsibility toward all activities, are actuated by the highest moral purpose and their newly constructed world will be one of greater civic and personal morality, far greater kindness, charity, and justice, and considerably greater happiness per person.

The personnel of these feminist leaders is invariably beyond reproach. It is very amusing to note that the public always insists that women reformers are unhappily married, and therefore are discontented and bitter, arguing that women think only in terms of personalities. I have in mind, at the moment, three beautiful young radicals in the thirties. Each has a handsome, intelligent husband whom she adores.

There is something rather noble and lofty in women who might be lazy and live by their sex, as their ancestors for centuries have done, deliberately putting themselves to work. There is a growing feeling among sensible women that alimony is absurd and unfair to men. Most people are fairly greedy, and it would seem natural that a disgruntled woman who obtained a divorce because her husband was at fault might be glad to secure all the "financial reparation" the court would allow her. Many women believe, however, that it is sufficiently absurd for an able-bodied woman to be supported by a man while living with him, but doubly so during long years after they have ceased to be on speaking terms!

The support of children is another matter. Of course there is a grain of justice in the alimony idea, founded on the fact that if a woman has lived with a man for twenty years she probably has fallen behind in the race for a livelihood, and cannot make a place for herself in the economic struggle, and so, as marriage has deprived her of her earning capacity, some restitution should be made. In the future, when women continue to make money after marriage, they will not be a drag (should they become divorced) on an ex-husband!

Such are a few of the claims and beliefs and hopes of a surprising number of women all over the world. They are not always brave enough to speak them openly. Many a man would be amazed if he could turn an X-ray on the brain of his demure little helpmeet! I hasten to say that suffrage is not responsible for these radical opinions. It might, and probably would, repudiate many of them. But I will tell you a little secret. Although woman suffrage does not know it, it is a part of the social revolution that is surely sweeping every civilized country, and is the prophecy of the dawn of a tomorrow far brighter and better than yesterday or today.

II FEMINISM IN THE 1910's

Feminism, the philosophy that accepts the basic humanness of women, had many articulate and thoughtful spokesmen and women during the 1910's. Charlotte Perkins Gilman, the leading writer on the subject, discussed the relationship of industrialization to the home and found it to be the most inefficiently run enterprise in the country. Taking an economic point of view, Mrs. Gilman argued that women's productivity was not being maximized; she was not paid for her labor, and society (male capitalists) only recognized and rewarded productive people. Thus, she developed some ideas and followers to deal with this problem. Margaret Sanger, Emma Goldman, as well as many other Greenwich Village feminists, campaigned for the right to distribute birth-control pamphlets to working- and middle-class women. Margaret Drier Robbins, Henrietta Rodman, Josephine Goldmark, and others organized the Women's Trade Union League to help working women improve their lot. And when war came, many feminists, most notably Crystal Eastman, worked for peace as a necessary and essential part of any feminist campaign.

The General Attack on the Subordination of Women

Florence Guy Seabury

STEREOTYPES

Florence Guy Seabury attacked the woman problem, as it was sometimes called, from the literary perspective. She deals with the questions: How have fictional writers viewed the woman? What have their conclusions been? In what ways do imaginative writers reflect or influence general opinions? What, therefore, can fiction tell us about the role of women?

If Clarissa Harlow could have stepped out of her pre-Victorian world to witness some of the women stevedores and "longshoremen" now at work along the New York waterfront, she would certainly have fainted so abruptly that no masculine aid could have restored consciousness. If we can believe the 1920 census, a goodly number of Clarissa's timid and delicate sex are toiling gloriously in the most dangerous and violent occupations. Nor are they only engaged in handling steel beams and freight, running trucks and donkey engines, but as miners and steeplejacks, aviators and divers, sheriffs and explorers—everything, in fact that man ever did or thought of doing. They have proved, moreover, as successful in such a new occupation as capturing jungle tigers as in the old one of hunting husbands, as deft in managing big business as in running a little household.

But the census bureau, compiling all the facts of feminine industry, forgot to note that woman might perform these amazingly varied operations, outside the home, without changing in any measurable degree the rooted conception of her nature and activities. She may step out of skirts into knickers, cut her hair in a dozen short shapes and even beat a man in a prize fight, but old ideas as to her place and qualities endure. She changes nothing as

From *Our Changing Morality*, edited by Freda Kirchwey (New York: Charles Boni and Son, 1924), pp. 219–231.

set as the stereotyped image of her sex which has persisted since Eve.

The Inquiring Reporter of the New York *Sun* recently asked five persons whether they would prefer to be tried by a jury of men or women. "Of men," cried they all—two women and three men. "Women would be too likely to overlook the technical points of the law." "Women are too sentimental." "They are too easily swayed by an eloquent address." "Women are by nature sentimental." Almost anybody could complete the list. Ancient opinions of women's characteristics have been so widely advertised that the youngest child in the kindergarten can chirp the whole story. Billy, aged ten, hopes fervently that this country may never have a woman president. "Women haven't the brains—it's a man's job." A. S. M. Hutchinson, considerably older than Billy, has equally juvenile fears: that the new freedom for women may endanger her functions in the home. Whatever and wherever the debate, the status and attributes of women are settled by neat and handy generalizations, passed down from father to son, and mother to daughter. For so far, most women accept the patterns made for them and are as likely as not to consider themselves the weaker vessel, the more emotional sex, a lay figure of biological functioning.

Optimists are heralding a changed state in the relationship of men and women. They point to modern activities and interests as evidence of a different position in the world. They say that customs and traditions of past days are yielding to something freer and finer. The old order, as far as home life is concerned, has been turned topsy-turvy. Out of this chaos, interpreters of the coming morality declare that already better and happier ways have been established between man and maid.

It sounds plausible enough, but the trouble remains that, so far, it isn't true. The intimate relationship of men and women is about as it was in the days of Cleopatra or Xanthippe. The most brawny stevedorette leaves her freight in the air when the whistle blows and rushes home to husband as if she were his most sheltered possession. Following the tradition of the centuries, the business woman, whose salary may double that of her mate, hands him her pay envelope and asks permission to buy a new hat. Busts and bustles are out, flat chests and orthopedic shoes are in, while the waistline moves steadily toward the thigh—but what of it? Actualities of present days leave the ancient phantasies unchanged.

Current patterns for women, as formulated by the man in the street, by the movies, in the women's clubs and lecture halls can be boiled down to one general cut. Whatever she actually is or does, in the stereotype she is a creature specialized to function. The girl on the magazine cover is her symbol. She holds a mirror, a fan, a flower and—at Christmas—a baby. Without variety, activity, or individuality her sugary smile pictures satisfying femininity. Men are allowed diversity. Some are libertines, others are husbands; a few are lawyers, many are clerks. They wear no insignia of masculinity or badge of paternity and they are never expected to live up to being Man or Mankind. But every woman has the whole weight of formulated Womanhood upon her shoulders. Even in new times, she must carry forward the design of the ages.

One of the quaint hang-overs of the past is that men are the chief interpreters of even the modern woman. It may be that the conquest of varied fields and the strain of establishing the right to individuality has taken all her time and energy. Or it may be that the habit of vicarious expression has left her inarticulate. Whatever it is, in the voluminous literature of the changing order, from the earnest tracts on "How It Feels to Be a Woman," by a leading male educator to the tawdry and flippant syndicated views of W. L. George, masculine understanders take the lead. And the strange part of their interpretations is that they run true to ancient form. Old adages are put in a more racy vernacular, the X-ray is turned on with less delicacy. . . .

Take the intimate life story of a girl of the younger generation—Janet March—written by that good friend of women, Floyd Dell. The blurb on the jacket of the book announces that she moves toward "not a happy ending but an intelligent one." And the end? Janet finds her mate and the curtain falls to the soft music of maternity. "One has to risk something," Janet cries. "All my life I've wanted to *do* something with myself. Something exciting. And this is the one thing I can do. I can"—she hesitated. "I can create a breed of fierce and athletic girls, new artists, musicians, and singers."

As a conclusion this is acceptable to anyone with a heart, but wherein is it intellectual and not happy? Queen Victoria, the Honorable Herbert Asquith, or the Reverend Lyman Abbott would be equally pleased by its one hundred percent womanliness. And how does it differ from our cherished slogan, "Woman's place is in the home"? Only because Floyd Dell cuts Janet in a large, free-hand design. The advance pattern calls for a wealth of biological and gynecological explanation, pictures the girl as a healthy young animal who "smoked but drew the line on grounds of health at inhaling," and, following the fashion of peasants in foreign countries, consummated the marriage before it was celebrated. Yet Janet, who claimed her right to all experience and experiment, finally raises her banner on the platform of fireside and nursery.

Despite its unquestionable orthodoxy, Janet March was retired from circulation. But no one has successfully dammed the flowing tide of W. L. George. He draws with somewhat futuristic effect, at times, but his conclusions are those of the old masters. "No woman," he enunciates authoritatively, "values her freedom until she is married and then she is proud to surrender it to the man she has won." Or take this: "All women are courtesans at heart, living only to please the other sex." Wherein does this differ from the sentiment of Alexander Pope who, one hundred and fifty or more years before the birth of W. L. George, declared:

> *Men, some to business, some to pleasures take,*
> *But every woman is at heart a rake.*

H. L. Mencken, stirred by debates about the intelligence of woman and her newer activities, essayed "In Defense of Women," to put his old wine in a fancy bottle, but it was the same home brew. Generously conceding brains to women, he proves his point on the evidence that they are used to ensnare men, who weak-minded and feeble in flight are usually bowled over in the battle of wits. "Marriage," he says, "is the best career a woman can reasonably aspire to—and in the case of very many women, the only one that actually offers a livelihood." . . . "A childless woman remains more than a little ridiculous and ill at ease." . . . "No sane woman has ever actually muffed a chance." . . . "The majority of inflammatory suffragettes of the sex hygiene and birth-control species are simply those who have done their best to snare a man and failed."

In H. L. Mencken's favor is his absence of the usual gush about feminine beauty. He declares with refreshing honesty that in contrast to the female body a milk jug or even a cuspidor is a thing of intelligent and gratifying design. Of woman's superior mental ability he says, "A cave man is all muscle and mush. Without a woman to think for him, he is truly a lamentable spectacle, a baby with whiskers, a rabbit with the frame of an aurochs, a feeble and preposterous caricature of God." What a pity that women use all these advantages of superior mentality and ability only in the age-old game of man-hunting. But do they?

D. H. Lawrence shares this philosophy of the chief business of women, and he is much more gloomy about it. In fact, he is decidedly neurotic in his fear of the ultimate absorption of man. Woman he describes perpetually as a great, magnetic womb, fecund, powerful, drawing, engulfing. Man he sees as a pitiful, struggling creature, ultimately devoured by fierce maternal force. "You absorb, absorb," cries Paul to Miriam in *Sons and Lovers,* "as if you must fill yourself up with love because you've got a shortage somewhere." The Lawrence model, madly, fiercely possessive, differs from older forms in the abundance of physiological and pathological trimming. His conclusion, as voiced again by Paul to Miriam is, "A woman only works with part of herself; the real and vital part is covered up." And this hidden reality is her terrific, destructive, fervid determination to drown man in her embrace.

So it goes. To Floyd Dell woman is a Mother, to H. L. Mencken a Wife, to W. L. George a Courtesan, and to D. H. Lawrence a Matrix —always specialized to sex. There may be men who are able to think of woman apart from the pattern of function, but they are inarticulate. Most of them spend their lives associating with a symbol. The set pieces they call Mary, Martha, Elaine, or Marguerite may follow the standardized design of grandmother, mother, or aunt. Or in more advanced circles, the pattern may call for bobbed hair, knickers, and cigarette case. Under any form of radicalism or conservatism the stereotype remains.

The old morality was built upon this body of folklore about women. Whether pictured as a chaste and beautiful angel, remote and untainted by life's realities, or more cynically regarded as a devil and the source of sin, the notion was always according to pattern. Naturally, the relationship of men and women has been built upon the design, and a great many of our social ideals and customs follow it. The angel concept led, of course, to the so-called double standard which provides for a class of Victorian dolls who personify goodness, while their sisters, the prostitutes, serve as sacrificial offerings to the wicked ways of men. The new morality, as yet rather nebulous and somewhat mythical, has fewer class distinctions. The angel picture, for instance, has had some rude blows. As portrayed by the vanguard of radicals and interpreters, however, the changing conventions have their roots in the old generalizations and phantasies.

Perhaps this is only to be expected, for the man or woman does not exist whose mind has not become so filled with accepted ideas of human beings and relationships before maturity, or even adolescence, that what is seen thereafter is chiefly a fog of creeds and patterns. If several hundred babies, children of good inherited backgrounds, could be brought up on an isolated island, without a taint of superimposed custom and never hearing generalizations about themselves—never having standardized characteristics laid heavily upon their shoulders, perhaps a different type of relationship founded upon actualities, would be evolved. Without a mythology of attributes, based chiefly upon biological functions, real human beings might discover each other and create new and honest ways of comradeship and association. As it is today, we do not know what the pristine reactions of individuals, free from the modifications of stereotype, would be like.

It was the development of means by which beliefs could be separated from actual facts which brought modern science into being and freed the world from the quaint superstitions of the ages. Not until the nature of substance could be proved and classified in contrast with the mass of ignorant notions which clogged ancient thought was the amazing mechanical, economic, and scientific advance of the last century possible. The world of antiquity had standardized life and tied thought down to speculative creeds. Empirical science discarded all supposition and centered itself upon building up another picture—life as an examination of its actual nature proved it to be.

In the creating of a new order which will bring with it a different type of social and personal contact, something similar must take place. For most of our ideas, even those classified as liberal and advanced, are built upon the reactions of an alleged, not an actual human being. Men have suffered from pattern-making, but never have they been burdened with the mass of generalizations that are heaped upon women from birth. Nobody knows what women are really like because our minds are so filled with the stereotype of Woman. And this picture, even in the interpretations of those who claim to understand the modern woman, is chiefly of function, not character. It is impossible to create a satisfying relationship between a red-blooded individual and a symbol. A changed morality cannot successfully emerge when half of those who participate are regarded not as people but functions. As long as women are pictured chiefly as wife, mother, courtesan—or what not—defining merely a relationship to men—nothing new or strange or interesting is likely to happen. The old order is safe.

Floyd Dell

THE NATURE OF WOMAN

Floyd Dell was a well-known Greenwich Village writer during the 1910's. He was also a self-proclaimed feminist. To Dell, the emancipation of American women (and the Bohemian feminists he knew in the Village were living examples of liberated womanhood) was an exciting and highly desirable goal of the twentieth century. Emancipated women, Dell believed, would free men as well as women. It would enable all human beings to work and play together without one sex dominating the other. The Masses, a radical magazine with Dell as a coeditor, frequently discussed feminism in its pages. What kind of evidence is he presenting in the following book review to support feminism? What particular negative claim is he trying to repudiate? How successful, in your judgment, is he? What may be the ultimate consequence of "biological equality"?

If the value of a book is in its power to release those who read it

From *The Masses*, Vol. 8 (January 1916), p. 16.

from the tyranny of old ideas, then the three books I am going to mention in this column are among the most valuable books I have ever read. If I had a shelf devoted to the literature of intellectual emancipation, I should put these books alongside of Haeckel, Stirner, Havelock Ellis, and Bernard Shaw.

Let me confess. Although I am a feminist, and believe in the high destiny of women, I have never been unable to disregard the historical fact that men and not women have in general been the inventors, discoverers, poets, artists, in short the creative geniuses of the world—I have not been able to regard this as an accident, due to environment and education. I have believed that there was an inherent difference in the nature of men and women which would make this generally true in the future, as it had been in the past. I believed that women would be happier, and the world better off, if women were free, but I did not believe that women would ever successfully compete with men in distinctly creative activities.

The reason I believed this was that I had been informed, in the most convincing manner, by the scientific authorities whom I held in most respect, including Havelock Ellis, himself a feminist, that women were nearer to the racial norm, and that men had a greater "variability" than women. This greater male variability has made great criminals and great geniuses—so I believed.

It was a pamphlet by Leta Stetter Hollingworth, reprinted from the American Journal of Sociology, on "Variability as Related to Sex Differences in Achievement" which first enlightened me. I do not mind confessing, for the whole sociological world is still apparently in the dark. From this pamphlet I learned that this inherent variability, which I had taken as a scientific fact, was as raw an assumption as was ever put forward, without a shred of evidence to support it. It was pointed out that there was not, and could not be in the nature of the case, any scientific test of "inherent" variability. The only thing in the nature of a scientific basis for the assertion was the alleged, and disputed, fact that new-born male babies have a greater physical variability than female babies. Upon this uncertain basis had been reared a whole elaborate scientific hypothesis which has been handed on from one sociologist to another as the gospel truth.

But this was not all. In another pamphlet, Helen Montague and Leta Stetter Hollingworth went into the subject of "The Comparative

Variability of the Sexes at Birth." They made 20,000 measurements of new-born infants at a New York hospital—the most elaborate experiment ever made in this field—and analyzed the results. The conclusion is that there is no perceptible difference in the anatomical variability of males and females. So the whole reasoning by analogy from physical to intellectual variability falls flat.

I had wanted to believe that it was only, as this author says, because "nearly 100 percent of their energy is expended in the performance and supervision of domestic and allied tasks, a field where eminence is impossible," that women have not been eminent. I wanted to believe that not merely the practical genius but the creative genius of woman would add new splendors to the future achievement of mankind. I was restrained by the weight of pseudo-scientific authority. I have been freed from that obsession.

The third book, also by Leta Stetter Hollingworth, is entitled "Functional Periodicity: An Experimental Study of the Mental and Motor Abilities of Women During Menstruation." We know how the "reverberations of her physiological emergencies" has been adduced by a noted British surgeon as a reason why women should not be allowed to vote. That was going a little too far. But it is an extreme type of the superstitious prejudice which this book aims to destroy.

Here is a fairer example, and it is from Havelock Ellis:

> It is but the outward manifestation of a monthly physiological cycle, which influences throughout the month the whole of woman's physical and psychic organism. Whatever organic activity we investigate with any precision, we find traces of this rhythm. . . . Woman always lives on the upward or downward slope of a curve.

The general medical and sociological opinion is certainly that this period, which year by year occupies nearly the fourth part of woman's life, is a period of mental and physical incapacity.

Now this book is an account of the first scientific experiment on a large scale to determine the facts. Twenty-three women and two men were subjected for an hour a day every day for a period of several months to tests of muscular control, steadiness, speed and accuracy of perception, and fatiguability. The subjects were of various ages from 23 to 45 years of age. The results are elaborately listed, analyzed, and charted. It sums up the result of this experiment to say that not only is it impossible to tell by the chart of any given case when the menstrual period is occurring, but it is impossible to tell whether a given chart is that of a man or a woman!

"Careful and exact measurement," as the experimenter puts it, "does not reveal a periodic mental or motor inefficiency in normal women." The reverberations of her physiological emergencies appear to be a product of the male imagination, stimulated by "the tradition emanating from mystic and romantic novelists, that woman is a mysterious being, half hysteric, half angel."

To quote again: "From whatever source or sources the idea of woman's periodic irresponsibility may have arisen, it is certainly very widespread. Men of the most varied interests and professional equipment have written on the matter—historians, physicians, lawyers, philosophers, physiologists, novelists, and educators." And all that they have written is, in the light of experimental science, not true.

Charlotte Perkins Gilman

THE WASTE OF PRIVATE HOUSEKEEPING

In the following selection Mrs. Gilman summarizes one of her principal arguments for feminism; namely, that at this stage in the industrial development of our country, the home stands alone as an obsolete institution. What is the relationship, in Mrs. Gilman's mind, between industrialization and the home? In what ways can the home implement industrial principles? Why don't hardheaded businessmen apply principles of efficiency and specialization to their homes? What are men implicitly saying about their wives? In a profit-oriented society, how will an unpaid household worker be viewed?

The principal waste in our "domestic economy" lies in the fact that it is domestic.

Domestic industry is the earliest form of labor. Its original type

From *The Annals of the American Academy of Political and Social Science,* Vol. XLVIII (July 1913), pp. 91–95.

is mother-service, to which was soon added wife-service and slave-service, often embodied in the same person. This primitive labor type increased in numbers where more than one slave, or wife, or slave-wife was possessed, and was slightly raised in grade as slave labor became serf labor, and that gradually turned to contract labor in a modified form.

The domestic servant is still expected to take part wage in barter, food and shelter being given instead of the full price in money; to live in the house of the employing family, to show the virtues of the earlier status, humility, loyalty, faithfulness, and, as belonging to that earlier status, no high degree of skill is expected.

Where no servants are employed, which in our country is the case in fifteen families out of sixteen, domestic industry is still at its first stage, mother-service. As such it is not regarded as labor, in any economic sense, but as a sex-function proper to the woman. She is expected to do the work because she is a woman, without any regard to special fitness or experience, this view being frequently expressed in the words "every girl should know how to cook," while no single trade is ever so mentioned as necessary to every boy.

Industrial efficiency grows along lines of specialization, organization and interchange. In the stage of industrial evolution when each man provided for himself by his own unaided exertions we find the maximum of effort with the minimum of product.

Domestic industry is the only survival of that stage in our otherwise highly differentiated economic system. While every woman is expected to follow one trade the grade of efficiency must remain at the lowest possible average.

The servant is but a shade higher in specialization, and this advantage is nullified by two conditions: first, that owing to its status few persons are willing to perform this service except those incompetent for more highly evolved duties; and second, that owing to the natural tendency of women to marry, the grade of domestic service is that of a perpetual apprenticeship.

Neither the labor of the overworked average mother, nor the labor of the perpetual low-grade apprentice, can ever reach high efficiency. This element of waste is inherent in domestic industry and cannot be overcome. No special training can be applied to every girl and produce good results in all; no psychological gymnastics can elevate housework when housework, in economic status, is at the very bottom of industrial evolution.

This is the first element of waste in domestic industry—permanent inefficiency. The second is in the amount of labor required.

While each man, however poor, requires one whole woman to cook for him, we have a condition in which half the people of the world are engaged in house-service.

Today some seven million women in the United States are working at gainful occupations, but several million of these are employed as house-servants, and the general division of labor is that women as a whole, 50 percent of the world's workers, are in domestic industry.

The waste here is between this proportion and the proportion such work really requires, which is about 10 percent. For fifty women to spend all their time doing what ten women could do in the same, or even less time, is a waste of 40 percent of the world's labor.

Estimating the present market value of women's labor at charwoman's wages, $1.50 a day, and assuming that we have 15,000,000 working housewives, their labor is worth, per year, some $7,500,000,-000. One-fifth of them could do the work at a cost of $1,500,000,000, making an annual saving of $6,000,000,000, about $300 per family. This element of waste has not been considered because we are not accustomed to consider women's work as having any cash value. Our lack of perception does not however alter the economic facts. While wasting, in house-service, 40 percent of the productive industry of the woman world, we thus lose not only by the low average of capacity here stated, but all the higher potentiality of many women for the more valuable forms of world-service. In this connection no one should be allowed to claim that house-service is in itself noble, high, supremely valuable, while at the same time willing to leave its performance to the lowest grade of labor in the world.

The third element of waste in domestic industry is in the repetition of plant.

Under this head we will group the building expense involved in attaching a kitchen and laundry to every house (the smaller the house the greater the proportion of space given to this purpose; if but one room it must serve as the workshop), the furnishing of each kitchen with its stove, tubs, boilers, sink, and all the dishes, ironware, and utensils appurtenant, and the further supplying of each kitchen with water, light and fuel; also the amounts due for break-age and depreciation.

No definite figures can be given in estimates based on such widely varying conditions as those here considered, but it is shown from ample experience that one properly constituted kitchen can provide food for five hundred people, equal to one hundred families, and with space, fittings and supplies certainly not exceeding those of ten private kitchens.

A waste of 90 percent is a conservative estimate here. If this seems too great we should hold in mind not only the reduction in original expense, between building one large kitchen and a hundred small ones, between the one outfit and the hundred in boilers, tubs, sinks, ranges, tables, refrigerators, pantrys, cupboards, etc., and not only the difference in the amount of fuel and other supplies needed, but the difference in the bills for breakage and repairs. Ten skilled experts, working under the proper conditions with proper tools, are not so expensive as a hundred clumsy beginners in a hundred necessarily imperfect average kitchens.

Beyond this comes the fourth great element of waste in domestic industry—that involved in the last and least extreme of retail pur-chasing.

Our economists should establish for us the difference between the "cost" and the "price" of living; what it really costs to raise and deliver our food, and what we are charged for it.

Here again the field of study is too wide, too varying in conditions, for exact tabulation in figures, but the amount wasted may be roughly suggested by the difference between apples by the barrel at $3, and apples by the quart at 15 cents, or $12 a barrel—a waste of three-fourths.

In some commodities it is higher than this, in others much lower; but it is more than safe to say that we expend full twice as much as we need to for our food, by our small private purchasing. The poorer the purchaser the higher the price and the lower the value obtained.

We must remember that the high cost of living is not only in what we pay, but in what we buy; we are taxed not merely in the increased price, but in the decreased value. Ten cents a quart for good milk is high price. Ten cents a quart for a medicated, half-cooked, repulsive white fluid that does not sour but reeks instead, is a higher price.

We are striving in many ways, from federal laws to local inspection, to improve the quality of our food supplies, but no one seems to see that the one permanent continuing cause of poor food is the helplessness of the private purchaser.

The working housewife is not only the cook but the purchaser of food. She has little time and less money, and almost no knowledge. She has no machinery for testing the products offered her, no time to search widely, no cash to pay for the better grades. She must buy and buy quickly, close at home—for the baby is heavy to carry or left to uncertain risks.

Even if, by some gross miracle, all these millions of poor women could be taught to know bad food, that would not give them the means to pay for the good.

We have, of course, our Housewives' League, doing excellent work, but remember that the women who keep servants are but one-sixteenth of the whole; fifteen-sixteenths of our families are poor. This condition of ignorance and financial helplessness is what enables the bad food products to be kept on the market.

Now look at the difference in purchasing power when one skilled experienced buyer orders, at wholesale, for hundreds, perhaps thousands, of customers. Such a person would have the special knowledge and wide experience to recognize the best, and the power to demand it. No one condition would more promptly raise the standard of our food supply than this knowledge and power in the purchaser.

It is of no use to urge that "all women should be so trained." You could not make a skilled "tea-taster" of all men, nor a skilled caterer of all women. Specialization is necessary to develop skill. The domestic worker, wife, or servant is eternally unspecialized.

This study is one of criticism, devoted to pointing out the wastes in our system of living, and to showing that they are inherent in that system. It is not possible at the same time and in the same space to present a convincing revelation as to how we might live otherwise. This much, however, may be stated: that the specialization of those industries now lumped together as "domestic" will no more injure "the privacy of the home," the "sanctity of the family," than has the specialization of the spinning-wheel. Neither maid nor matron may be now assailed with, "Go spin, you jade, go spin!" They do not spin—yet the home and family endure. This trade was once considered so wholly, so essentially a "feminine function" that we still have the term "spinster" to prove it. Similarly we might call a woman "a cookster" long after she had ceased to cook. But the integrity of the family, the happiness and wholesomeness of home life, are no more dependent on the private cook-stove than they were on the private spinning-wheel.

To conclude our list of wastes we ought to indicate a little of the waste of human life involved in this process, the waste of health, of energy, of the growing power of the world.

While the women waste four-fifths of their labor on this department of work, the men must make up by extra earnings. They are saddled with this extravagant and inefficient low-grade private industry, must pay its expenses and suffer from its deficiencies.

Our general food habits, and standard of health in the alimentary processes, are not such as to justify the dragging anachronism of domestic industry. If the world were kept healthy, happy, and well-fed, we might be willing to do it wastefully, but such is by no means the case.

The professionalization of cooking, cleaning and laundry work should be hailed not only by the economist but by the hygienist, the eugenist, and the social psychologist as a long upward step in world progress.

For the specific purposes of this paper it is enough to show that of all waste and extravagance in the cost of living none can equal this universal condition in which we waste four-fifths of the world's labor, more than half of our living expenses, and call it "domestic economy."

Women and Birth Control

Margaret Sanger
THE CASE FOR BIRTH CONTROL

Margaret Sanger is the best-remembered advocate of the long struggle for promoting birth-control information. In 1910, before Mrs. Sanger began her crusade, it was a crime in New York City to distribute birth-control pamphlets. To middle-class America, sex, conception, and pregnancy were not even words openly used in polite society. While many middle- and upper-class women discreetly practiced the crude and inefficient birth-control methods available at the time, working-class mothers were burdened with large families because of their sexual ignorance. What were Mrs. Sanger's major reasons for advocating birth control? Are her reasons feminist ones? Do you think Mrs. Sanger would support liberal abortion laws? To which class in our society was she aiming her birth-control message?

Everywhere we look, we see poverty and large families going hand in hand. We see hordes of children whose parents cannot feed, clothe, or educate even one half of the number born to them. We see sick, harassed, broken mothers whose health and nerves cannot bear the strain of further child-bearing. We see fathers growing despondent and desperate, because their labor cannot bring the necessary wage to keep their growing families. We see that those parents who are least fit to reproduce the race are having the largest number of children; while people of wealth, leisure, and education are having small families.

It is generally conceded by sociologists and scientists that a nation cannot go on indefinitely multiplying without eventually reaching the point when population presses upon means of subsistence. While in this country there is perhaps no need for immediate alarm on this account, there are many other reasons for demanding birth control. At present, for the poor mother, there is only one alternative to the necessity of bearing children year after year, regardless of her health, of the welfare of the children she

From the *Woman Citizen*, Vol. 8 (February 23, 1924), pp. 17–18.

42

already has, and of the income of the family. This alternative is abortion, which is so common as to be almost universal, especially where there are rigid laws against imparting information for the prevention of conception. It has been estimated that there are about one million abortions in the United States each year.

To force poor mothers to resort to this dangerous and health-destroying method of curtailing their families is cruel, wicked, and heartless, and it is often the mothers who care most about the welfare of their children who are willing to undergo any pain or risk to prevent the coming of infants for whom they cannot properly care.

There are definite reasons when and why parents should not have children, which will be conceded by most thoughtful people.

First—Children should not be born when either parent has an inheritable disease, such as insanity, feeble-mindedness, epilepsy, or syphilis.

Second—When the mother is suffering from tuberculosis, kidney disease, heart disease, or pelvic deformity.

Third—When either parent has gonorrhea. This disease in the mother is the cause of 90 percent of blindness in newborn babies.

Fourth—When children already born are not normal, even though both parents are in good physical and mental condition.

Fifth—Not until the woman is twenty-three years old and the man twenty-five.

Sixth—Not until the previous baby is at least three years old. This gives a year to recover from the physical ordeal of the birth of the baby, a year to rest, be normal and enjoy her motherhood, and another year to prepare for the coming of the next.

We want mothers to be fit. We want them to conceive in joy and gladness. We want them to carry their babies during the nine months in a sound and healthy body and with a happy, joyous, hopeful mind. It is almost impossible to imagine the suffering caused to women, the mental agony they endure, when their days and nights are haunted by the fear of undesired pregnancy.

Seventh—Children should not be born to parents whose economic circumstances do not guarantee enough to provide the children with the necessities of life.

A couple who can take care of two children and bring them up decently in health and comfort, give them an education and start them fairly in life, do more for their country and for mankind than the couple who recklessly reproduce ten or twelve children, some of them to die in infancy, others to survive but to enter the mill or factory at an early age, and all to sink to that level of degradation where charity, either state or private, is necessary to keep them alive. The man who cannot support three children should not have ten, notwithstanding all pleas of the militarists for numbers.

Eighth—A woman should not bear children when exhausted from labor. This especially applies to women who marry after spending several years in industrial or commercial life. Conception should not take place until she is in good health and has overcome her fatigue.

Ninth—Not for two years after marriage should a couple undertake the great responsibility of becoming parents. Thousands of young people enter marriage without the faintest idea of what marriage involves. They do not know its spiritual responsibilities. If children are born quickly and plentifully, people consider that the marriage is justified. I claim that this is barbaric and wrong. It is wrong for the wife, for the man, for the children.

It is impossible for two young people to really know each other until they have lived together in marriage. After the closeness and intimacy of that relation there often comes to the woman a rude awakening; the devoted lover becomes careless and dissatisfied. If she becomes pregnant immediately, she becomes physically disturbed, nervous, and irritable. The girl has changed, and the boy who knew her as a happy smiling sweetheart finds her disagreeable and disgruntled. Of course thousands of people learn to adjust themselves. Nevertheless, I maintain that young people should marry early and wait at least two years to adjust their own lives, to play and read together and to build up a cultural and spiritual friendship. Then will come the intense desire to call into being a little child to share their love and happiness. When children are conceived in love and born into an atmosphere of happiness, then will parenthood be a glorious privilege, and the children will grow to resemble gods. This can only be obtained through the knowledge and practice of Birth Control.

P.S.—The American Birth Control League desires that the instruction in birth control should be given by the medical profession. Only through individual care and treatment can a woman be given the best and safest means of controlling her offspring. We do not favor the indiscriminate diffusion of unreliable and unsafe birth control advice.

Max Eastman

REVOLUTIONARY BIRTH CONTROL

Max Eastman, coeditor of The Masses, *was a self-proclaimed feminist along with Floyd Dell. He was also a Socialist who believed in the class struggle. How does his defense of birth control reflect his radical philosophy? What is the relationship between class warfare and birth control? In what ways are his views similar to and different from Margaret Sanger's?*

The interesting objectors to birth control seem to be of two kinds: those who find it libidinous, or at least a violation of something sacred, and those who think it is not revolutionary enough, it is a palliative, a method of promoting contentment in poverty.

Of these two positions the latter is more interesting to us, but we wish to meet the former also on its own grounds. For from the standpoint of knowledge as well as of revolution, we believe in this fight.

Whether society were built on the exploitation of the workers or not, whether society needed revolution or not (if we can imagine a society that didn't), it would be the heart of moral wisdom that the bearing and rearing of children should always be a deliberate and therefore responsible act. The direction of instinctive activities by intelligence *is* wisdom, and "wisdom is virtue," and those who hesitate to direct intelligently this most momentous of activities, through a superstitious subjection whether to "God's law" or "Nature's" are no more virtuous than they are wise.

They are, in fact, more like salmon than like saints. . . .

The unskilled worker is never free, but an unskilled worker with a large family of half-starving children *cannot even fight for freedom.*

From *The Masses*, Vol. 6 (July 1915), pp. 21–22.

That for us is the connection between birth control and the working-class struggle. Workingmen and women ought to be able to feed and rear the children they want—that is the end we are seeking. But the way to that end is a fight; a measure of working-class independence is essential to that fight; and birth control is a means to such independence.

Radical Feminism

George MacAdam

HENRIETTA RODMAN: AN INTERVIEW WITH A FEMINIST

Henrietta Rodman was a leading Greenwich Village feminist of the 1910's. She participated in many women's causes such as the campaign for birth control and the Women's Trade Union League. She also organized the Feminist Alliance in 1914 to implement her plans. The following interview with Miss Rodman, published in The New York Times *of 1915, presents many of her ideas. Do Miss Rodman's ideas sound dated today? Do they appear to be practical? What are the values upon which she bases her feminist philosophy?*

"The care of the baby is the weak point in feminism."

No, it wasn't a woman with old-fashioned ideas of motherhood who said that: nor was it a mere man with conservative—antiquated, should I say?—notions of woman's place in our social system. The phrase was coined by a feminist, a woman feminist, a practical, actual feminist—a woman who wants all the rights of man, who earns her own living, who has a husband and two children (both adopted, by the by), who calls herself "Miss" and retains her maiden name.

Strange as it may seem, this woman is Miss Henrietta Rodman, the Wadleigh high school teacher who was recently suspended for eight months without pay for having written an open letter in which she labeled the majority members of the Board of Education "mother baiters" because they dismissed from the service public school teachers who became mothers. If the care of the baby is the weak point in feminism, it would seem that, judging it not as a question of individual right but as one of public policy to which individual right must yield, the baby is also the weak point in the demands of the

From George MacAdam, "Feminist Apartment House to Solve Baby Problem," *The New York Times,* January 24, 1915, Part V, p. 9.

teacher-mothers. In this long, bitterly fought controversy, which, through the recent decision of Dr. John H. Finley, State Commissioner of Education, has apparently ended in a victory for the teacher-mothers, Miss Rodman has been an influential leader.

In justice to Miss Rodman, it must be noted here that she did not coin the phrase anent babies and feminism recently. That was done last Spring at the first regular meeting of the Feminist Alliance, of which she is President. The meeting had been called to discuss the projected feminist apartment house, and Miss Rodman was the first spokesman of the evening.

Briefly, this new home for feminists, as outlined by Miss Rodman, is to contain about 400 rooms, and is to be divided into suites of from one to four rooms, with baths. It is designed primarily for the benefit of "married professional women, such as teachers and doctors," who, it is expected, will be at work most of the day, like their husbands. Therefore they are to be relieved of the "four primitive industries of women—care of house, clothes, food, and children." These details are to be looked after by "trained staffs."

For the children, there are to be nurseries and playgrounds and schoolrooms on the roof. Montessori teachers and expert attendants are to be in charge. All the cooking for the entire house will be done in a large kitchen in the basement, and the meals will be served to the tenants from electric service-elevators. Family mending will be done by a trained staff, the laundry work will be in charge of another trained staff, and so, also, will the sweeping and dusting and tidying up. All these conveniences, including the care of the children, will be supplied to the feminist tenants at cost price. The house is intended to fit the purse of families having incomes between $1,800 and $3,000 a year.

In the course of the discussion several persons asked if bachelors or childless couples would be permitted to engage apartments. It was explained that they would be. Miss Rodman continued: "Of course the real aim and purpose of the house is to enable people to have children who cannot afford it now. The average professional or business woman cannot as an independent individual employ the grade of nurse or governess that she would be content to leave her children with. The majority of professional and business women can only accomplish this by pooling their interests, by uniting under some such plan as that of the feminist apartment house. At the present time the care of the baby is the weak point in feminism. The care of children, particularly those under 4 or 5 years of age, is the point at which feminism is most open to attack. We must have this apartment house before we can be honest feminists."

Getting Something Definite

Now, in spite of the fact that during the last year or two we have heard a great deal about feminism, many of us are still puzzling over the exact meaning of this new "ism." Like so many other advocates of radical cures for the ills that afflict civilized society, the prophets of feminism have, for the most part, indulged in rose-colored predictions, based on airy generalities, in highfalutin talk that will not boil down into hard, concrete fact.

But here in this projected feminist apartment house we begin to get something tangible, something definite—an appreciable picture of what life would be like should feminism come to pass. (Let it be noted here that, according to Miss Rodman, the feminist apartment house is really to be erected; that the plans have been drawn, the site chosen; that the project is simply in abeyance because of the wartime tightness in the building loan and mortgage market.)

There are, however, many blank spaces in the picture projected by this unique scheme of pooled domestic cares. It was in the hope of filling these that I called on Miss Rodman one day last week. Here is the record of our talk. If for no other reason, it is valuable as the psychologic portrait of a feminist.

"A home," said Miss Rodman, the conversational preliminaries over, "a home is just as demoralizing a place to stay in all day as is a bed. See what the characteristics of a home are: Rest, peace, love, tenderness, withdrawal from the harsh realities of life outside, withdrawal from the complexities of modern social and economic life. If a woman stays in the home she fails to develop courage, initiative, and resourcefulness; she fails to make those contributions to society that society has a right to expect her to make. Feminism is a movement by women of the upper classes to save their own souls."

"It is a class movement, then?"

"No. It is simply a conscious movement in the upper classes. As a matter of fact, our sisters of the poorer class have the most fundamental right for which we are struggling—the right for economic independence, the right to continue their chosen work after marriage. As a matter of fact, talking this over as man to man—"

I'm afraid I smiled too visibly at this wistful figure of speech.

"What I mean by that is that I desire to be perfectly frank and straight in this matter."

"Then you believe that women are not frank and straight?"

"Certainly it is not characteristic of women who have not grown up. These are the women who have not been required to face the realities of life, who are protected in their homes from the necessity of meeting the economic struggle. They are thus kept from developing an appreciation and understanding of life as it is, from developing a broad social consciousness. These child-women are dependents, and dependents or subordinates cannot afford to be perfectly frank and straight. You find the same thing in servants and dependents everywhere; one cannot be frank and straight where one is obliged to be pleasant.

Definition of Feminism

"Feminism is the attempt of women to grow up, to accept the responsibilities of life, to outgrow those characteristics of childhood—selfishness and cowardliness—that we require our boys to outgrow, that we give them every opportunity to outgrow, but that we permit and by our social system encourage our girls to retain."

"Don't you think that your indictment of the home-staying, home-keeping woman, the 'child-woman,' as you label her, is a trifle sweeping? Don't you think that in bringing a family into existence, in raising it, in nursing it through the ills of babyhood and childhood, in being the home partner of her husband through both adversity and prosperity—don't you think that in doing this a woman is required to 'face the realities of life,' to develop courage and unselfishness?"

Miss Rodman's answer was a counter-question:

"Do you know how many children there are in the average well-to-do home? Two or three, that's all. The woman who manages her home and raises two or three children has not done her duty to society. The reason I say that is because so many women are doing more than that.

"I would have the question put to each woman to say for herself just how much she can do. Feminism does not demand that every woman should be a wage earner; but it does demand that no woman who desires to be a wage earner shall be prevented from doing her work because she has taken up the other responsibilities of women, such as marriage and child bearing.

"The feminist apartment house is a deliberate attempt of women who want to carry what they believe are the full responsibilities of womanhood, homemaking, childbearing—no, childbearing is included in homemaking—wage-earning, and citizenship. As a matter of fact, these are not the responsibilities of womanhood; they are the responsibilities of a human being.

"No, we women who are trying to do these things—take on the new duties of wage-earning and citizenship—do not want to neglect the old duties. We do not want our homes to be less happy and comfortable than were the old-fashioned homes, any less a place where the children will grow up to face life honestly, bravely, and kindly. We believe that because we have had more opportunities to develop our minds than our grandmothers had, our homes should be just so much better."

"But if I understand you aright," said I, "some such institution as the feminist apartment house is a necessary factor in the feminist program. In other words, the feminist cannot carry what she considers her full responsibilities unless she has some other women to help her; while she tends to wage-earning and citizenship, some other woman must tend to her home and children. Or, as you yourself have expressed it, 'the baby is the weak point in feminism.'"

"The baby," answered Miss Rodman, "is the weak point in economic independence." A moment's silence. Then: "Oh, I hate to say that the baby is the weak point in anything! I hardly believe that I did use that phrase. Anyhow, it does not represent my belief now."

"What is the need, then, of the feminist apartment house, with its elaborate system of nursery and kindergarten and school?"

"I will say that the baby is the great problem of the woman who attempts to carry the new responsibilities of wage-earning and citizenship. We must have babies for our own happiness, and we must give them the best of ourselves—not only for their own good, not only for the welfare of society, but for our own self-expression.

The bringing up of a child is the greatest creative work of the average man or woman."

"And yet you feminists demand that it be turned over to employes —experts, perhaps, but still employes. You seem to believe that a mother's duty ends with childbearing. How about mothering?"

"There's the point: what we feminists believe in is real mothering, in intelligent mothering, as opposed to instinctive mothering. By real mothering I do not mean washing the baby's clothes, preparing its food, watching over its sleep, nursing it through its baby illnesses, nor, in later years, darning the children's stockings, making, or even mending, their clothes, preparing their food, or supervising their education. All these things can be done better by experts. It is simply a question of efficiency versus instinct. By real mothering I mean an intimate spiritual relation between mother and child which enables the mother to give to the child all that she has gained from life, so that the new generation is started in advance of the old.

More Time for Fatherhood

"And I mean exactly the same thing by fathering. We have not only specialized women on motherhood, but we have made woman almost the unique parent. I maintain that every child has a right to a real father, one who has sufficient leisure to take a creative interest in his children. The average American man is specialized on wage-earning. One of the results of feminism, I believe, will be that by dividing the economic responsibility of the family between husband and wife, the father will be given more leisure in which he may take up the responsibility of fatherhood."

"You state specifically the things the feminist mother will not do, but you say nothing about the things she will do other than to establish an 'intimate spiritual relation' between herself and child. Just what do you mean by that? How is a mother to go at it?"

"By that I mean that a mother should know her child, not subjectively, as the mother of the past knew hers—her idea of the child colored by her love and her desire that her child should be what she had failed to be. The mother of the future must know her child as he really is—that is, as he is studied by experts, spiritually and mentally. She must see her child as an identity distinct from herself, and not as an idealized reflection of her own personality.

"The value of this spiritual relation is that the mother should be the genuine companion of her child, able to help him in his relations toward and conflicts with life, for she will know life. The mother of the past has known neither her child nor the experiences he will meet, and therefore she has been unable to go out with him in sympathy and understanding to meet them."

"But don't you think that it is through the material things that the spiritual relation between mother and child is really established? Doesn't instinctive mother love glorify into sacred privileges the things that otherwise would be menial nursemaid tasks? Isn't it the person who washed it and dresses it and feeds it and coos it to sleep that wins the baby's love and that has the greatest formative influence upon it? Why, I have known women who became jealous of the problematic smiles that a trained nurse has won from a few weeks' old baby."

"No, I do not think that a mother should want to express her love through material things. She should desire to express it through spiritual things. I often think that the material things are a degradation of the spiritual. A mother may overfeed her child instead of understanding his needs. You see, if women do put emphasis on the material things, it's only natural that they won't want another woman to wash baby's bottles.

"This is the point: the modern woman is seeking to understand the real needs of her child and to minister to them in the most effective way. That is why she so often employs experts. They do well what the old-fashioned mother did poorly. If the baby is sick, the modern mother does not go to her chest full of remedies; she telephones for the doctor. If the child shows spiritual or mental defects —and most of them do—she has the child cared for by an expert who has worked with hundreds of other children."

This "spiritual relationship" still seemed a trifle vague.

"Will you please give the daily program of a feminist mother living in a feminist apartment house, so far as children are concerned?"

"Montessori schools," answered Miss Rodman, "will take the children at 2 years of age. We feminists, I think, all maintain that from 6 months to 2 years of age a baby can be cared for better perhaps for six hours a day by a trained nurse than by its own mother. Now, let us see what a practical feminist would do. In the morning—if the baby had slept in mother's apartment instead of the house-nursery during the night—mother would ring for nurse, who would come and bathe and dress baby and give it its breakfast. The mother meanwhile, perhaps while she is doing up her hair, will play with and enjoy her baby.

"That enjoying of baby is one of the most important points of the mother of the future. The babies loved to be enjoyed. But the mother of the past has been so busy with her children that she hasn't had time to enjoy them. The point is not how long but how intensely a mother does it.

Sympathy Between Them

"I, for instance, never feel jealous of how much others take care of Joan" (the younger of Miss Rodman's adopted children), "she would never get to care for them more than she does for me, because none of them can enjoy her more than I do. The moment we come together a real, intense relationship of sympathy, understanding, and delight is established between us.

"And yet I could not bring up Joan without tremendous effort. She is very active, and therefore noisy, and most of the time she naturally wants other children about her. A little group of happy, noisy youngsters is a charming thing for a short time. But unless you have a special taste for it, it becomes very wearing after an hour or two.

"You see, most children are not allowed self-expression in the home because it is too destructive of furniture and of the parents' nerves. We propose to have a baby world in which the youngsters may be themselves.

"Now, when mother returns from work, six or seven hours later, she'll go up on the roof, into the baby world, which will be equipped with every possible delight—growing things and toys, especially the active toys that children love. She'll watch baby at play for a while, and then she'll take her home to her apartment, where they will have a quiet hour together. And father may be there, too."

"His workday also is to consist of six or seven hours?"

"Yes; because the economic responsibility of the family is divided. If the weather is good, mother and father may go out with baby for the afternoon."

"Rather idealistic," I commented.

"Well, there are women who have positions that enable their husbands to get home in the afternoon.

Attendants Night and Day

"But to get back to the daily program; it will now be time for baby to go to supper and bed. Mother may tend to these things herself, or she may ring for nurse, who will put baby to bed in a little crib in mother's room or in a crib in the nursery. In this nursery there will be a sufficient number of trained attendants in charge night and day.

"This arrangement will give the parents an opportunity to go out together at night to places of entertainment and public instruction. It will mean that domestic servitude no longer alienates a mother from her husband in what should be the hours of recreation. Also it will mean that if baby is sick, baby will get expert care, and mother and father get the sleep necessary to fit them, mentally and physically, for the next day's work."

"Just where are you to get the women who will take charge of this nursery?"

"There are some women of far greater maternal instinct—no, maternal instinct is too loose a term—say there are some women who have a far greater instinctive desire to be with babies than have others. With most women this instinctive desire to be with and care for children is not aroused by children of all ages. With each woman this instinct is aroused only by children of a certain age. I, for instance, haven't much desire to be with babies or young children for long; but I have a great liking and apparently an instinctive understanding of adolescent girls. Mothers often come to me for advice about their daughters.

"Under the feminist program, the women who desire to take up mothercraft will be trained by experts, and this training will be supplemented by experience. They will be the ones who will be put in charge of children of different ages, so that each will have under her care children suitable to her particular type of maternal instinct.

"Those having charge of the youngest children—children under 2 years of age—would each have not more than six children in her care, and each would be assisted by two young girls who are studying mothercraft. Just to scale up roughly: From 2 to 6 years of age, about twelve to each teacher and two assistants in training; from 6 to 9 or 10 years old, about twenty to each teacher and two assistants. After reaching 9 or 10 years of age the children would go out of the house to school. There we meet the problem of the public schools; and although this is not a feminist problem, but a humanist problem, nevertheless, I believe that we feminists must deal with it if it is to be done effectively."

"And the boys and the girls would be brought up together?"

"Absolutely. The boys and the girls would mix right straight through. We feminists believe that coeducation is one of the essentials of civilization. This mixing makes the girls brave and resourceful and the boys courteous and helpful."

"And the boys would play with dolls and dishes and the girls would take part in the rough-and-tumble games of the boys?"

Boys Might Play with Dolls

"I don't know whether the boys would play with dolls and dishes or not. They would if they wanted to. Certainly the boys would not be taught to be ashamed to play with dolls and dishes because they have been considered girls' toys. And the girls would not be told that they can't play vigorous games because they must keep their dresses clean and they must be ladylike."

"And would this mixing together continue after adolescence— would the young men attend sewing societies and afternoon card parties and the young women club smokers?"

"This is asking me for a prophecy. And my prophecy is that neither the young men nor the young women would attend sewing societies or card parties or club smokers. These are primitive forms of pleasure. They have been well described as a form of intellectual chewing-gum.

"What will be the recreations of the future? Oh, any number of splendid things. Dancing, for instance, is going to be one of our commonest forms of activity. People will go to the parks, and immense phonographs will be turned on, and they'll dance on the grass. No, none of the present dances, no tangoes nor one-steps; but beautiful, free dancing, dancing that gives expression to the spirit, the kind of dancing that is taught by Isadora Duncan.

"And there'll be all kinds of out-of-door sports. Yes, both sexes will take part in them indiscriminately. Of course, they won't play football; football will go the way of the sewing societies—it is a primitive form of sport, brutal and stupid."

"And you do not think that this constant association would make the men effeminate and the women masculine, that it would tend to efface the distinctive characteristics that we now consider not only desirable but even necessary in each sex?"

"That's where we split," exclaimed Miss Rodman emphatically. "There is no quality good in one sex that is not good in the other. We women have acquired some unfortunate characteristics to please the men—we're coquettish and coy and kittenish."

"And you don't believe that a feminist woman would be kittenish if she thought that it would please the man that she wanted to please?"

"No. I believe that we'll leave it to our children to be kittenish."

"And women won't be coquettish in the matter of dress?"

"There'll be a shift, an adjustment. The women will dress much more simply than at present, and the men far more beautifully."

"Wouldn't all this mean an approximation of the two sexes? Under the feminist program wouldn't it be but a comparatively short time before the only difference between men and women was the comparatively negligible one of anatomy?"

"Here again you are asking for a prophecy. My prophecy is that men and women will be much more like each other, mentally and physically, than they are at present, both approximating a type far higher than the distinct sex types of today. I believe that sex will be far less important than it is at present; that the great interest of the race will be in the development of the human qualities. By this I mean the love of neighbor, of community, of State. Of course we shall still have sexual love; but it won't be the overwhelming, dominant force in our lives that it is today."

Here I grasped the bull by both horns.

"Without speculation as to the future effects of feminism, isn't it a fact, Miss Rodman, that the feminist husband of today—the one who is willing that his wife go out and earn a living—lacks virility, lacks force, lacks the stand-up-and-fight quality? Isn't he the kind that needs assistance in the rough and tumble of the world?"

"If you are making money the test of these qualities, my answer is that feminist husbands are no less able to support their wives than are other husbands. But a frequent feminist arrangement is that the husband or wife that has a job that he or she is satisfied with will support the other while that other is preparing to do the work, or seeking the opportunity to do the work, which he or she desires. I have known instances where the wife has supported her husband for a year while he prepared himself to take up the work for which he believed himself best fitted. Then during the next year the husband supported his wife, so that she had the same opportunity. This turn-and-turn-about arrangement works out very satisfactorily."

"A little while back, Miss Rodman, you said that you would have the question put to each woman to say for herself just how much she can do, that feminism does not demand that every woman should be a wage earner. Now let me ask: Does feminism demand that every man shall be a wage earner, or is he to have the right—I suppose it is a right, since feminist women spurn privileges and demand only rights—is each man to have the right to say just how much he can do?"

"Certainly. Feminism does not demand that every man be a wage earner. It doesn't say whether a man shall work or not. It simply says that every self-respecting woman must do her share of the world's work, and naturally such a woman would not marry a man who is not doing his share."

"But if a man should feel that his talent lay in housework and child culture, would it be all right for such a man to stay at home and tend to things there while his wife went out and earned the wherewithal?"

"Any work that is fit for a self-respecting woman is fit for a self-respecting man. But the vital defect in your question is that it is based on the assumption that society is to continue in its present condition. Now, we feminists object to women being prisoners in the home, and there is no reason why men should be prisoners there, either. Feminism means that the home as it is known today, the industrially isolated home, must go; that the old home industries must be pooled under some cooperative scheme, of which our feminist apartment house is a forecast.

"With such a system in practice, of course men would take part in what is now regarded as the home work of women. Why not? In the big hotels today men do the cooking and dishwashing and food serving. When it comes to the care of the children under feminism, I doubt if a man is naturally fitted to care for a child under two years of age. But even today men wash bottles in laboratories and men prepare baby food in big quantities, and there are some remarkably successful men kindergartners. Under feminism such men would undoubtedly assist with child culture; but on the whole, I believe that mothercraft would remain largely the study and work of women.

"One of the greatest obstacles to the progress of feminism among men," continued Miss Rodman, "is their fear of what they'll have to give up. I believe their greatest treasure of this kind is the sense of their own superiority. This sense of superiority comes from the fact that they maintain a little world that they call 'home,' in which there is a little dependent that they call 'wife.' A man measures himself with his dependent. The more charming she is and the finer the little world that he has provided for her, the greater his feeling of superiority. Maintaining a dependent! Bah! That is no achievement. Men should get their sense of superiority by achieving in the big world and not in these little self-made worlds."

"How many of us, Miss Rodman, can achieve anything in the big world? Aren't you forgetting that in the very nature of things most of us have got to be underlings—laborers, motormen, mechanics, clerks, shopkeepers—men who feel that if they do their day's work and maintain a home and a wife and a family and pay their bills they have achieved no mean thing? You feminists and suffragists talk as though the social pyramid can be made all apex, as though all of us can become leaders in thought and action."

"Exactly, exactly. The possibilities in each human being are amazing, glorious! Have you ever looked at a classroom of boys or girls and thought of the possibilities there are in that young, unmolded material? It is one of the most inspiring things I know. Who can say just what are the limitations of any one of us? So why estimate it meanly?

Wants Equal Opportunities

"Now, there are just a few points about feminism that I would like you to bring out. What we women want is equality of opportunity with men. We do not ask the privilege of bearing arms, because we have the privilege of bearing children. The latter is quite as heavy a burden as is that of military service. This has been proved by statistics. In the United States alone 10,000 women die every year in childbirth, a greater number than there were men killed in battle in the Spanish-American war, and the women pay their toll every year.

"We feminists are accused of advocating free love. I deny it. Our attitude may be expressed in this form: We demand that no civil or political right be refused to any person on account of sex. The right to form sex unions without the control of the State has never been granted to men, and therefore is no part of the demand of women.

"I do not believe that women should smoke or drink; I see no reason why we should adopt men's blunders because of a new freedom. But I would put no heavier penalty upon the girl who blunders—I am now speaking of sex blunders—than I would on the man. Society has no right to treat the girl who blunders more brutally than it does the man."

Survey Report
WOMEN'S PEACE PARTY ORGANIZED

Survey, the magazine of American social workers in the 1910's, often reported the activities of leading liberal groups in New York City. The following news story describes the formation of the Woman's Peace Party at the beginning of World War I. What are the unique features of women described in the party's preamble that makes them suited for peace work? How realistic is a woman's peace party? What were the methods of the organization? How does this group differ from the suffrage movement? In what ways is peace propaganda work part of feminism?

The conference at Washington on January 9–10, referred to in the last number of *The Survey*, resulted in the organization of the Woman's Peace Party with a definite program for constructive peace and a vigorous platform. The form of organization was purposely left elastic. Jane Addams, the president, is to choose her own secretary

From *Survey*, Vol. 33 (January 23, 1915), pp. 433–434.

and treasurer in Chicago. The other members of the executive board are the four vice-presidents, Mrs. White of Washington, Mrs. Spencer of Meadville, Pa., Mrs. Post of Washington, and Mrs. Henry Villard of New York.

Further details in regard to organization may be secured direct from Miss Addams at Hull House. Any woman's organization desiring to organize also as a peace circle may join the Woman's Peace Party on annual payment of $5 and sustaining membership is also open to all women, the annual fee being $1.

The conference was made up of a hundred and more representatives of national women's associations. They came from all parts of the country and held diverse points of view, but they did their work with a constructive quality of mind and an enthusiasm which had in it a strong note of spiritual distinction.

The degree of public interest in the matter was amply demonstrated at the open meeting on Sunday. The ballroom of the New Willard hotel was filled, there was an overflow meeting, and still 500 people had to be turned away. At this meeting, presided over by Carrie Chapman Catt, addresses were made by Jane Addams, Mrs. Pethick Lawrence, of England, Madam Rosika Schwimmer, of Hungary, the Rev. Anna Howard Shaw, Harriet Stanton Blatch, and Janet Richards. Mrs. Catt was chairman of the program committee, which was made up of representatives from different sections of the country.

The preamble to the program, presented by the Rev. Anna Garlin Spencer, reads as follows:

> We women of the United States, assembled in behalf of world peace, grateful for the security of our own country, but sorrowing for the misery of all involved in the present struggle among warring nations, do hereby band ourselves together to demand that war should be abolished.
>
> Equally with men pacifists, we understand that planned-for, legalized, wholesale, human slaughter is today the sum of all villainies. As women, we feel a peculiar moral passion of revolt against both the cruelty and the waste of war.
>
> As women, we are especially the custodians of the life of the ages. We will no longer consent to its reckless destruction. As women we are particularly charged with the nurture of childhood and with the care of the helpless and the unfortunate. We will not longer accept without protest

that added burden of maimed and invalid men and poverty-stricken widows and orphans which war places upon us.

As women we have builded by the patient drudgery of the past the basic foundation of the home and of peaceful industry. We will not longer endure without a protest which must be heard and heeded by men that hoary evil which in an hour destroys the social structure that centuries of toil have reared.

As women we are called upon to start each generation onward toward a better humanity. We will not longer tolerate without determined opposition that denial of the sovereignty of reason and justice by which war and all that makes for war today renders impotent the idealism of the race.

Therefore, as the mother half of humanity, we demand that our right to be considered in the settlement of questions concerning not alone the life of individuals but of nations be recognized and respected.

We demand that women be given a share in deciding between war and peace in all the courts of high debate; within the home, the school, the church, the industrial order, and the state.

So protesting, and so demanding, we hereby form ourselves into a national organization to be called the Woman's Peace Party.

We hereby adopt the following as our platform of principles, some of the items of which have been accepted by a majority vote, and more of which have been the unanimous choice of those attending the conference which had initiated the formation of this organization. We have sunk all differences of opinion on minor matters and given freedom of expression to a wide divergence of opinion in the details of our platform and in our statement of explanation and information in a common desire to make our woman's protest against war and all that makes for war vocal, commanding and effective. We welcome to our membership all who are in substantial sympathy with that fundamental purpose of our organization whether or not they can accept in full our detailed statement of principles. [Emphasis ours.]

The purpose of this organization is to enlist all American women in arousing the nations to respect the sacredness of human life and to abolish war.

The platform, as adopted, is given in another column. It was supplemented by a statement of information and explanation, which will be sent out to still further elucidate the Program for Constructive Peace, in four main parts, which may be summarized as follows:

I. To secure the cessation of hostilities, the party urges our government to call a conference of neutral nations, or failing to secure such an official conference, the party itself will call an unofficial conference of pacifists from the world over.

II. To insure such terms of settlement as will prevent this war from being but the prelude to new wars: no province should be transferred against the will of its people; no indemnities assessed save when recognized international law has been violated; no treaty or international arrangement of any sort should be entered upon unless ratified by representatives of the people.

III. To place the peace of the world on securer foundations: foreign policies should not be aimed at creating alliances to maintain the "balance of power" but to establish a "concert of nations," with courts for the settlement of all disputes, an international congress possessed of legislative and administrative powers over international affairs and an international police force; the first step in this direction should be a permanent league of neutral nations, or league of peace; the league of peace and national disarmament should be effected as soon as this peace program is subscribed to by nations of sufficient power to insure protection to those disarmed; pending general disarmament all manufactures of war material should be national property; neutralization of the sea with complete protection of private property at sea; national and international action to remove the economic causes of war; and "the democracies of the world should be extended and re-enforced by general application of the principle of self-government including the extension of suffrage to women."

IV. As an immediate national program: the organization approves the peace treaties negotiated by the United States with thirty nations, stipulating delay and investigation for a year before war may be declared; protesting against increase of armament by the United States; and recommends to the President that he create a commission, with adequate appropriation, "to work for the prevention of war and the formulation of the most compelling and practical methods of world organization."

The conference further adopted the following resolution:

Resolved: That we denounce with all the earnestness of which we are capable the concerted attempt now being made to force this country into still further preparedness for war. We desire to make a solemn appeal to the higher attributes of our common humanity to help us unmask this menace to our civilization.

A committee on plan of action, whose report was adopted, recom-

mended the formation of a national legislative committee and local
legislative committee, the endorsement of the Crosser bill, the pre-
sentation of the embassies of the program, and the sending abroad
of a commission on the effects of war on women.

It further recommended the holding of mass meetings throughout
the country, preferably simultaneously, to arouse interest in the program. It suggested the promotion of a peace propaganda through
existing organizations, especially women's organizations, and in the
public schools. It adopted a plan of cooperation both with the press
and with artists as a means to adequate publicity.

Crystal Eastman
NOW WE CAN BEGIN

*In 1920 radical feminists looked to the future. While the suffragists applauded
the passage of the Nineteenth Amendment and organized the League of
Women Voters in order to educate women to use the vote wisely, a few
thoughtful feminists considered their future course. Crystal Eastman was
one of them. What does Crystal Eastman think the primary focus of a
feminist campaign should be? How pragmatic and realizable is her program?
Why is economic independence so important to Miss Eastman's view of
feminism? What does she say about the psychological and cultural freedom
of the woman?*

Most women will agree that August 23, the day when the Tennessee
legislature finally enacted the Federal suffrage amendment, is a day
to begin with, not a day to end with. Men are saying perhaps "Thank
God, this everlasting woman's fight is over!" But women, if I know
them, are saying, "Now at last we can begin." In fighting for the
right to vote most women have tried to be either non-committal or
thoroughly respectable on every other subject. Now they can say
what they are really after; and what they are after, in common with
all the rest of the struggling world, is *freedom*.

Freedom is a large word.

From *The Liberator*, Vol. 3 (December 1920), pp. 23–24.

Many feminists are socialists, many are communists, not a few are active leaders in these movements. But the true feminist, no matter how far to the left she may be in the revolutionary movement, sees the woman's battle as distinct in its objects and different in its methods from the workers' battle for industrial freedom. She knows, of course, that the vast majority of women as well as men are without property, and are of necessity bread and butter slaves under a system of society which allows the very sources of life to be privately owned by a few, and she counts herself a loyal soldier in the working-class army that is marching to overthrow that system. But as a feminist she also knows that the whole of woman's slavery is not summed up in the profit system, nor her complete emancipation assured by the downfall of capitalism.

Woman's freedom, in the feminist sense, can be fought for and conceivably won before the gates open into industrial democracy. On the other hand, woman's freedom, in the feminist sense, is not inherent in the communist ideal. All feminists are familiar with the revolutionary leader who "can't see" the woman's movement. "What's the matter with the women? My wife's all right," he says. And his wife, one usually finds, is raising his children in a Bronx flat or a dreary suburb, to which he returns occasionally for food and sleep when all possible excitement and stimulus have been wrung from the fight. If we should graduate into communism tomorrow this man's attitude to his wife would not be changed. The proletarian dictatorship may or may not free women. We must begin now to enlighten the future dictators.

What, then, is "the matter with women"? What is the problem of women's freedom? It seems to me to be this: how to arrange the world so that women can be human beings, with a chance to exercise their infinitely varied gifts in infinitely varied ways, instead of being destined by the accident of their sex to one field of activity—housework and child-raising. And second, if and when they choose housework and child-raising, to have that occupation recognized by the world as work, requiring a definite economic reward and not merely entitling the performer to be dependent on some man.

This is not the whole of feminism, of course, but it is enough to begin with. "Oh, don't begin with economics," my friends often protest, "Woman does not live by bread alone. What she needs first of all is a free soul." And I can agree that women will never be great until they achieve a certain emotional freedom, a strong healthy egotism, and some un-personal sources of joy—that in this inner sense we cannot make woman free by changing her economic status. What we can do, however, is to create conditions of outward freedom in which a free woman's soul can be born and grow. It is these outward conditions with which an organized feminist movement must concern itself.

Freedom of choice in occupation and individual economic independence for women: How shall we approach this next feminist objective? First, by breaking down all remaining barriers, actual as well as legal, which make it difficult for women to enter or succeed in the various professions, to go into and get on in business, to learn trades and practice them, to join trades unions. Chief among these remaining barriers is inequality in pay. Here the ground is already broken. This is the easiest part of our program.

Second, we must institute a revolution in the early training and education of both boys and girls. It must be womanly as well as manly to earn your own living, to stand on your own feet. And it must be manly as well as womanly to know how to cook and sew and clean and take care of yourself in the ordinary exigencies of life. I need not add that the second part of this revolution will be more passionately resisted than the first. Men will not give up their privilege of helplessness without a struggle. The average man has a carefully cultivated ignorance about household matters—from what to do with the crumbs to the grocer's telephone number—a sort of cheerful inefficiency which protects him better than the reputation for having a violent temper. It was his mother's fault in the beginning, but even as a boy he was quick to see how a general reputation for being "no good around the house" would serve him throughout life, and half-consciously he began to cultivate that helplessness until today it is the despair of feminist wives.

A growing number of men admire the woman who has a job, and, especially since the cost of living doubled, rather like the idea of their own wives contributing to the family income by outside work. And of course for generations there have been whole towns full of wives who are forced by the bitterest necessity to spend the same hours at the factory that their husbands spend. But these bread-winning wives have not yet developed homemaking husbands. When the two come home from the factory the man sits down while his wife gets supper, and he does so with exactly the same sense of fore-ordained right as if he were "supporting her." Higher up in the economic scale the same thing is true. The business or professional woman who is married, perhaps engages a cook, but the responsibility is not shifted, it is still hers. She "hires and fires," she orders meals, she does the buying, she meets and resolves all domestic crises, she takes charge of moving, furnishing, settling. She may be, like her husband, a busy executive at her office all day, but unlike him, she is also an executive in a small way every night and morning at home. Her noon hour is spent in planning, and too often her Sundays and holidays are spent in "catching up."

Two business women can "make a home" together without either one being over-burdened or over-bored. It is because they both know how and both feel responsible. But it is a rare man who can marry one of them and continue the homemaking partnership. Yet if there are no children, there is nothing essentially different in the combination. Two self-supporting adults decide to make a home together: if both are women it is a pleasant partnership, more fun than work; if one is a man, it is almost never a partnership—the woman simply adds running the home to her regular outside job. Unless she is very strong, it is too much for her, she gets tired and bitter over it, and finally perhaps gives up her outside work and condemns herself to the tiresome half-job of housekeeping for two.

Cooperative schemes and electrical devices will simplify the business of homemaking, but they will not get rid of it entirely. As far as we can see ahead people will always want homes, and a happy home cannot be had without a certain amount of rather monotonous work and responsibility. How can we change the nature of man so that he will honorably share that work and responsibility and thus make the homemaking enterprise a song instead of a burden? Most assuredly not by laws or revolutionary decrees. Perhaps we must cultivate or simulate a little of that highly prized helplessness ourselves. But fundamentally it is a problem of education, of early training—we must bring up feminist sons.

Sons? Daughters? They are born of women—how can women be free to choose their occupation, at all times cherishing their economic independence, unless they stop having children? This is a further question for feminism. If the feminist program goes to pieces on the arrival of the first baby, it is false and useless. For ninety-nine out of every hundred women want children, and seventy-five out of every hundred want to take care of their own children, or at any rate so closely superintend their care as to make any other full-time occupation impossible for at least ten or fifteen years. Is there any such thing then as freedom of choice in occupation for women? And is not the family the inevitable economic unit and woman's individual economic independence, at least during that period, out of the question?

The feminist must have an answer to these questions, and she has. The immediate feminist program must include voluntary motherhood. Freedom of any kind for women is hardly worth considering unless it is assumed that they will know how to control the size of their families. "Birth control" is just as elementary an essential in our propaganda as "equal pay." Women are to have children when they want them, that's the first thing. That ensures some freedom of occupational choice; those who do not wish to be mothers will not have an undesired occupation thrust upon them by accident, and those who do wish to be mothers may choose in a general way how many years of their lives they will devote to the occupation of child-raising.

But is there any way of insuring a woman's economic independence while child-raising is her chosen occupation? Or must she sink into that dependent state from which, as we all know, it is so hard to rise again? That brings us to the fourth feature of our program—motherhood endowment. It seems that the only way we can keep mothers free, at least in a capitalist society, is by the establishment of a principle that the occupation of raising children is peculiarly and directly a service to society, and that the mother upon whom the necessity and privilege of performing this service naturally falls is entitled to an adequate economic reward from the political government. It is idle to talk of real economic independence for women unless this principle is accepted. But with a generous endowment of motherhood provided by legislation, with all laws against voluntary motherhood and education in its methods repealed, with the feminist ideal of education accepted in home and school, and with all special barriers removed in every field of human activity, there is no reason why woman should not become almost a human thing.

It will be time enough then to consider whether she has a soul.

III FEMINISM IN THE 1960's

Betty Friedan's The Feminine Mystique *(1963) is often viewed as the opening cry in the 1960's feminist battle. Mrs. Friedan's attack upon male publishers in the women's magazine business and her conspiratorial view of how domesticity was foisted upon an unsuspecting female population after World War II may sound overdone and underdocumented to some, but it raised the issue of the woman's role in a decade that had seemingly considered her already free. American men considered their wives independent, or so they said. And American women had also considered their increased affluence, their comfortable home in the suburbs with all of its time-saving devices, and the freedom to play bridge, to smoke, and to drink, as the evidences of freedom. American women were better educated and more of them were working than ever before. So what was Mrs. Friedan's complaint? After studying her generation of Vassar graduates, she found that unhappiness, a rising divorce rate, and a rising alcoholism rate marred the public relations image of the contented and emancipated American woman.*

Mrs. Friedan's book, however, did not begin a major revolt or a profound reexamination of the role of women in American society. Rather, the organization she formed in 1967, NOW (National Organization for Women) concentrated upon lobbying activities in Congress for child-care centers and Social Security provisions for mothers. The revolt, rather, began by the generation of young women who would be the age of the daughters of the 1948 Vassar graduates. These girls came to women's liberation, not from a reading of The Feminine Mystique, *but often from a stint in radical student groups. They rediscovered the relationship between other social problems and the position of women that the nineteenth-century feminists had understood.*

The Revival of Feminism

Brigid Brophy

WOMEN ARE PRISONERS OF THEIR SEX

In the same year that Betty Friedan published The Feminine Mystique *(1963), Brigid Brophy, a novelist and essayist, wrote an article for the staid* Saturday Evening Post *that captured the contemporary feminist's major complaint. In what ways does Miss Brophy begin the argument where Crystal Eastman left it off in 1920? What new awareness does she display? Why is the focus on psychology rather than law?*

All right, nobody's disputing it. Women are free. At least, they *look* free. They even feel free. But in reality women in the western, industrialized world today are like the animals in a modern zoo. There are no bars. It appears that cages have been abolished. Yet in practice women are still kept in their place just as firmly as the animals are kept in their enclosures. The barriers which keep them in now are invisible.

It is about 40 years since the pioneer feminists raised such a rumpus by rattling the cage bars that society was at last obliged to pay attention. The result was that the bars were uprooted, the cage thrown open: whereupon the majority of the women who had been held captive decided that they would rather stay inside the cage anyway.

To be more precise, they *thought* they decided; and society, which can with perfect truth point out, "Look, no bars," *thought* it was giving them the choice. There are no laws and very little discrimination to prevent western, industrialized women from voting, being voted for or entering the professions. If there are still few women lawyers and engineers, let alone women Presidents of the United States, what are women to conclude except that this is the result

From the *Saturday Evening Post,* November 2, 1963, pp. 10, 12. Reprinted with special permission of the *Saturday Evening Post* © 1963 The Curtis Publishing Company.

either of their own free choice or of something inherent in female nature?

Many of them do draw just this conclusion. They have come back to the old argument of the antifeminists that women are unfit by nature for life outside the cage. And in letting this old wheel come full cycle, women have fallen victim to one of the most insidious and ingenious confidence tricks ever perpetrated.

In point of fact, neither female nature nor women's individual free choice has been put to the test. As American Negroes have discovered, to be officially free is by no means the same as being actually and psychologically free. A society as adept at propaganda as ours has become should know that "persuasion," which means the art of launching myths and artificially inducing inhibitions, is every bit as effective as force of law. No doubt the reason society eventually agreed to abolish its anti-women laws was that it had become confident of a commanding battery of hidden dissuaders which would do the job just as well. Cage bars are clumsy methods of control, which excite the more rebellious personalities inside to rattle them. Modern society, like the modern zoo, has contrived to get rid of the bars without altering the fact of imprisonment. All the zoo architect needs to do is run a zone of hot or cold air, whichever the animal concerned cannot tolerate, round the cage where the bars used to be. Human animals are not less sensitive to social climate.

The ingenious point about the new-model zoo is that it deceives both sides of the invisible barrier. Not only cannot the animal see how it is imprisoned; the visitor's conscience is relieved of the unkindness of keeping animals shut up. He can say, "Look, no bars round the animals," just as society can say, "Look, no laws restricting women," even while it keeps women rigidly in place by zones of fierce social pressure.

There is, however, one great difference. A woman, being a thinking animal, may actually be more distressed because the bars of her cage cannot be seen. What relieves society's conscience may afflict hers. Unable to perceive what is holding her back, she may accuse herself and her whole sex of craven timidity because women have not jumped at what has the appearance of an offer of freedom. Evidently quite a lot of women have succumbed to guilt of this sort, since in recent years quite an industry has arisen to assuage it.

Comforting voices make the air as thick and reassuring as cotton wool while they explain that there is nothing shameful in not wanting a career, that to be intellectually unadventurous is no sin, that taking care of home and family may be personally "fulfilling" for a woman and socially valuable.

This is an argument without a flaw—except that it is addressed exclusively to women. Address it to both sexes and instantly it becomes progressive and humane. As it stands, it is merely anti-woman prejudice revamped.

That many women would be happier not pursuing careers or intellectual adventures is only part of the truth. The whole truth is that many people would be. If society had the clear sight to assure men as well as women that there is no shame in preferring to stay non-competitively and nonaggressively at home, many masculine neuroses and ulcers would be avoided, and many children would enjoy the benefit of being brought up by a father with a talent for the job of child-rearing instead of a mother with no talent for it but a sense of guilt about the lack.

But society does nothing so sensible. Blindly it goes on insisting on the tradition that men are the ones who go out to work and adventure—an arrangement which simply throws talent away. All the homemaking talent born inside male bodies is wasted; and our businesses and governments are staffed largely by people whose aptitude for the work consists solely of their being what is, by tradition, the right sex for it.

The pressures society exerts to drive men out of the house are very nearly as irrational and unjust as those by which it keeps women in. The mistake of the early reformers was to assume that men were emancipated already and that therefore reform need ask only for the emancipation of women. What we ought to do now is go right back to scratch and demand the emancipation of both sexes.

The zones of hot and cold air which society uses to perpetuate its uneconomic and unreasonable state of affairs are the simplest and most effective conceivable. Society is playing on our sexual vanity. Tell a man that he is not a real man, or a woman that she is not 100 percent woman, and you are threatening both with not being attractive to the opposite sex. No one can bear not to be attractive to the opposite sex. That is the climate which the human animal cannot tolerate.

So society has us all at its mercy. It has only to murmur to the man that staying home is a feminine characteristic, and he will be out of the house like a bullet. It has only to suggest to the woman that logic and reason are the exclusive province of the masculine mind, whereas "intuition" and "feeling" are the female forte, and she will throw her physics textbooks out of the window, barricade herself into the house and give herself up to having wishy-washy poetical feelings while she arranges the flowers.

She will, incidentally, take care that her feelings *are* wishy-washy. She has been persuaded that to have cogent feelings, of the kind which really do go into great poems—most of which are by men—would make her an unfeminine woman, a woman who imitates men. In point of fact, she would not be imitating men as such, most of whom have never written a line of great poetry, but poets, most of whom so far happen to be men. But the bad logic passes muster with a woman because part of the mythology she has swallowed ingeniously informs her that logic is not her forte.

Should a woman's talent or intelligence be so irrepressible that she insists on producing cogent works of art or water-tight meshes of argument, she will be said to have "a mind like a man's."

What is more, this habit of thought actually contributes to perpetuating a state of affairs where most good minds really do belong to men. It is difficult for a woman to want to be intelligent when she has been told that to be so will make her like a man. She inclines to think an intelligence would be as unbecoming to her as a moustache; and, pathetically, many women have tried in furtive privacy to disembarrass themselves of intellect as though it were facial hair.

Discouraged from growing "a mind like a man's," women are encouraged to have thoughts and feelings of a specifically feminine tone. Women, it is said, have some specifically feminine contribution to make to culture. Unfortunately, as culture had already been shaped and largely built up by men before the invitation was issued, this leaves women little to do. Culture consists of reasoned thought and works of art composed of cogent feeling and imagination. There is only one way to be reasonable, and that is to reason correctly; and the only kind of art which is any good is good art. If women are to eschew reason and artistic imagination in favor of "intuition" and "feeling," it is pretty clear what is meant. "Intuition" is just a polite name for bad reasoning, and "feeling" for bad art.

In reality, the whole idea of a specifically feminine—or, for the matter of that, masculine—contribution to culture is a contradiction of culture. A contribution to culture is not something which could not have been made by the other sex; it is something which could not have been made by any other *person*. The arts are a sphere where women seem to have done well; but really they have done too well—too well for the good of the arts. Rather than women sharing the esteem which ought to belong to artists, art is becoming smeared with femininity. We are approaching a Philistine state of affairs where the arts are something which it is nice for women to take up in their spare time—men having slammed out of the house to get on with society's "serious" business, like making money, running the country and the professions.

In that "serious" sphere it is still rare to encounter a woman. A man sentenced to prison would probably feel his punishment was redoubled by indignity if he were to be sentenced by a woman judge under a law drafted by a woman legislator—and if, on admission, he were to be examined by a woman prison doctor. If such a thing happened every day, it would be no indignity but the natural course of events. It has never been given the chance to become the natural course of events and never will be so long as women remain persuaded it would be unnatural of them to want it.

So brilliantly has society contrived to terrorize women with this threat that certain behavior is unnatural and unwomanly, that it has left them no time to consider—or even sheerly observe—what womanly nature really is. For centuries arrant superstitions were accepted as natural law. The physiological fact that only women can secrete milk for feeding babies was extended into the pure myth that it was women's business to cook for and wait on the entire family. The kitchen became woman's "natural" place because, for the first few months of her baby's life, the nursery really was. To this day a woman may fear she is unfeminine if she can discover in herself no aptitude or liking for cooking. Fright has thrown her into such a muddle that she confuses having no taste for cookery with having no breasts, and conversely assumes that nature has unfailingly endowed the human female with a special handiness with frying pans.

Even psychoanalysis, which in general has been the greatest benefactor of civilization since the wheel, has unwittingly reinforced the terrorization campaign. The trouble was that it brought with it from its origin in medical therapy a criterion of normality instead of rationality. On sheer statistics every pioneer, genius and social reformer, including the first woman who demanded to be let out of the kitchen and into the polling booth, is abnormal, along with every lunatic and eccentric. What distinguishes the genius from the lunatic is that the genius's abnormality is justifiable by reason or aesthetics. If a woman who is irked by confinement to the kitchen merely looks around to see what other women are doing and finds they are accepting their kitchens, she may well conclude that she is abnormal and had better enlist her psychoanalyst's help toward "living with" her kitchen. What she ought to ask is whether it is rational for women to be kept to the kitchen, and whether nature really does insist on that in the way it insists women have breasts.

And in a far-reaching sense to ask that question is much more normal and natural than learning to "live with" the handicap of women's inferior social status. The normal and natural thing for human beings is not to tolerate handicaps but to reform society and to circumvent or supplement nature. We don't learn to live minus a leg; we devise an artificial limb.

That, indeed, is the crux of the matter. Not only are the distinctions we draw between male nature and female nature largely arbitrary and often pure superstition, they are completely beside the point. They ignore the essence of *human* nature. The important question is not whether women are or are not less logical by nature than men, but whether education, effort and the abolition of our illogical social pressures can improve on nature and make them— and, incidentally, men as well—more logical. What distinguishes human from any other animal nature is its ability to be unnatural. Logic and art are not natural or instinctive activities; but our nature includes a propensity to acquire them. It is not natural for the human body to orbit the earth; but the human mind has a natural adventurousness which enables it to invent machines whereby the body can do so.

Civilization consists not necessarily in defying nature but in making it possible for us to do so if we judge it desirable. The higher we can lift our noses from the grindstone of nature, the wider the area we have of choice; and the more choices we have freely made, the more individualized we are. We are at our most civilized when nature does not dictate to us, as it does to animals and peasants, but when we can opt to fall in with it or better it. If modern civilization has invented methods of preparing baby foods and methods of education which make it possible for men to feed babies and for women to think logically, we are betraying civilization itself if we do not set both sexes free to make a free choice.

Paula Stern
THE WOMANLY IMAGE

Paula Stern, a free-lance writer who has done graduate study in international relations at the Fletcher School of Law and Diplomacy, extends the feminist argument in modern terms. What is her view of the Freudian contribution to the womanly image? What role do child-raising practices play in determining women's roles? What part do the popular media play in stereotyping the female sex?

I had a job interview several weeks ago. Friends warned me not to be too aggressive. During the interview, I tried to present myself as a competent candidate, able to "think like a man" and yet not to be a "masculine" female. After fielding several questions relevant to the job, I suddenly heard, "Miss Stern, are you in love?"

Do you think they asked my competition—seven men—the same question? No, for a cultureful of reasons. Jacqueline Kennedy Onassis was quoted once as saying, "There are two kinds of women:

those who want power in the world and those who want power in bed." And the majority seem to agree with Jackie that the latter is socially more acceptable. That's how many women in America have been taught to think. And that's how many men think women ought to think.

Children are taught sexual stereotypes early, as well as the appropriate behavior for a sex-determined role in life. Asking a little boy, "What do you want to be when you grow up?" implies to him unlimited possibilities in his future. But most often we ask a little girl, "Where did you get that pretty dress?" suggesting she has only one real option open to her. If we do ask her what she wants to be, she's likely to give the conditioned female response—"A mother." Why? So she can replace her dolls with real babies.

The inspiration for teaching girls to expect less than boys comes from a range of cultural sources, religious, literary, psychiatric, and pop. Even in the Bible, exceptional, independent women like Rebecca, Sarah, Deborah, or Ruth are practically "unknowns" compared with infamous Eve or Delilah.

Eve was made from one of Adam's spare parts, almost as an afterthought, to help him out on earth: "And the Lord God said: 'It is not good that the man should be alone; I will make him a helpmeet for him.'"

There is a contrary legend of the first female, Lilith, who was created equal to man.

> When the Lord created the world and the first man, he saw that man was alone, and quickly created a woman for him, made like him from the earth, and her name was Lilith. Right away, they began to quarrel. He would say "You sleep on the bottom," and she would say "No, you sleep on the bottom, since we are equals and both formed from the earth. . . ." When Lilith saw what the situation was, she pronounced the Ineffable Name and disappeared into thin air.

But Eve, not Lilith, is the prototypal woman—man's little helper, and his temptress.

Today the heirs to the Bible in America—Jews and Christians— have formalized biblical biases in laws and ceremonies and thereby elevated folklore to religious truths. Among the Orthodox Jews, for example, discrimination against women is so blatant that they are forced to sit segregated behind a curtain or in a balcony. The rationale is that women will distract men from their prayers. It is no wonder that men thank God every morning in their ritual prayer "that Thou has not made me a woman."

The majority of Jews have modified most traditional formalities, but independent female expression is still discouraged if outside the confines of the home or not channeled through husband and children.

A Jewish wife is less subservient to her husband than a gentile wife; so say comparative studies on the subject. That's somewhat understandable since Christianity owes much to a prominent classical heritage, that held the second sex in even lower esteem. Utopia for the male chauvinist is Demosthenes' description of Hellenic male-female arrangements: "We have hetairae for the pleasure of the spirit, concubines for sensual pleasure, and wives to bear our sons."

Aristotle's definition of femininity was "a certain lack of qualities; we should regard the female nature as afflicted with a natural defectiveness." And his disciple Saint Thomas Aquinas echoed him religiously: ". . . a female is something deficient and by chance."

Contempt for women helps explain why they can't become Catholic priests, and why theologians, religious education courses, and Catholic marriage manuals highlight the supposedly inferior and passive qualities of women, who "naturally" subordinate themselves to men.

Traditional Protestant marriage services also perpetuate the attitude that the female is a second-class human being. Like a piece of property, the bride is "given" by her father to the groom, whom she promises to "obey." (Although formally removed from the liturgy, this vow still persists in the popular image of the wedding ceremony.) The clergyman reminds her of her proper place when he says, "I pronounce that they are man and wife." Not husband and wife. Not man and woman. The man keeps his status, while she takes on a new one. Her identity vanishes when she sheds her maiden name for his identification. (Blackstone's *Commentaries* on the law strips a married woman of her rights altogether as she legally dies on her wedding day and becomes "incorporated and consolidate with her husband." Accordingly, "A man cannot grant anything to his wife for the grant would be to suppose her separate existence.")

Although reputedly "progressing" beyond the attitudes of antiquity and the Middle Ages, our enlightened European ancestors continued furnishing us some not too enlightened guidelines on a woman's place—or lack of it—in the world.

High school English students learn from Shakespeare that "Frailty, thy name is woman." Rousseau's contribution to the ideas of man's equality and natural goodness makes one exception: "Woman was made to yield to man and put up with his injustice."

Samuel Johnson's word to the wise woman is that "a man is in general better pleased when he has a good dinner upon his table, than when his wife talks Greek." Honoré de Balzac adds, "A woman who is guided by the head and not the heart is a social pestilence: she has all the defects of a passionate and affectionate woman with none of her compensations: she is without pity, without love, without virtue, without sex."

When in 1776 in America, Abigail Adams asked her husband, John Adams, to "be more generous and favorable to them [women] than your ancestors" and to see to it that the new government not "put such unlimited power into the hands of the husbands," John reportedly chuckled. The Continental Congress ignored her. Two hundred years later Spiro Agnew said: "Three things have been difficult to tame—the ocean, fools, and women. We may soon be able to tame the ocean; fools and women will take a little longer."

America's twentieth-century gospel is the work of Freud. Although Freud supposedly has altered the entire course of Western intellectual history, many of his ideas about women are simply male chauvinism. Letters he wrote his fiancée reveal that he, too, wanted his woman kept relatively docile and ignorant so she couldn't compete with him.

His theories have given scientific status to prejudice. The Freudians—psychiatrists, clinical psychologists, psychiatric social workers, marriage counselors, pastoral counselors, educators, writers, literary critics, historians, anthropologists, sociologists, criminologists, and just plain subway psychiatrists in the newspapers, magazines, and on TV—all subscribe to the belief that "anatomy is destiny." In other words, biological differences between the sexes determine personality differences; standards of mental health depend on the sex of the sick.

How? Dr. Judd Marmor, clinical professor of psychiatry at UCLA, has summarized Freud's views on feminine psychology:

> *The most significant of the biological factors . . . is the lack of the penis, which inevitably leads to "penis envy" in the woman. Freud considered penis envy to be a dominant theme in all feminine life, and one that inevitably causes women to feel inferior to men. These deep-seated feelings of inadequacy can be compensated for only partially by giving birth to a male child. . . .*
>
> *Masochism and passivity . . . are natural aspects of normal femininity and whenever a woman behaves in non-passive or aggressive ways or competes with men, she is being neurotically unfeminine. . . .*
>
> *The most complicated sequence of personality development that women are subject to . . . leads inevitably . . . to less adequate superego formation than in men. This presumably is reflected in women having a poorer sense of justice and weaker social interests than men have.*

The myths of marriage counselor G. C. Payetter (from his book *How To Get and Hold a Woman*) have been praised by a number of psychiatrists, and he is consulted in earnest by troubled people. Payetter counsels:

> *Feelings, moods, and attitude . . . rule a woman, not facts, reason, nor logic.*
>
> *By herself woman is all mixed-up but superb as an auxiliary (Genesis: helper).*
>
> *Woman is inanimate or on the defensive until you create a feeling such as a praise. Then she goes all out.*
>
> *Never scold or explain when she is angry, remember she is feeling not thinking. . . .*
>
> *Stop bossing; just manipulate her in her feelings. . . .*
>
> *The acquisition of knowledge or responsibilities does not lessen women's need for support, guidance, and control. Quite the contrary.*
>
> *Why ask women when they only need to be told? Why ask women when they hope to be taken?*

Any resemblance between women and pet dogs or mute concubines is purely coincidental. No doubt, Payetter's model woman is the runner-up to this year's Miss America, who said women shouldn't try to run things "because they are more emotional and men can overcome their emotions with logic."

Even more objectionable are psychiatrist-authors who pronounce final judgment on the mental health of thousands of women reading books like *The Power of Sexual Surrender*. Featured in the book, which has had at least ten paperback printings and been excerpted in *Pageant* magazine, is "The Masculine Woman." (Doctor, how can a woman be a female and be masculine simultaneously?) She's "frigid"—"a driving, competitive woman who was very successful in the business world, having graduated from a leading woman's college." "Clear thinking and logical mind, her emotionless almost masculine forthrightness in expressing herself belied her softly feminine appearance." Surrendering to her "real nature," the doctor's cure, is the only way she can be mentally healthy. Then miraculously

> . . . those details of life that once seemed so difficult become simple.
> And because they are feminine tasks, household work, planning and
> getting dinners, keeping the children busy or in line—whatever life de-
> mands—soon lose their irksome and irritating quality and become easy,
> even joyful. . . . At this juncture, or closely following on it, a woman
> begins to feel her full power; the power that comes to her for her
> surrender to her destiny.

The spuriously Freudian vision of a truly "feminine" female serves the purposes of admen who woo women to spend millions on clothes and cosmetics in vain pursuit of their "real nature." To sell a new product, industry need only simultaneously make the product and manufacture anxiety in gals, pressing them to consume or be consumed in a female identity crisis. For example, featured in every women's magazine, including those for teen-agers, are the latest advertising campaigns for vaginal deodorants, a "female necessity." One called Cupid's Quiver comes in four flavors—Orange Blossom, Raspberry, Champagne, or Jasmine. Madison Avenue courts the female, even seducing minors. Teenform, Inc., manufacturers of bras for teen-agers, estimates that nine-year-olds spend $2 million on bras annually.

Ingenue magazine pushes teen-agers into adult posturing. The format is peppered with advertisements for engagement rings, pictures of desirable adolescent boys, and occasionally a plan of attack such as dinners for two. The ads for cosmetics and clothes are practically identical to those in magazines designed for their mothers. Typical of women's magazines, *Ingenue* includes at least one psychologically centered article. Recently, it explained in "The Hardest Thing About Growing Up" that "inevitably, relationships with boys affect relationships with girls." It condoned the statement, "I don't trust other girls in the same way anymore. They become rivals." This is how girls learn the platitudes: women can't work with other women when men are around, and never work for a woman.

If a girl manages to survive *Ingenue* without succumbing to marriage, *Glamour* picks her up. ("How Five Groovy Men Would Make You Over Into Their Dream Girls") Where the boys are is where it's at for the reader who is shunted from high school to college to career to marriage to motherhood—"Find Your New Look. College Into Career Make-over. Job Into Mother Make-over."

The lucky gal who's made the grade by landing a man is promoted to *Modern Bride,* which induces her to buy "utterly feminine" wedding gowns, bride-and-groom matching wedding rings, silver, china, furniture, ad nauseam. The wedding itself is big business; Wediquette International, Inc., offers total planning—the place, time, invitations, gown, caterers, florist, photographer . . . .

Ah, then conjugal bliss—and of course, a magazine for mothers. *Redbook* boasts its biggest year because it knows "Young Mamas Spend More Than Big Daddies" and so talks "to that 18–34 year old the way she wants to be talked to," which means in baby talk or kitchen chatter.

McCall's claims 16 million matrons who "buy more than the readers of any other woman's service magazine." Its reader "buys more cosmetics and toiletries, more prepared foods, owns more life insurance, more automobiles . . . ."

Although *Cosmopolitan* says its reader is the career woman who desires success in her own right, it is pitched to the gal who missed the marriage boat the first time around. Female passivity is still the accepted mode of behavior. She can be assertive in the office, but when man-hunting after five, she must be seductively submissive. Who knows? She might hook a divorced man or married man looking for an affair.

Cosmo repeats an old tip from Jackie and Delilah—sex is a woman's hidden arsenal. Under a pseudonym, "a well-known American gynecologist" instructs readers "How to Love Like a Real Woman." "If your man bawls at you and you know you are in the right, what should you do?" "You should take your clothes off. Sex is a woman's strongest weapon. It is her proper weapon."

Taking a cue from *The Power of Sexual Surrender,* the expert explains, "Women must give and give and give again because it is their one and only way to obtain happiness for themselves." Further, "To argue is a male activity. To fight is a male activity. I say to women: 'Don't become a man in skirts. Don't fight. Don't argue. . . .'" Any female who would practice this advice must be masochistic —typical of a "normal" female, according to Freudian thought.

A popular misconception is that in time education will erase all the ill effects of thinking in stereotypes. But the educational system takes over where cultural myths, Freudian folklore, and the media leave off in depressing a girl's aspirations and motivations. All along, she's taught to accept a double standard for success and self-esteem: It's marriage and motherhood for girls, while it's education and career for boys. She's pushed to be popular, date, and marry young (more than half of all American women are married before the age of twenty-one). Success in school only inhibits her social life. Intellectual striving, a necessity for academic success, is considered competitively aggressive; that is unnatural and unladylike behavior, since the essence of femininity, she has learned, is repressing aggressiveness. Telling her she thinks like a man is a backhanded compliment, which is discouraging if she has tried to be a woman using her brains, not sex, in the classroom and office.

While girls outperform boys intellectually in prepuberty, attrition in IQ sets in during adolescence when they learn from new, extracurricular lessons that looks, not brains, are what counts. After high school, achievement in terms of productivity and accomplishment drops off even more. More than 75 percent (some say as high as 95 percent) of all qualified high-schoolers not entering college are girls. Those who go attend more for husband-hunting than for educational self-advancement; one study at a Midwestern university revealed 70 percent of the freshmen women were there for an MRS. Women BA's are less than half as likely to try for a graduate degree as equally qualified men.

Women should not be given an even break in education and

careers, says a clichéd argument, because they will get married and quit anyway. But that's because they are given an arbitrary, unfair option which men aren't forced to accept—either career or marriage. Career opportunities and salary levels for women are so poor that a calculating female would figure marriage is a better bargain. Once married, she can stop fighting the stereotypes and start teaching them to her children.

Alice S. Rossi

EQUALITY BETWEEN THE SEXES: AN IMMODEST PROPOSAL

Alice S. Rossi, an associate professor of sociology, is an experienced campaigner for women's rights. She was an active and early supporter of the National Organization for Women (NOW) and has written extensively on discrimination against women, especially in academia. What is Alice Rossi's view of psychological and sociological teachings of the last thirty years? What kind of evidence does she present to refute the view that a woman cannot have both a career and a home? How do the various institutions in our society (home, school, job) need reconstructing to achieve a status of sex equality?

> . . . *the principle which regulates the existing relations between the two sexes . . . is wrong in itself and [is] now the chief hindrance to human improvement; and . . . it ought to be replaced by a principle of perfect equality, admitting no power or privilege on the one side, nor disability on the other.*
>
> *John Stuart Mill, 1869*

Introduction

When John Stuart Mill wrote his essay on "The Subjection of Women" in 1869, the two major things he argued for with elegance and persuasion were to extend the franchise to women, and to end

From *The Woman in America,* edited by Robert Jay Lifton, *Daedalus,* Vol. 93 (Spring 1964). Reprinted by permission of *Daedalus,* Journal of the American Academy of Arts and Sciences, Boston, Massachusetts.

the legal subordination of married women to their husbands. The movement for sex equality had already gathered considerable momentum in England and the United States by 1869, reaching its peak fifty years later, when the franchise was won by American women in 1920. In the decades since 1920, this momentum has gradually slackened, until by the 1960's American society has been losing rather than gaining ground in the growth toward sex equality. American women are not trying to extend their claim to equality from the political to the occupational and social arenas and often do not even seem interested in exercising the rights so bitterly won in the early decades of the twentieth century in politics and higher education. The constitutional amendment on equal rights for men and women has failed to pass Congress for seventeen consecutive years, and today a smaller proportion of college graduates are women than was true thirty years ago.

There is no overt antifeminism in our society in 1964, not because sex equality has been achieved, but because there is practically no feminist spark left among American women. When I ask the brightest of my women college students about their future study and work plans, they either have none because they are getting married in a few months, or they show clearly that they have lowered their aspirations from professional and research fields that excited them as freshmen, to concentrate as juniors on more practical fields far below their abilities. Young women seem increasingly uncommitted to anything beyond early marriage, motherhood and a suburban house. There are few Noras in contemporary American society because women have deluded themselves that the doll's house is large enough to find complete personal fulfillment within it.

It will be the major thesis of this essay that we need to reassert the claim to sex equality and to search for the means by which it can be achieved. By sex equality I mean a socially androgynous conception of the roles of men and women, in which they are equal and similar in such spheres as intellectual, artistic, political and occupational interests and participation, complementary only in those spheres dictated by physiological differences between the sexes. This assumes the traditional conceptions of masculine and feminine are inappropriate to the kind of world we can live in in the second half of the twentieth century. An androgynous conception of sex role means that each sex will cultivate some of the characteristics usually associated with the other in traditional sex role definitions. This means that tenderness and expressiveness should be cultivated in boys and socially approved in men, so that a male of any age in our society would be psychologically and socially free to express these qualities in his social relationships. It means that achievement need, workmanship and constructive aggression should be cultivated in girls and approved in women so that a female of any age would be similarly free to express these qualities in her social relationships. This is one of the points of contrast with the feminist goal of an earlier day: rather than a one-sided plea for women to adapt a masculine stance in the world, this definition of sex equality stresses the enlargement of the common ground on which men and women base their lives together by changing the social definitions of approved characteristics and behavior for both sexes.

It will be an assumption of this essay that by far the majority of the differences between the sexes which have been noted in social research are socially rather than physiologically determined. What proportion of these sex differences are physiologically based and what proportion are socially based is a question the social and physiological sciences cannot really answer at the present time. It is sufficient for my present purpose to note that the opportunities for social change toward a closer approximation of equality between the sexes are large enough within the area of sex differences now considered to be socially determined to constitute a challenging arena for thought and social action. This is my starting point. I shall leave to speculative discourse and future physiological research the question of what constitutes irreducible differences between the sexes.

There are three main questions I shall raise in this essay. Why was the momentum of the earlier feminist movement lost? Why should American society attempt to reach a state of sex equality as I have defined it above? What are the means by which equality between the sexes can be achieved?

Why Feminism Declined

I shall discuss three factors which have been major contributors to the waning of feminism. The chief goals of the early leaders of the feminist movement were to secure the vote for women and to change the laws affecting marriage so that women would have equal rights to property and to their own children. As in any social reform movement or social revolution, the focus in the first stage is on change in the legal code, whether this is to declare independence from a mother country, establish a constitution for a new nation, free the slaves, or secure the right of women to be equal citizens with men. But the social changes required to translate such law into the social fabric of a society are of a quite different order. Law by itself cannot achieve this goal. It is one thing to declare slaves free or to espouse a belief in racial equality; quite another matter to accept racial integration in all spheres of life, as many northern communities have learned in recent years. In a similar way, many people accept the legal changes which have reduced the inequality between men and women and espouse belief in sex equality, but resist its manifestation in their personal life. If a social movement rests content with legal changes without making as strong an effort to change the social institutions through which they are expressed, it will remain a hollow victory.

This is one of the things which occurred in the case of the feminist movement. Important as the franchise is, or the recent change in Civil Service regulations which prevents the personnel specification of "male only," the new law or regulation can be successful only to the extent that women exercise the franchise or are trained to be qualified for and to aspire for the jobs they are now permitted to hold. There is no sex equality until women participate on an equal basis with men in politics, occupations and the family. Law and administrative regulations must permit such participation, but women must want to participate and be able to participate in politics and the occupational world; to be able to participate depends primarily on whether home responsibilities can be managed simultaneously with work or political commitments. Since women have had, and probably will continue to have, primary responsibility for child-rearing, their participation in politics, professions or the arts cannot be equal to that of men unless ways are devised to ease the combination of home and work responsibilities. This is precisely what has not occurred; at the same time, since fewer women today choose a career over marriage, the result has been a reduction in women's representation in the more challenging and demanding occupations.

By itself, the stress on legal change to the neglect of institutional change in the accommodations between family and work does not go very far in explaining why the feminist movement has lost momentum. There is an important second factor which must be viewed in conjunction with this first one. The feminist movement has always been strongest when it was allied with other social reform movements. In the nineteenth century its linkage was with the antislavery movement, and in the early twentieth century it was allied to the social welfare movement. There is an interesting and a simple explanation of this: unlike any other type of social inequality, whether of race, class, religion or nationality, sex is the only instance in which representatives of the unequal groups live in more intimate association with each other than with members of their own group. A woman is more intimately associated with a man than she is with any woman. This was not the case for lord-serf, master-slave, Protestant-Roman Catholic, white-Negro relationships unless or until the social groups involved reach a full equality. By linking the feminist cause to the antislavery or social welfare movement, women were able to work together with men of similar sympathies and in the process they enlisted the support of these men for the feminist cause. To a greater extent than any other underprivileged group, women need not only vigorous spokesmen and pacesetters of their own sex, but the support of men, to effect any major change in the status of women, whether in the personal sphere of individual relationships or on the level of social organization. The decline of political radicalism and the general state of affluence and social conservatism in American society since World War II have contributed in subtle ways to the decline of feminism, for women are not joined with men in any movement affecting an underprivileged group in American society. At the present time, marriage remains the only major path of social mobility for women in our society.

The general conservatism of the total society has also penetrated the academic disciplines, with side effects on the motivation and ability of women to exercise the rights already theirs or to press for an extension of them. Feminism has been undermined by the conservatism of psychology and sociology in the postwar period. Sociologists studying the family have borrowed heavily from selective findings in social anthropology and from psychoanalytic theory and have pronounced sex to be a universally necessary basis for role differentiation in the family. By extension, in the larger society women are seen as predominantly fulfilling nurturant, expressive functions and men the instrumental, active functions. When this viewpoint is applied to American society, intellectually aggressive women or tender expressive men are seen as deviants showing signs of "role conflict," "role confusion," or neurotic disturbance. They are not seen as a promising indication of a desirable departure from traditional sex role definitions. In a similar way, the female sphere, the family, is viewed by social theorists as a passive, pawnlike institution, adapting to the requirements of the occupational, political or cultural segments of the social structure, seldom playing an active role either in affecting the nature of other social institutions or determining the nature of social change. The implicit assumption in problem after problem in sociology is that radical social innovations are risky and may have so many unintended consequences as to make it unwise to propose or support them. Although the sociologist describes and analyzes social change, it is change already accomplished, seldom anticipated purposive social change. When the changes are in process, they are defined as social problems, seldom as social opportunities.

Closely linked to this trend in sociology and social anthropology and in fact partly attributable to it, is the pervasive permeation of psychoanalytic thinking throughout American society. Individual psychoanalysts vary widely among themselves, but when their theories are popularized by social scientists, marriage and family counselors, writers, social critics, pediatricians and mental health specialists, there emerges a common and conservative image of the woman's role. It is the traditional image of woman which is popularized: the woman who finds complete self-fulfillment in her exclusive devotion to marriage and parenthood. Women who thirty years ago might have chosen a career over a marriage, or restricted their family size to facilitate the combination of family and work roles, have been persuaded to believe that such choices reflect their inadequacy as women. It is this sense of failure as a woman that lies behind the defensive and apologetic note of many older unmarried professional women, the guilt which troubles the working mother (which I suspect goes up in direct proportion to the degree to which she is familiar with psychoanalytic ideas), the restriction of the level of aspiration of college women, the early plunge into marriage, the closed door of the doll's house.

Our society has been so inundated with psychoanalytic thinking that any dissatisfaction or conflict in personal and family life is considered to require solution on an individual basis. This goes well with the general American value stress on individualism, and American women have increasingly restored to psychotherapy, the most highly individualized solution of all, for the answers to the problems they have as women. In the process the idea has been lost that many problems even in the personal family sphere, cannot be solved on an individual basis, but require solution on a societal level by changing the institutional contexts within which we live.

The consequences of this acceptance of psychoanalytic ideas and conservatism in the social sciences have been twofold: first, the social sciences in the United States have contributed very little since the 1930's to any lively intellectual dialogue on sex equality as a goal or the ways of implementing that goal. Second, they have provided a quasi-scientific underpinning to educators, marriage counselors, mass media and advertising researchers, who together have partly created, and certainly reinforced, the withdrawal of millions of young American women from the mainstream of thought and work in our society.

*   *   *

. . . What has not been seen is the more general point that *for the first time in the history of any known society, motherhood has become a full-time occupation for adult women.* In the past, whether a woman lived on a farm, a Dutch city in the seventeenth century, or a colonial town in the eighteenth century, women in all strata of society except the very top were never able to be full-time mothers as the twentieth-century middle-class American woman has become. These women were productive members of farm and craft teams along with their farmer, baker or printer husbands and other adult kin. Children either shared in the work of the household or were left to amuse themselves, their mothers did not have the time to organize their play, worry about their development, discuss their problems. These women were not lonely because the world came into their homes in the form of customers, clients or patients in villages and towns, or farmhands and relatives on the farm; such women had no reason to complain of the boredom and solitude of spending ten-hour days alone with babies and young children because their days were peopled with adults. There were no child specialists to tell the colonial merchant's wife or pioneer farmer's wife that her absorption in spinning, planting, churning and preserving left her children on their own too much, that how she fed her baby would shape his adult personality, or that leaving children with a variety of other adults while she worked would make them insecure.

There are two important questions this analysis raises: why has full-time motherhood been accepted by the overwhelming majority of American women, and how successful has been the new pattern of full-time motherhood of the past forty years or so? I believe the major answer to the first question is that the American woman has been encouraged by the experts to whom she has turned for guidance in child-rearing to believe that her children need her continuous presence, supervision and care and that she should find complete fulfillment in this role. If, for example, a woman reads an article by Dr. Spock on working mothers, she is informed that any woman who finds full-time motherhood produces nervousness is showing a "residue of difficult relationships in her own childhood"; if irritability and nervousness are not assuaged by a brief trip or two, she is probably in an emotional state which can be "relieved through regular counseling in a family social agency, or, if severe, through psychiatric treatment"; and finally, "any mother of a preschool child who is considering a job should discuss the issues with a social worker before making her decision." Since the social worker shares the same analytic framework that Dr. Spock does, there is little doubt what the advice will be; the woman is left with a judgment that wanting more than motherhood is not natural but a reflection of her individual emotional disturbance.

The fundamental tenet of the theory underlying such advice is that the physically and emotionally healthy development of the infant requires the loving involvement of the mother with the child. If an infant does not receive stable continuous mothering there is almost invariably severe physical and emotional disturbance. There is apparently ample clinical evidence to support these points. Studies

have suggested that prolonged separation from parents, and particularly from the mother, has serious effects upon infants and young
children. However, practitioners make unwarranted extrapolations
from these findings when they advise that *any* separation of mother
and child is risky and hazardous for the healthy development of the
child. Despite the fact that the empirical evidence stems from instances of prolonged, traumatic separation caused by such things as
the death or serious illness of the mother, or the institutionalization
of the child, this viewpoint is applied to the situation of an employed mother absent from the home on a regular basis. No one
predicts that any dire consequences will flow from a woman's
absence from home several afternoons a week to engage in a shop-
ping spree, keep medical appointments or play bridge; nor is a
father considered to produce severe disturbance in his young children even if his work schedule reduces contact with them to the
daylight hours of a weekend. But women who have consulted
pediatricians and family counselors about their resuming work are
firmly told that they should remain at home, for the sake of their
children's emotional health.

What effect *does* maternal employment have upon children?
Many sociologists of the family have raised this question during the
past fifteen years, expecting to find negative effects as psychoanalytic theory predicted. In fact, the focus of most maternal
employment studies has been on the effect of mothers' working
upon the personalities of their children, somewhat less often on the
tensions and strains between the mother role and the occupational
role, seldom on the question of how maternal employment affects
the woman's satisfactions with herself, her home and marriage. To
date, *there is no evidence of any negative effects traceable to
maternal employment;* children of working mothers are no more likely
than children of non-working mothers to become delinquent, to
show neurotic symptoms, to feel deprived of maternal affection, to
perform poorly in school, to lead narrower social lives, etc. Many
of the researchers in the 1950's frankly admitted surprise at their
negative findings. In a study reported in 1962, the only significant
difference found between working and non-working mothers was
the mother's confidence about her role as mother: 42 percent of
the working mothers but only 24 percent of the non-working mothers

expressed concern about their maternal role, "often by explicit questioning and worry as to whether working is interfering with their relationships and the rearing of their children." Yet these working women did not actually differ from the at-home mothers in the very things that concerned them: there were no differences between these women in the emotional relationships with their children, household allocation of responsibilities, principles of child-rearing, etc. The working mothers appeared to share the prevailing view that their children would suffer as a result of their employment, though in fact their children fare as well as those of non-working mothers.

It would appear, therefore, that the employment of women when their children are eight years of age or older has no negative effect on the children. What about the earlier years, from infancy until school age? In the American literature, there is little to refer to as yet which bears directly upon the effect of maternal employment on the infant or toddler, partly because employment of mothers with preschool children is so negligible in the United States, partly because the measurement of "effects" on young children is difficult and cannot be done with the research tools which have been used in most studies of maternal employment effects—questionnaires administered to mothers and to their school-age children.

There is, however, one significant body of data which is of considerable relevance to the question of the effect of maternal employment upon infants and very young children. Maternal employment is a regular pattern of separation of mother and child: the Israeli kibbutzim are collective settlements with several decades of experience in precisely this pattern. On the kibbutz, infants live in children's houses where their physical care and training are largely handled. During the infancy months the mother visits the house to feed the infant; as toddlers, children begin a pattern of visiting with their parents for a few hours each day, living in the children's houses for the remaining portions of their days and nights. A number of studies have been conducted to investigate the effect of this intermittent multiple mothering on the young child. They all point to essentially the same conclusion; the kibbutz child-rearing practices have no deleterious effects upon the subsequent personality development of the children involved. In fact, there are a number of respects in which the kibbutz-reared Israeli children exceed those reared in the traditional farm family: the kibbutz children showed a more accurate perception of reality, more breadth of interest and cultural background, better emotional control and greater overall maturity.

Continuous mothering, even in the first few years of life, does not seem to be necessary for the healthy emotional growth of a child. The crux of the matter appears to be in the nature of the care which is given to the child. If a child is reared by a full-time mother who is rejecting and cold in her treatment of him, or if a child is reared in an institutional setting lacking in warmth and stimulation and with an inadequate staff, both children will show personality disturbances in later years. If the loving care of the biological mother is shared by other adults who provide the child with a stable loving environment, the child will prosper at least as well as and potentially better than one with a good full-time mother. In the section below on child care and careers, I shall suggest institutional innovations which would ensure good quality care for children and ease the combination of work and child-rearing for women.

Turning now to the second question raised above: how successful has the new pattern of full-time motherhood been? Are women more satisfied with their lives in the mid-twentieth century than in the past? Does motherhood fulfill them, provide them with a sufficient canvas to occupy a lifetime? Are contemporary children living richer lives, developing greater ego strength to carry them through a complex adulthood? Are children better off for having full-time mothers?

I think the answer to all the questions posed above is a firm no. Educators, child psychologists and social analysts report an increasing tendency for American middle-class children to be lacking in initiative, excessively dependent on others for direction and decision, physically soft. Our children have more toys and play equipment than children in any other society, yet they still become bored and ask their mothers for "something to do." No society has as widespread a problem of juvenile delinquency and adolescent rebellion as the United States. Alcoholism, compulsive sex-seeking and adolescent delinquency are no longer social problems confined to the working class, socially disorganized sections of our cities, but have been on the increase in the middle-class suburb in the past twenty years, and involve more women and girls than in the past. There is a strong strand of male protest against the mother or "matriarch" in both our beatnik culture and our avant-garde literature: social and artistic extremes are seldom fully deviant from the middle range in a society, but show in an exaggerated heightened way the same though less visible tendencies in the social majority.

In a large proportion of cases, the etiology of mental illness is linked to inadequacy in the mother-child relationship. A high proportion of the psychoneurotic discharges from the army during World War II was traced to these young soldiers' overly dependent relationships to their mothers. This has been the subject of much earnest discussion in the years since the war, but the focus has remained on the mother-*son* relationship, I suspect only because as a fighter, a professional man or a worker, male performance is seen to be more crucial for society than female performance. But dependence, immaturity and ego diffusion have been characteristic of daughters as well as sons. The only difference is that, in the case of daughters, this less often reaches the overt level of a social problem because young women move quickly from under their mothers' tutelage into marriage and parenthood of their own: female failures are therefore not as socially visible, for they are kept within the privacy of family life and psychoanalytic case records. It is a short-sighted view indeed to consider the immature wife, dominating mother or interfering mother-in-law as a less serious problem to the larger society than the male homosexual, psychoneurotic soldier or ineffectual worker, for it is the failure of the mother which perpetuates the cycle from one generation to the next, affecting sons and daughters alike.

Disturbing trends of this sort cannot all be traced to the American woman's excessive and exclusive involvement with home and family. We live in turbulent times, and some part of these trends reflects the impact of world tension and conflict. But there is no reason to assume that world tension is relevant to many of them. Emotional and physical difficulties after childbirth or during the menopause years, the higher incidence of college girl than college boy breakdowns, the shrunken initiative and independence of children, are clearly not explained by world conflict. Besides, vast sections of American society remain totally unmoved and unaffected by international political and military events until they directly impinge on their own daily lives. Since history is both written and produced more by men than by women, the fact that our writers are preoccupied with the relationship to the mother points to difficulties in our family system more than the course of world events.

It is a paradox of our social history that motherhood has become a full-time occupation in precisely the era when objectively it could, and perhaps should, be a part-time occupation for a short phase of a woman's life span. I suspect that the things women do for and with their children have been needlessly elaborated to make motherhood a full-time job. Unfortunately, in this very process the child's struggle for autonomy and independence, for privacy and the right to worry things through for himself are subtly and pervasively reduced by the omnipresent mother. As a young child he is given great permissive freedom, but he must exercise it under supervision. As an adolescent he is given a great deal of freedom, but his parents worry excessively about what he does with it. Edgar Friedenberg has argued that there is entirely too much parental concentration on adolescent children, with the result that it has become increasingly difficult to *be* an adolescent in American society. He suggests that parents are interested in youth to the extent that they find their own stage of life uninteresting. Middle-class children are observed and analyzed by their mothers as though they were hothouse plants psychologically, on whose personalities any pressure might leave an indelible bruise. If a woman's adult efforts are concentrated exclusively on her children, she is likely more to stifle than broaden her children's perspective and preparation for adult life. Any stress or failure in a child becomes a failure of herself, and she is therefore least likely to truly help her child precisely when the child most needs support. In myriad ways the mother binds the child to her, dampening his initiative, resenting his growing independence in adolescence, creating a subtle dependence which makes it difficult for the child to achieve full adult stature without a rebellion which leaves him with a mixture of resentment and guilt that torments him in his mother's declining years.

It seems to me no one has linked these things together adequately. Psychiatric counselors of college students frequently have

as their chief task that of helping their young patients to free themselves from the entangling web of dependence upon their parents,
primarily their mothers, and encouraging them to form stable independent lives of their own. In other words, if the patient is eighteen
years old the analyst tries to help her free herself from her mother,
but if the next patient is twenty-five years old with young children
at home, the analyst tells her the children would suffer emotional
damage if she left them on a regular basis to hold down a job. The
very things which would reduce the excessive dependency of children before it becomes a critical problem are discouraged by the
counselor or analyst during the years when the dependency is being
formed. If it is true that the adult is what the child was, and if we
wish adults to be assertive, independent, responsible people, then
they should be reared in a way which prevents excessive dependence on a parent. They should be cared for by a number of adults in
their childhood, and their parents should truly encourage their independence and responsibility during their youthful years, not merely
give lip service to these parental goals. The best way to encourage
such independence and responsibility in the child is for the mother
to be a living model of these qualities herself. If she had an independent life of her own, she would find her stage of life interesting,
and therefore be less likely to live for and through her children. By
maintaining such an independent life, the American mother might
finally provide her children with something she can seldom give
when she is at home—a healthy dose of inattention, and a chance
for adolescence to be a period of fruitful immaturity and growth. If
enough American women developed vital and enduring interests
outside the family and remained actively in them throughout the
child-bearing years, we might then find a reduction in extreme
adolescent rebellion, immature early marriages, maternal domination of children, and interference by mothers and mothers-in-law in
the lives of married children.

There remains one further general characteristic of our industrial
society which has relevance to the question of why American society
should achieve full sex equality. Our family unit is small, for the
most part geographically if not socially isolated from its kin. This
small family unit is possible because of the increased longevity in
highly industrialized societies. In agricultural societies, with their

high rate of mortality, many parents die before they have completed the rearing of their young. The extended family provided substitutes for such parents without disturbing the basic lines of kin affiliation and property rights of these children. In our modern family system it is an unusual event for women or men to be widowed while they have young dependent children. This also means, however, that American families must fend for themselves in the many emergencies less critical than the death of a spouse: army service, long business or professional trips, prolonged physical or emotional illness, separation or divorce often require that one spouse carry the primary responsibility for the family, even if this is cushioned or supplemented by insurance, government aid, paid helpers or relatives. The insurance advertisements which show fathers bending over a cradle and begin "what would happen if?" evoke a twinge of fear in their readers precisely because parents recognize the lonely responsible positions they would be in if serious illness or death were to strike their home. In our family system, then, it is a decided asset if men and women can quickly and easily substitute for or supplement each other as parents and as breadwinners. I believe these are important elements in the structure of our economy and family system which exert pressure toward an equality between men and women. It is not merely that a companionate or equalitarian marriage is a desirable relationship between wife and husband, but that the functioning of an urban industrial society is facilitated by equality between men and women in work, marriage and parenthood.

The conclusions I have drawn from this analysis are as follows: full-time motherhood is neither sufficiently absorbing to the woman nor beneficial to the child to justify a contemporary woman's devoting fifteen or more years to it as her exclusive occupation. Sooner or later—and I think it should be sooner—women have to face the question of who they are besides their children's mother.

A major solution to this quest would be found in the full and equal involvement of women in the occupational world, the culmination of the feminist movement of the last one hundred and fifty years. This is not to overlook the fact that involvement as a volunteer in politics or community organizations or a serious dedication to a creative art can be a solution for many women. These areas of participation and involvement provide innumerable women with a keen sense of life purpose, and women are making significant and often innovative contributions in these pursuits. A job per se does not provide a woman, or a man either, with any magical path to self-fulfillment; nor does just any community volunteer work, or half-hearted dabbling in a creative art.

Women are already quite well represented in volunteer organizations in American communities. However, broadening the range of alternatives open to women and chosen by women for their life patterns is still to be achieved in the occupational world. It is also true that at the most challenging reaches of both political and community volunteer work, the activities have become increasingly professionalized. Thus while many women have and will continue to make innovative contributions to these fields as volunteers, such opportunities have become limited. Furthermore, many such women often find themselves carrying what amounts to a full-time job as a "volunteer executive," yet neither the recognition nor the rewards are equivalent to what they would receive in comparable positions in the occupational system. Hence, the major focus in this essay will be on the means by which the full and equal involvement of well-educated women in the occupational world may be achieved. For reasons which will become clear later, I believe that the occupational involvement of women would also be the major means for reducing American women's dominance in marriage and parenthood, and thus for allowing for the participation of men as equal partners in family life.

*   *   *

Institutional Levers for Achieving Sex Equality

In turning to the problem of how equality between the sexes may be implemented as a societal goal, I shall concentrate on the three major areas of child care, residence and education. Institutional change in these areas in no sense exhausts the possible spheres in which institutional change could be effected to facilitate the goal of sex equality. Clearly government and industry, for example, could effect highly significant changes in the relations between the sexes. But one must begin somewhere, and I have chosen these three topics, for they all involve questions of critical significance to the goal of equality between men and women.

1. It is widely assumed that rearing children and maintaining a career is so difficult a combination that except for those few women with an extraordinary amount of physical strength, emotional endurance and a dedicated sense of calling to their work, it is unwise for women to attempt the combination. Women who have successfully combined child-rearing and careers are considered out of the ordinary, although many men with far heavier work responsibilities who yet spend willing loving hours as fathers, and who also contribute to home maintenance, are cause for little comment. We should be wary of the assumption that home and work combinations are necessarily difficult. The simplified contemporary home and smaller sized family of a working mother today probably represent a lesser burden of responsibility than that shouldered by her grandmother.

This does not mean that we should overlook the real difficulties that are involved for women who attempt this combination. Working mothers do have primary responsibility for the hundreds of details involved in home maintenance, as planners and managers, even if they have household help to do the actual work. No one could suggest that child-rearing and a career are easy to combine, or even that this is some royal road to greater happiness, but only that the combination would give innumerable intelligent and creative women a degree of satisfaction and fulfillment that they cannot obtain in any other way. Certainly many things have to "give" if a woman works when she also has young children at home. Volunteer and social activities, gardening and entertaining may all have to be curtailed. The important point to recognize is that as children get older, it is far easier to resume these social activities than it is to resume an interrupted career. The major difficulty, and the one most in need of social innovation, is the problem of providing adequate care for the children of working mothers.

If a significant number of American middle-class women wish to work while their children are still young and in need of care and supervision, who are these mother-substitutes to be? In the American experience to date, they have been either relatives or paid domestic helpers. A study conducted by the Children's Bureau in 1958 outlines the types of child-care arrangements made by women working full time who had children under twelve years of age. The study showed that the majority of these children (57 percent) were cared for by relatives: fathers, older siblings, grandparents and others. About 21 percent were cared for by nonrelatives, including neighbors as well as domestic helpers. Only 2 percent of the children were receiving group care—in day nurseries, day-care centers, settlement houses, nursery schools and the like. Of the remainder, 8 percent were expected to take care of themselves, the majority being the "latchkey" youngsters of ten and twelve years of age about whom we have heard a good deal in the press in recent years.

These figures refer to a national sample of employed mothers and concern women in blue collar jobs and predominantly low-skill white collar jobs. Presumably the proportion of middle-class working mothers who can rely on either relatives or their husbands would be drastically lower than this national average, and will probably decline even further in future years. Many of today's, and more of tomorrow's American grandmothers are going to be wage earners themselves and not baby-sitters for their grandchildren. In addition, as middle-class women enter the occupational world, they will experience less of a tug to remain close to the kinswomen of their childhood, and hence may contribute further to the pattern of geographic and social separation between young couples and both sets of their parents. Nor can many middle-class husbands care for their children, for their work hours are typically the same as those of their working wives: there can be little dovetailing of the work schedules of wives and husbands in the middle class as there can be in the working class.

At present, the major child-care arrangement for the middle-class woman who plans a return to work has to be hired household help. In the 1920's the professional and business wife-mother had little difficulty securing such domestic help, for there were thousands of first generation immigrant girls and women in our large cities whose first jobs in America were as domestic servants. In the 1960's, the situation is quite different: the major source of domestic help in our large cities is Negro and Puerto Rican women. Assuming the continuation of economic affluence and further success in the American Negro's struggle for equal opportunity in education, jobs and housing, this reservoir will be further diminished in coming decades. The daughters of many present-day Negro domestic servants will be able to secure far better paying and more prestigeful jobs than their mothers can obtain in 1964. There will be increasing difficulty of finding adequate child-care help in future years as a result.

The problem is not merely that there may be decreasing numbers of domestic helpers available at the same time more women require their aid. There is an even more important question involved: are domestic helpers the best qualified persons to leave in charge of young children? Most middle-class families have exacting standards for the kind of teachers and the kind of schools they would like their children to have. But a working mother who searches for a competent woman to leave in charge of her home has to adjust to considerably lower standards than she would tolerate in any nursery school program in which she placed her young son or daughter, either because such competent help is scarce, or because the margin of salary left after paying for good child care and the other expenses associated with employment is very slight.

One solution to the problem of adequate child care would be an attempt to upgrade the status of child-care jobs. I think one productive way would be to develop a course of study which would yield a certificate for practical mothering, along the lines that such courses and certificates have been developed for practical nursing. There would be several important advantages to such a program. There are many older women in American communities whose lives seem empty because their children are grown and their grandchildren far away, yet who have no interest in factory or sales work, for they are deeply committed to life and work within the context of a home. Indeed, there are many older women who now work in factories or as cashiers or salesclerks who would be much more satisfied with child-care jobs, if the status and pay for such jobs were upgraded. These are the women, sometimes painfully lonely for contact with children, who stop young mothers to comment on the baby in the carriage, to talk with the three-year-old and to discuss their own distant grandchildren. I think many of these women would be attracted by a program of "refresher" courses in first aid, child development, books and crafts appropriate for children of various ages, and the special problems of the mother substitute-child relationship. Such a program would build upon their own experiences as mothers but would update and broaden their knowledge, bringing it closer to the values and practices of the middle-class woman who is seeking a practical mother for her family. Substitute motherhood for which she earns a wage, following active motherhood of her own, could provide continuity, meaning and variety to the life span of those American women who are committed to the traditional conception of woman's role. Such a course of study might be developed in a number of school contexts—a branch of a college department of education, an adult education extension program or a school of nursing.

A longer-range solution to the problem of child care will involve the establishment of a network of child-care centers. Most of the detailed plans for such centers must be left for future discussion, but there are several important advantages to professionally run child-care centers which should be noted. Most important, better care could be provided by such centers than any individual mother can provide by hiring a mother's helper, housekeeper or even the practical mother I have just proposed. In a child-care center, there can be greater specialization of skills, better facilities and equipment, and play groups for the children. Second, a child-care center would mean less expense for the individual working mother, and both higher wages and shorter hours for the staff of the center. Third, these centers could operate on a full-time, year-round schedule, something of particular importance for women trained in professional or technical fields, the majority of which can be handled only on a full-time basis. Except for the teaching fields, such women must provide for the afternoon care of their nursery school and kindergarten-age children, after-school hours for older children and three summer months for all their children. Fourth, a child-care center could develop a roster of home-duty practical mothers or practical nurses to care for the ill or convalescent child at home, in much the way school systems now call upon substitute teachers to cover the classes of absent regular teachers.

A major practical problem is where to locate such child-care centers. During the years of experimentation which would follow acceptance of this idea, they might be in a variety of places, under a variety of organizational auspices, as a service facility offered by an industrial firm, a large insurance company, a university, the federal or a state government. Community groups of women interested in such service might organize small centers of their own much as they have informal pooled baby-sitting services and cooperatively run nursery schools at the present time.

I believe that one of the most likely contexts for early experimentation with such child-care centers is the large urban university. As these universities continue to expand in future years, in terms of the size of the student body, the varied research institutes associated with the university and the expansion of administrative, technical and counseling personnel, there will be increasing opportunity and increasing need for the employment of women. A child-care center established under the auspices of a major university would facilitate the return for training of older women to complete or refresh advanced training, forestall the dropping out of younger graduate married women with infants and young children to care for, and attract competent professional women to administrative, teaching or research positions, who would otherwise withdraw from their fields for the child-rearing years. It would also be an excellent context within which to innovate a program of child care, for the university has the specialists in psychology, education and human development on whom to call for the planning, research and evaluation that the establishment of child-care centers would require. If a university-sponsored child-care program were successful and widely publicized, it would then constitute an encouragement and a challenge to extend child-care centers from the auspices of specific organizations to a more inclusive community basis. A logical location for community child-care centers may be as wings of the elementary schools, which have precisely the geographic distribution throughout a city to make for easy access between the homes of very young children and the centers for their daytime care. Since school and center would share a location, it would also facilitate easy supervision of older children during the after-school hours. The costs of such care would also be considerably reduced if the facilities of the school were available for the older children during after-school hours, under the supervision of the staff of the child-care center. There are, of course, numerous problems to be solved in working out the details of any such program under a local educational system, but assuming widespread support for the desirability of community facilities for child care, these are technical and administrative problems well within the competence of school and political officials in our communities. . . .

2. The preferred residential pattern of the American middle class in the postwar decades has been suburban. In many sections of the country it is difficult to tell where one municipality ends and another begins, for the farm, forest and waste land between towns and cities have been built up with one housing development after another. The American family portrayed in the mass media typically occupies a house in this sprawling suburbia, and here too, are the American women, and sometimes men, whose problems are aired and analyzed with such frequency. We know a good deal about the characteristics and quality of social life in the American suburb and the problems of the men and women who live in them. We hear about the changing political complexion of the American suburbs, the struggle of residents to provide sufficient community facilities to meet their growing needs. But the social and personal difficulties of suburban women are more likely to be attributed to their early family relationships or to the contradictory nature of the socialization of girls in our society than to any characteristic of the environment in which they now live. My focus will be somewhat different: I shall examine the suburban residence pattern for the limitations it imposes on the utilization of women's creative work abilities and the participation of men in family life. Both limitations have important implications for the lives of boys and girls growing up in the suburban home.

The geographic distance between home and work has a number of implications for the role of the father-husband in the family. It reduces the hours of possible contact between children and their fathers. The hour or more men spend in cars, buses or trains may serve a useful decompression function by providing time in which to sort out and assess the experiences at home and the events of the work day, but it is questionable whether this outweighs the disadvantage of severely curtailing the early morning and late afternoon hours during which men could be with their children.

The geographic distance also imposes a rigid exclusion of the father from the events which highlight the children's lives. Commuting fathers can rarely participate in any special daytime activities at home or at school, whether a party, a play the child performs in or a conference with a teacher. It is far less rewarding to a child to report to his father at night about such a party or part in a play than to have his father present at these events. If the husband-father must work late or attend an evening function in the city, he cannot sandwich in a few family hours but must remain in the city. This is the pattern which prompted Margaret Mead to characterize the American middle-class father as the "children's mother's husband," and partly why mother looms so oversized in the lives of suburban children.

Any social mixing of family-neighborhood and job associates is reduced or made quite formal: a work colleague cannot drop in for an after-work drink or a Saturday brunch when an hour or more separates the two men and their families. The father-husband's office and work associates have a quality of unreality to both wife and children. All these things sharpen the differences between the lives of men and women—fewer mutual acquaintances, less sharing of the day's events, and perhaps most importantly, less simultaneous filling of their complementary parent roles. The image of parenthood to the child is mostly motherhood, a bit of fatherhood and practically no parenthood as a joint enterprise shared at the same time by father and mother. Many suburban parents, I suspect, spend more time together as verbal parents—discussing their children in the children's absence—than they do actively interacting with their children, the togetherness cult notwithstanding. For couples whose relationship in courtship and early marriage was equalitarian, the pressures are strong in the suburban setting for parenthood to be highly differentiated and skewed to an ascendant position of the mother. Women dominate the family, men the job world.

* * *

It is for these reasons that I believe any attempt to draw a significant portion of married women into the mainstream of occupational life must involve a reconsideration of the suburban pattern of living. Decentralization of business and industry has only partly alleviated the problem: a growing proportion of the husbands living in the suburbs also work in the suburbs. There are numerous shops and service businesses providing job opportunities for the suburban wife. Most such jobs, however, are at skill levels far below the ability potential and social status of the suburban middle-class wife. Opportunities for the more exacting professional, welfare and business jobs are still predominantly in the central sections of the city. In addition, since so many young wives and mothers in this generation married very young, before their formal education was completed, they will need more schooling before they can hope to enter the fields in which their talents can be most fruitfully exercised, in jobs which will not be either dull or a status embarrassment to themselves and their husbands. Numerous retail stores have opened suburban branches; colleges and universities have yet to do so. A woman can spend in the suburb, but she can neither learn nor earn.

That some outward expansion of American cities has been necessary is clear, given the population increase in our middle- to large-sized cities. But there are many tracts in American cities between the business center and the outlying suburbs which imaginative planning and architectural design could transform and which would attract the men and women who realize the drawbacks of a suburban residence. Unless there is a shift in this direction in American housing, I do not think there can be any marked increase in the proportion of married middle-class women who will enter the labor force. That Swedish women find work and home easier to combine than American women is closely related to the fact that Sweden avoided the sprawling suburban development in its postwar housing expansion. The emphasis in Swedish housing has been on inner-city housing improvement. With home close to diversified services for schooling, child care, household help and places of work, it has been much easier in Sweden than in the United States to draw married women into the labor force and keep them there.

In contrast, the policy guiding the American federal agencies which affect the housing field, such as the FHA, have stressed the individual home, with the result that mortgage money was readily available to encourage builders to develop the sprawling peripheries of American cities. Luxury high-rise dwellings at the hub of the city and individual homes at the periphery have therefore been the pattern of middle-class housing development in the past twenty years. A shift in policy on the part of the federal government which would embrace buildings with three and four dwelling units and middle-income high-rise apartment buildings in the in-between zones of the city could go a long way to counteract this trend toward greater and greater distance between home and job. Not everyone can or will want to live close to the hub of the city. From spring through early fall, it is undoubtedly easier to rear very young children in a suburban setting with backyards for the exercise of healthy lungs and bodies. But this is at the expense of increased dependence of children on their mothers, of minimization of fathers' time with their youngsters, of restriction of the social environment of women, of drastic separation of family and job worlds and of less opportunity for even part-time schooling or work for married women.

3. Men and women must not only be able to participate equally; they must want to do so. It is necessary, therefore, to look more closely into their motivations, and the early experiences which mold their self-images and life expectations. A prime example of this point can be seen in the question of occupational choice. The goal of sex equality calls for not only an increase in the extent of women's participation in the occupational system, but a more equitable distribution of men and women in all the occupations which comprise that system. This means more women doctors, lawyers and scientists, more men social workers and school teachers. To change the sex ratio within occupations can only be achieved by altering the sex-typing of such occupations long before young people make a career decision. Many men and women change their career plans during college, but this is usually within a narrow range of relatively homogeneous fields: a student may shift from medicine to a basic science, from journalism to teaching English. Radical shifts such as from nursing to medicine, from kindergarten teaching to the law, are rare indeed. Thus while the problem could be attacked at the college level, any significant change in the career choices men and women make must be attempted when they are young boys and girls. It is during the early years of elementary school education that young people develop their basic views of appropriate characteristics, activities and goals for their sex. It is for this reason that I shall give primary attention to the sources of sex-role stereotypes and what the elementary school system could do to eradicate these stereotypes and to help instead in the development of a more androgynous conception of sex role.

[Editor's note: In a section omitted here, Mrs. Rossi recommends

conscious educational programs in the elementary schools to combat sex role differentiations; for example, lectures by prominent
women professionals and equal opportunity for both sexes to take
sex, family living, and craft courses.]

The Old and the New Ideas in the New Feminism

Pat Mainardi

THE POLITICS OF HOUSEWORK

Pat Mainardi's discussion of the politics of housework is one of the most popular examples of women's liberation literature. Many militant feminists use the word "politics" to denote the basic power relationships in our culture. Why have women, according to Miss Mainardi, always been assigned the task of housework? Why should women object to this work? What kind of household would women liberationists envision as the desired model?

> *Though women do not complain of the power of husbands, each complains of her own husband, or of the husbands of her friends. It is the same in all other cases of servitude; at least in the commencement of the emancipatory movement. The serfs did not at first complain of the power of the lords, but only of their tyranny.*
> —*John Stuart Mill,* On the Subjection of Women

Liberated women—very different from Women's Liberation! The first signals all kinds of goodies, to warm the hearts (not to mention other parts) of the most radical men. The other signals—*Housework.* The first brings sex without marriage, sex before marriage, cozy housekeeping arrangements ("I'm living with this chick") and the self-content of knowing that you're not the kind of man who wants a doormat instead of a woman. That will come later. After all, who wants that old commodity anymore, the Standard American Housewife, all husband, home and kids. The New Commodity, the Liberated Woman, has sex a lot and has a Career, preferably something that can be fitted in with the household chores—like dancing, pottery, or painting.

On the other hand is Women's Liberation—and housework. What? You say this is all trivial? Wonderful! That's what I thought. It seemed perfectly reasonable. We both had careers, both had to work a couple of days a week to earn enough to live on, so why shouldn't we share the housework? So I suggested it to my mate and he agreed—most men are too hip to turn you down flat. You're right, he said. It's only fair.

Then an interesting thing happened. I can only explain it by stating that we women have been brainwashed more than even we can imagine. Probably too many years of seeing television women in ecstasy over their shiny waxed floors or breaking down over their dirty shirt collars. Men have no such conditioning. They recognize the essential fact of housework right from the very beginning. Which is that it stinks.

Here's my list of dirty chores: buying groceries, carting them home and putting them away; cooking meals and washing dishes and pots; doing the laundry, digging out the place when things get out of control; washing floors. The list could go on but the sheer necessities are bad enough. All of us have to do these things, or get someone else to do them for us. The longer my husband contemplated these chores, the more repulsed he became, and so proceeded the change from the normally sweet considerate Dr. Jekyll into the crafty Mr. Hyde who would stop at nothing to avoid the horrors of—housework. As he felt himself backed into a corner laden with dirty dishes, brooms, mops and reeking garbage, his front teeth grew longer and pointier, his fingernails haggled and his eyes grew wild. Housework trivial? Not on your life! Just try to share the burden.

So ensued a dialogue that's been going on for several years. Here are some of the high points:

"I don't mind sharing the housework, but I don't do it very well. We should each do the things we're best at." *Meaning:* Unfortunately I'm no good at things like washing dishes or cooking. What I do best is a little light carpentry, changing light bulbs, moving furniture (how often do *you* move furniture?) *Also meaning:* Historically the lower classes (black men and us) have had hundreds of years experience doing menial jobs. It would be a waste of manpower to train someone else to do them now. *Also meaning:* I don't like the dull stupid boring jobs, so you should do them.

"I don't mind sharing the work, but you'll have to show me how to do it." *Meaning:* I ask a lot of questions and you'll have to show me everything every time I do it because I don't remember so good. Also don't try to sit down and read while *I'm* doing my jobs because I'm going to annoy hell out of you until it's easier to do them yourself.

"We used to be so happy!" (Said whenever it was his turn to do something.) *Meaning:* I used to be so happy. *Meaning:* Life without housework is bliss. No quarrel here. Perfect Agreement.

"We have different standards, and why should I have to work to your standards? That's unfair." *Meaning:* If I begin to get bugged by the dirt and crap I will say, "This place sure is a sty" or "How can anyone live like this?" and wait for your reaction. I know that all women have a sore called "Guilt over a messy house" or "House-hold work is ultimately my responsibility." I know that men have caused that sore—if anyone visits and the place *is* a sty, they're not going to leave and say, "He sure is a lousy housekeeper." You'll take the rap in any case. I can outwait you. *Also meaning:* I can provoke innumerable scenes over the housework issue. Eventually doing all the housework yourself will be less painful to you than trying to get me to do half. Or I'll suggest we get a maid. She will do my share of the work. You will do yours. It's women's work.

"I've got nothing against sharing the housework, but you can't make me do it on your schedule." *Meaning:* Passive resistance. I'll do it when I damned well please, if at all. If my job is doing dishes, it's easier to do them once a week. If taking out laundry, once a month. If washing the floors, once a year. If you don't like it, do it yourself oftener, and then I won't do it at all.

"I hate it more than you. You don't mind it so much." *Meaning:* Housework is garbage work. It's the worst crap I've ever done. It's degrading and humiliating for someone of *my* intelligence to do it. But for someone of *your* intelligence . . . .

"Housework is too trivial to even talk about." *Meaning:* It's even more trivial to do. Housework is beneath my status. My purpose in life is to deal with matters of significance. Yours is to deal with matters of insignificance. You should do the housework.

"This problem of housework is not a man-woman problem. In any relationship between two people one is going to have a stronger personality and dominate." *Meaning:* That stronger personality had better be *me*.

"In animal societies, wolves, for example, the top animal is usually a male even where he is not chosen for brute strength but on the basis of cunning and intelligence. Isn't that interesting?" *Meaning:* I have historical, psychological, anthropological and biological justification for keeping you down. How can you ask the top wolf to be equal?

"Women's Liberation isn't really a political movement." *Meaning:* The Revolution is coming too close to home. *Also meaning:* I am only interested in how I am oppressed, not how I oppress others. Therefore the war, the draft and the university are political. Women's Liberation is not.

"Man's accomplishments have always depended on getting help from other people, mostly women. What great man would have accomplished what he did if he had to do his own housework?" *Meaning:* Oppression is built into the system and I, as the white American male, receive the benefits of this system. I don't want to give them up.

Participatory democracy begins at home. If you are planning to implement your politics, there are certain things to remember:

1. He *is* feeling it more than you. He's losing some leisure and you're gaining it. The measure of your oppression is his resistance.

2. A great many American men are not accustomed to doing monotonous repetitive work which never issues in any lasting, let alone important, achievement. This is why they would rather repair a cabinet than wash dishes. If human endeavors are like a pyramid with man's highest achievements at the top, then keeping oneself alive is at the bottom. Men have always had servants (us) to take care of this bottom strata of life while they have confined their efforts to the rarefied upper regions. It is thus ironic when they ask of women—where are your great painters, statesmen, etc. Mme. Matisse ran a millinery shop so he could paint. Mrs. Martin Luther King kept his house and raised his babies.

3. It is a traumatizing experience for someone who has always thought of himself as being against any oppression or exploitation of one human being by another to realize that in his daily life he has been accepting and implementing (and benefiting from) this exploitation; that his rationalization is little different from that of the

LITTLE POLITICS OF HOUSEWORK QUIZ

1. The lowest job in the army, used as punishment is (a) *working 9–5* (b) *kitchen duty (K.P.)*.

2. When a man lives with his family, his (a) *father* (b) *mother* does his housework.

3. When he lives with a woman, (a) *he* (b) *she* does the housework.

4. (a) *His son* (b) *His daughter* learns preschool how much fun it is to iron daddy's handkerchief.

5. From *The New York Times,* 9/21/69: "Former Greek Official George Mylonas pays the penalty for differing with the ruling junta in Athens by performing household chores on the island of Amorgos where he lives in forced exile" (with hilarious photo of a miserable Mylonas carrying his own water). What the *Times* means is that he ought to have (a) *indoor plumbing* (b) *a maid*.

6. Dr. Spock said (Redbook, 3/69) "Biologically and temperamentally I believe, women were made to be concerned first and foremost with child care, husband care, and home care." Think about (a) *who made us* (b) *why?* (c) *what is the effect on their lives* (d) *what is the effect on our lives?*

7. From *Time*, 1/5/70, "Like their American counterparts, many housing project housewives are said to suffer from neurosis. And for the first time in Japanese history, many young husbands today complain of being henpecked. Their wives are beginning to demand detailed explanations when they don't come home straight from work and some Japanese males nowadays are even compelled to do housework." According to *Time,* women become neurotic (a) *when they are forced to do the maintenance work for the male caste all day every day of their lives or* (b) *when they no longer want to do the maintenance work for the male caste all day every day of their lives.*

racist who says "Black people don't feel pain" (women don't mind doing the shitwork); and that the oldest form of oppression in history has been the oppression of 50 percent of the population by the other 50 percent.

4. Arm yourself with some knowledge of the psychology of oppressed peoples everywhere, and a few facts about the animal kingdom. I admit playing top wolf or who runs the gorillas is silly but as a last resort men bring it up all the time. Talk about bees. If you feel really hostile bring up the sex life of spiders. They have sex. She bites off his head.

The psychology of oppressed peoples is not silly. Jews, immigrants, black men and all women have employed the same psychological mechanisms to survive: admiring the oppressor, glorifying the oppressor, wanting to be like the oppressor, wanting the oppressor to like them, mostly because the oppressor held all the power.

5. In a sense, all men everywhere are slightly schizoid—divorced from the reality of maintaining life. This makes it easier for them to play games with it. It is almost a cliché that women feel greater grief at sending a son off to a war or losing him to that war because they bore him, suckled him, and raised him. The men who foment those wars did none of those things and have a more superficial estimate of the worth of human life. One hour a day is a low estimate of the amount of time one has to spend "keeping" oneself. By foisting this off on others, man has seven hours a week—one working day more to play with his mind and not his human needs. Over the course of generations it is easy to see whence evolved the horrifying abstractions of modern life.

6. With the death of each form of oppression, life changes and new forms evolve. English aristocrats at the turn of the century were horrified at the idea of enfranchising workingmen—were such that it signalled the death of civilization and a return to barbarism. Some workingmen were even deceived by this line. Similarly with the minimum wage, abolition of slavery, and female suffrage. Life changes but it goes on. Don't fall for any line about the death of everything if men take a turn at the dishes. They will imply that you are holding back the Revolution (their Revolution). But you are advancing it (your Revolution).

7. Keep checking up. Periodically consider who's actually *doing*

the jobs. These things have a way of backsliding so that a year later once again the woman is doing everything. After a year make a list of jobs the man has rarely if ever done. You will find cleaning pots, toilets, refrigerators and ovens high on the list. Use time sheets if necessary. He will accuse you of being petty. He is above that sort of thing (housework). Bear in mind what the worst jobs are, namely the ones that have to be done every day or several times a day. Also the ones that are dirty—it's more pleasant to pick up books, newspapers, etc., than to wash dishes. Alternate the bad jobs. It's the daily grind that gets you down. Also make sure that you don't have the responsibility for the housework with occasional help from him. "I'll cook dinner for you tonight" implies it's really your job and isn't he a nice guy to do some of it for you.

8. Most men had a rich and rewarding bachelor life during which they did not starve or become encrusted with crud or buried under the litter. There is a taboo that says women mustn't strain themselves in the presence of men—we haul around 50 lbs. of groceries if we have to but aren't allowed to open a jar if there is someone around to do it for us. The reverse side of the coin is that men aren't supposed to be able to take care of themselves without a woman. Both are excuses for making women do the housework.

9. Beware of the double whammy. He won't do the little things he always did because you're now a "Liberated Woman," right? Of course he won't do anything else either . . . .

I was just finishing this when my husband came in and asked what I was doing. Writing a paper on housework. Housework? he said, *Housework*? Oh my god how trivial can you get. A paper on housework.

Midge Decter
THE PEACE LADIES

Just as peace or war was a major concern in the 1910's, so it has been in the 1960's. Vietnam consumes the time and attention of many peace groups, including women's groups. Early in the decade of the sixties, however, before Vietnam was the major issue, many women's peace groups, especially Women Strike for Peace, were concerned with nuclear fallout from atomic testing and with nuclear disarmament. How does Midge Decter view the goals and methods of the Women Strike for Peace group? Is WSP a feminist-oriented movement? How does it compare to the Women's Peace Party of the World War I period?

On the day following President Kennedy's announcement of the United States "quarantine" of Cuba, it was no surprise to find peace marchers gathered outside the United Nations. Nor was it surprising to anyone at all acquainted with the various peace groups that women representing an organization called Women Strike for Peace were among the first of these marchers to arrive. This particular group, during the year it has been in existence, had shown an impressive capacity for overnight mobilization, and by now its members well knew the way to Hammarskjold Plaza. Many of the women brought their babies and small children. They were opposed, they said, to unilateral action on the part of the United States; as for missile bases, they were against those all over the world; and they demanded that the Cuban question be brought immediately before the UN. They were demonstrating—as one of them explained—to help prevent a possible "nuclear holocaust."

In framing their proposals they had not seemed to find it necessary to consider either what Khrushchev was up to or whether the UN could in fact, as it had never done before, effectively settle a dispute between the Soviet Union and the United States. What they seemed mainly concerned to do was to register a protest against the dangers of the situation and to insist that these dangers must become the foremost consideration of American policy. This peculiar combination of energetic determination to act, political vagueness, and maternal emotionalism has characterized most of the activities of Women Strike for Peace.

The group came officially into being on November 1, 1961, with a demonstration in which some fifty thousand women in sixty communities throughout the United States took part. This first "strike" —or in the parlance of the peace movement, "action"—was a hastily, loosely put together affair, planned at the end of September by a small group in Washington who simply got in touch with acquaintances all over the country. The slogan for the demonstration was "End the Arms Race—Not the Human Race," and its main thrust was to announce that the mothers of America and undoubtedly those of the rest of the world were not going to stand idly by while governments deliberately pursued policies which threatened their children with disease and extinction.

No one who participated in this demonstration was asked to sign anything or commit herself to anything beyond the proposition that there must under no circumstances be a nuclear war. The demonstration in each community depended entirely on what the local group was willing and able to do. Some of them marched; some flooded Washington (and particularly Mrs. Kennedy) with telegrams and letters; some lobbied with local officials and government representatives; some took advertisements in the local press. All that was required was that they demonstrate simultaneously and call attention to this new voice of American womanhood.

Many of the women participating were already active members of established peace groups, like the Women's International League for Peace and Freedom, or SANE. A number gravitated toward the Women's Strike from other liberal causes, such as civil rights and school desegregation. Many of the women, on the other hand, had never before been involved in anything more far-reaching than the local PTA. Very few had ever taken part in any public demonstration.

In Washington, on that first Strike day, no less than 750 women and at some point as many as 1,500 joined in the walk from the Washington Monument to the White House and the Soviet Embassy. They delivered a letter to Mrs. Kennedy and one to Madam Khrushchev, from "the women of America," appealing to them to join in the women's struggle for the survival of mankind.

The scope of the Strike apparently caught everyone by surprise, particularly those who organized it. And indeed, to have activated fifty thousand women, even for one afternoon, by means of chain letters and telephone calls, without any formal membership lists, and in only a month's time, is a rather astonishing feat—one that in fact became the envy of the established peace groups. Nevertheless, if we look back to the late summer and early autumn of 1961, the women's response seems easily accountable.

It was a time for demonstrating. The world had just passed through the tensest moments of the Berlin crisis, moments that brought with them—for masses of citizens in the large metropolitan centers, at least—a new kind of hard confrontation with the possibility of war. During this time, many people first began concretely to visualize the consequences to themselves and their families of a nuclear attack. The air was filled with expressions of the feelings of powerlessness, and on the other hand, of the will to "*do* something." The government announced its shelter program; and this announcement, though obviously intended more as a gesture in foreign and military policy than as a serious effort to find some way to protect the American populace, roused people to consider very directly the question of their own survival. And then the Russians resumed nuclear testing. Apart from dashing briefly nursed hopes that Kennedy would soon be able to effect a test-ban agreement with the Russians, this meant that there was going to be fallout to think about once more.

No Crackpot Dream

It was to this general apprehension that the Strike made its appeal. "When I saw Dagmar Wilson's ad saying, 'Women Strike for Peace,'" explained Ruth Gage-Colby, a veteran member of the Women's International League for Peace and Freedom, "I said to myself, 'This is different.' If the ad had said Women for Peace, I'd have said, 'God bless the ladies,' and paid no further attention. But the word 'Strike' struck a chord with me." Peace, it seemed, was finally coming to be seen as a genuine mass concern. The push toward disarmament was no longer to be counted as the crackpot dream of that lonely, marginal band of pacifists, guilt-ridden scientists, agitators, and do-gooders that to the popular imagination made up the peace movement.

The mood which the Women Strikers exploited so effectively had at the same time found the established peace groups somewhat wanting. Their years of being thrown so much upon themselves, in the midst of a hostile or at best indifferent public, had left them without that looseness, that spirit of inclusiveness, that carelessness about specific issues which are necessary to attract masses of people in a state of high emotion and with a rather low level of political experience.

In addition, the women could count on the courtesy if not the sympathy of the press, police, and government officials: they were the mothers of America, acting out of anxiety for the welfare of their children. They might be considered misguided, but only a cad would impugn their motives.

Women Strike for Peace, then, was ideologically free to act quickly at the same time that it was sociologically in the position to remain respectable; and this gave it a very special opportunity. On November 8, 1961, a group of the leaders, with representatives from several cities, met and decreed that WSP would continue to exist in its present unorganized state. There would be "no national organization, no membership, no dues, no board; women [would] stay in touch informally and raise their own funds locally for local projects."

The enormous waste of time and energy involved in this kind of anarchy was to be more than offset by certain advantages. The women would be free to work at the things, and with the people, most congenial to them. No one would be burdened with going "through channels" or struggling to impose her ideas on a whole organization. If the women in Detroit wanted to keep on organizing street demonstrations and marches, they were able to do so without having to overcome the disapproval of the national leader who announced, "It is time to stop walking and start working." If the women of Evanston, Illinois, wanted to organize a project called "Pennies for Peace" whose beneficiary was to be the UN, they would not have to argue with someone who might feel this money could be better used elsewhere. If the women of Westchester decided to agitate for an eight-day consumers' strike against milk after each nuclear test, they need not be deterred by a Philadelphia leader who thinks milk strikes both foolish and unfair, because "nuclear weapons, after all, and not the dairies create fallout." In addition, members of WSP would be able to cooperate with other peace groups, or bring others in on their projects, without problems of jurisdiction.

By far the most decisive advantage lies in the fact that if there is nothing to join and nothing to sign, there are no official policies to approve or disapprove and therefore no internal dissension— such as that which nearly tore SANE apart a few years ago when its national board required an anti-Communist declaration of all participating groups. (As one of WSP's Washington leaders put it, "We have some women who will only demonstrate before the Russian Embassy and some who will only demonstrate before the White House, and we can happily contain them both.") A woman, then, would be known to "belong" to WSP[1] simply if she said she did.

Ideologies Unlimited

In January 1962, WSP "went" international, and became WISP. It is not exactly clear who its European affiliates are. By the women's account, international contacts, like the local ones, were made through letters and cables to personal friends abroad. WISP legend, however, appears to be carried a little too far at this point. The European "friends" are presumably leaders of peace groups in their respective countries and known through some established international group. In England, at any rate, the major contact has been Mrs. Diane Collins, the wife of Canon Collins, famous for his wide-ranging, if not promiscuous, sympathy with "worthy" causes.

On January 15 a year ago, there was an international women's "witness," celebrated as before in various ways in different places —but now including several European countries. The main demonstration was again in Washington, to which a peace train brought two thousand women, who marched around the White House in pouring rain, and then dispersed to visit their Congressmen. (Kennedy refused to meet them, but later said that he had seen them through the window and got their message.) Women in the rest of

---

[1] The principle of decentralization seems to have been carried so far as to apply even to the name of the movement: some refer to themselves as Women Strike for Peace; others call themselves Women for Peace. For convenience I refer to the group—it *is* a single group—as WSP or WISP.

the country and Europe cabled, wired, and wrote. For WISP to become an international movement was a perfectly obvious development. Women who speak *as* women and mothers speak—by a logical extension—for the whole of mankind: if one's children are the issue, then matters of geography, political system, or even ideology seem irrelevant.

With at least one hundred communities in the United States boasting adherents of WISP, late in January 1962, a national monthly newsletter appeared. A twelve-page, legal-size, mimeographed publication, each issue carries a long editorial, usually on the larger social, economic, or spiritual implications of peace work, reports of the past month's activities listed community by community, national requests or announcements, appeals for cooperation and/or advice.

The monthly reports cover the whole gamut of activities available for peace work: demonstrations, political lobbying, organizing research and study groups, placing material in the press, inviting lecturers, raising funds, petitioning the President and Capitol Hill, distributing leaflets, letter-writing campaigns, and door-to-door canvassing. Each group has engaged in virtually all of these activities, with some specializing in a pet project: for example, the women of Mount Vernon, New York, have concentrated on the problems of radiation and food contamination, and have prepared studies, fact sheets, petitions with a view, among other things, to pressuring dairies and certain food packagers to install decontamination equipment.

The specific political content of all these activities, however, is left to the discretion of the women themselves. Consequently for most of the women there is no such content. In the words of Mrs. Dagmar Wilson,[2] one of the founders of WISP and by acclaim, if not by election, its national president, "Most women would probably rather be active in areas that affect their daily lives—the PTA, the local art clubs, and the like. But when your destiny appears to be decided in ways opposite from the way you want it to go, you've got to get out there and concern yourself with it."

Some of the women, to be sure, operate from fully developed political attitudes. In certain communities a leading member of the

[2] As reported by Alvin Shuster in *The New York Times Magazine,* May 6, 1962.

group may be a long-standing member of SANE. Elsewhere one will find a woman imbued with the kind of personalist radicalism that informs the Committee for Nonviolent Action (whose work carries the implications of a pacifist social order), or a woman committed to thinking through the radical technological and economic consequences of disarmament. For these women, working in WISP represents an opportunity to direct the restless energy of thousands of their fellow women to serious and substantial goals.

But by and large the women of WISP admittedly concern themselves with nothing but the prevention of nuclear war. It is this absence of political engagement from below and political policy-making from above—one of the group's most attractive features to its members and leaders alike—that makes WISP peculiarly vulnerable to a certain kind of unrecognized political appeal.

On Sunday, February 18, 1962, Madam Khrushchev in a broadcast appeal for peace specifically hailed WISP. In reply to an inquiry by NBC, Mrs. Wilson said: "We think that Madam Khrushchev made a sincere speech. Why should we not take it at face value as she did our words to her, instead of labeling it as propaganda?" There is no reason to suppose that Madam Khrushchev and Russian women in general want peace and fear war any less than their American counterparts. There was, however, much reason for the women to understand that the Russians would quite naturally respond to communications from WISP in terms of their own interests. Such an understanding could quite properly make no difference to WISP's —or any other peace group's—activities for peace; but it might have chastened some of the confidence with which the Washington women had on January 8 received a message from a group of Soviet women in Moscow under the direction of Madam Olga Chechetkina. The language of that message could not, to any experienced eye, appear as anything but propaganda. Paragraph four says:

> Expressing the will and the interests of all Soviet people, our government, in recent years, has been bending every effort and continues to do so now in order to normalize the international situation and to put into effect general and complete disarmament under effective international control. The Soviet Union has repeatedly reduced its armed forces, liquidated its military bases in foreign countries, and did not conduct any nuclear weapons tests for a period of three years.

This is not the kind of message, one can safely assume, that WISP on its part would send to the women of Russia.

A further display of vulnerability—in this case, both political and female—took place among a WISP delegation to Geneva in April. This trip by fifty of its members from thirty-five communities in the United States was a crucial moment in the life of the group: there they came face to face with international politics and the problems of foreign policy.

In commenting on Madam Khrushchev's speech, Mrs. Wilson had also expressed her hope that Kennedy and Khrushchev would each appoint a woman to the Disarmament Conference at Geneva, the implication being that women could more easily communicate across bloc barriers than men. When no official appointment was forthcoming, the women elected to go to Geneva on their own, for one week, and canvass the delegations. The Geneva peace plane was yet another tribute to the commanding vitality of WISP. For an organization so new, even though so enthusiastic, to have sparked the local raising of fifty times the $350 fare (from New York City to Geneva) was no mean feat.

Biological Pacifism

The two "stars" of the delegation, at least for the press, were Mrs. Cyrus Eaton and Mrs. Martin Luther King. Each of them made a little statement before boarding the plane. Mrs. Eaton said that she had come to know many Russians and was confident that, with the right moves on our part, an agreement could be reached. Mrs. King, admitting that she had had no previous connection with WISP, explained that both she and her husband believed in the principle of nonviolent resistance. The fifty women were to be met in Geneva by fifty-one from England, France, Norway, Sweden, Switzerland, Canada, Austria, West Germany, and the Soviet Union.

They went to Geneva not so much as Americans, or as people holding certain beliefs, but as women. They went there to be heard from as representatives of more than half of the world's population; women, who are daily involved almost by biological definition in what are the true, deep issues of life—food, shelter, care of the young. Over and over again, WISP members use terms like this excerpt from a letter from Mrs. Christine Hughes of Claremont, California:

> *Before becoming a mother . . . I felt that the Hiroshima bomb was quite justified, that the Russians were pretty evil in intention. . . . After a while some doubt crept into my mind. . . . I sensed a futility about the situation and had nightmares about nuclear war. (This, after becoming a mother.)*

The women had, of course, briefed themselves about the particular issues at stake in Geneva; they were preparing to speak to power in the way that power would respect. Yet this way was clearly not one for which they themselves showed much respect. Their strength, however small or great it might prove to be, lay with the simplicities of life and death and not with the complexities of policy. They visited all seventeen delegations to the Disarmament Conference. They met with Ambassadors Zorin and Dean. They expressed their consternation at the mutual suspicion that was—so they were told by members of the neutral delegations—the major stumbling block to agreement between the Russians and Americans. They devised a plan for talking the American government into closing down a U.S. base near Russian territory ("Just one would give faith!" Semyon Tsarapkin was reported to have said in response to the idea) and converting it to an international cultural center. Madam Chechetkina was on hand to represent Russian women—still unrecognized in her time-honored and rather famous identity as an official of the secret police and the Party. And together with Madam Chechetkina and the Europeans, they drafted a statement which announced that they, "representatives of different ideologies and social systems," had met in Geneva to express the "hopes and fears of all women. . . ."

One cannot perhaps blame these women for their impatience with the details of policy and strategy, for putting things so simply. But behind this simplicity lies the possibility of another kind of simplicity—one well remembered from the thirties and early forties in this country and for which the liberal community subsequently paid a catastrophic price in disillusionment and demoralization. In a report on the Geneva trip which appeared in the *Independent*

Political Forum News of Rochester, New York, Mrs. Mary Grooms recorded this bit of "human interest":

> *Later that morning Olga [Chechetkina] marched with us the two miles to the Palais des Nations to present the International Statement. She had explained that, in the U.S.S.R., they don't march. Yet there she was, trudging along with us "capitalist" women, led by an American Quaker in complete Quaker silence. I thought it must be difficult for her.*

In addition to the tenderness of mind that is bred in a situation where everyone is equally free to make statements and everyone else free to feel no responsibility for them, there are certain intellectual indulgences that WISP members, simply as women, tend to claim for themselves. "We left Geneva," ends the account of the trip appearing in the newsletter for April 19, "feeling we had made Mr. Dean and Mr. Zorin, for a short while at any rate, aware of the grave responsibilities for mass survival."

Now, there is very little overt female chauvinism or "feminism" to be found in WISP. Naturally, some members like to point to the fact that men have always played irresponsibly with human life while women have always protected it. Most of the women, however —and particularly the leaders—say that they have very little use for "ladies' societies" as such. The femininity of WISP in their opinion, is simply an effective instrumentality; women have more free time for the work than men have and can make a more straightforward appeal; and, in the words of Mrs. Shirley Lens of Chicago, "They are not afraid of crying and don't have to take the posture of being 'strong.' And furthermore, they don't have to be logical, but can be emotional. This is an accepted image."

Nevertheless, collectively WISP has often brought itself to that pitch of rhetoric at which it can speak of bringing men and the world back to reality—or of having made the ambassadors of two contending great powers "aware" of "grave responsibilities." Any movement that speaks for mothers, it seems, is bound in some way or other to leave rather ragged the question of fathers. (At Idlewild on send-off day one placard bore the inscription, "Our Mommy Is Going to Geneva 'Cause She Wants Us to Grow Up Not Blow Up. P.S. Our Daddy Feels the Same Way.")

In the end, their being a women's movement has not only served to make their motives unimpeachable in the eyes of, say, the press and police; it has come to make them so in their own eyes as well. It was a simple matter for WISP to send a letter of appeal to Soviet women and receive a reply; they did not have to consider that in their eagerness to sound the voice of womankind they might be offering an opportunity for the dissemination of someone else's rather crude propaganda. For them, all that mattered was that women who were "representatives of different ideologies and social systems" were able to get together and reaffirm their common humanity. Somewhere in all this there is the hint that the issues of international conflict are not only not women's business, but are something of a fraud.

What Makes Them Strong

The deliberate abdication of political responsibility that is exemplified in the "Geneva spirit" of WISP goes hand in hand with the group's immense vitality. By making the right demands—or rather, by leaving exactly the right demands unmade—the movement has been able to hook into the issues of war and peace some of that enormous hoard of civic energy that had been dormant in the U.S. for two decades.

The past couple of years have witnessed a rather sudden explosion of all those yearnings for activism that had been quelled by the complicated, gray years of the Cold War or sent into hiding by McCarthyism. Whatever the reasons for this—and there are several —it seems clear that WISP has hit on an old, familiar, and all too easily successful way of tapping this new source of energy.

Once before, in the declining days of the New Deal and during World War II, liberals depended on their good-heartedness and right-mindedness to take them through the knotty problems of domestic politics and foreign relations. At home, one could rest comfortably in the fervid support of such now firmly established social devices as trade unionism and government regulation; while abroad one had only to defeat fascism and further the causes of all those who spoke the language of social progress. Once before, liberals were complacent enough about the sheer nobility of their goals to permit everyone who called himself a friend to *be* a friend.

Once before, liberals lived in that political Eden in which good and bad were defined by God and one had only to opt for the good to be relieved of the need to make any further distinctions. (One of the more depressing aspects of the current situation is how much it reminds one of the almost pathological incredulity with which large segments of the liberal community greeted revelations about such things as the Moscow trials and over a decade later Soviet espionage in the U.S. in general, and Alger Hiss in particular.)

In any case, the end of World War II found most "liberals" of this variety unwilling to face the reality of Soviet expansionism, and therefore utterly unprepared to think productively about America's position in the long, hard contention for power that followed from it. And the result, when the cold facts of power could no longer be evaded, was the eventual attrition and demoralization of American liberalism that contributed so much to the career of Senator McCarthy. For the Senator could only have been able to work his kind of terror on people already cowed and weakened by their own inability to recognize and admit their mistakes. This inability stemmed then —as it stems now among so many members of the peace movement —from reliance on a system of total righteousness: with the very first error, the whole system collapses; error must therefore be denied or one must give up.

In the several months that have passed since the return of the WISP delegation from Geneva, members of the movement have busied themselves with such things as propagandizing about fallout, possible plans for disarmament, converting the national economy to peace, etc. Greater emphasis has been placed on distributing leaflets and literature—some of it the fruits of the women's own study—on these questions; sponsoring lectures, study groups, public discussions; and, in the recent elections, campaigning for the several "peace party" candidates.

Last December—probably as the aftermath of their posture during the Cuban crisis—some of WISP's leaders were summoned before a special subcommittee of the House Committee on Un-American Activities. Several women made headlines by declining, on constitutional grounds, to say whether they were or had been Communists. Mrs. Wilson calmly told a UPI reporter that in a group as large as hers there were bound to be some current or former

Communists taking part. But this didn't worry her, she said, because Communists "just like everyone else" are frightened over what might happen to the world if there is nuclear war.

Whatever one may think of HUAC's or WISP's position on this occasion, neither has helped illuminate the question that must trouble anyone in basic sympathy with the impulses behind the current peace movement—namely, what can such movements do that is both meaningful and beneficial?

One has heard it remarked, for instance, that even if the Russians were to accept the United States disarmament proposals, it is far from certain that the President could rely on the United States Senate's doing so. Under such circumstances, nothing less than a firm and enlightened and vocal public opinion could provide him with the necessary mandate. The creation of such a public voice in these times, however, is serious and responsible work—requiring at least as much of the dispassionateness that comes with knowing the conditions are real and the alternatives few as of the moral passion that comes with knowing *some* alternative must be found. The hurry, and the intellectual ease, with which the women responded last fall to the delicate and complicated question of Cuba will not serve to make them the kind of salutary influence on the public mind that they wish to be; more important, neither hurry nor ease is likely in the nature of things to serve the cause of peace in any way at all.

Precisely because the issue is one of life and death, the liberal dream of Eden becomes all the more dangerous. And least of all does it behoove Eve to claim the right of return to that vanished paradise of innocence.

Naomi Weisstein

WOMAN AS NIGGER

Naomi Weisstein when she wrote the following was assistant professor of psychology at Loyola University in Chicago. In her review of professional psychological studies, what does she find? What is a "social context" and how important is it to the psychological makeup of an individual? Does Miss Weisstein find evidence to support the view that there are immutable psychological differences between the sexes?

Psychology has nothing to say about what women are really like, what they need and what they want, for the simple reason that psychology does not know. Yet psychologists will hold forth endlessly on the true nature of woman, with dismaying enthusiasm and disquieting certitude.

Bruno Bettelheim, of the University of Chicago, tells us:

We must start with the realization that, as much as women want to be good scientists or engineers, they want first and foremost to be womanly companions of men and to be mothers.

Erik Erikson, of Harvard University, explains:

Much of a young woman's identity is already defined in her kind of attractiveness and in the selectivity of her search for the man (or men) by whom she wishes to be sought.

Some psychiatrists even see in women's acceptance of woman's role the solution to problems that rend our society. Joseph Rheingold, a psychiatrist at Harvard Medical School, writes:

. . . when women grow up without dread of their biological functions and without subversion by feminist doctrine and . . . enter upon motherhood with a sense of fulfillment and altruistic sentiment, we shall attain the goal of a good life and a secure world in which to live it.

These views reflect a fairly general consensus among psycholo-

Reprinted from *Psychology Today Magazine*, October 1969. Copyright © Communications/Research/Machines/Inc.

gists, and the psychologists' idea of woman's nature fits the common prejudice. But it is wrong. There isn't the tiniest shred of evidence that these fantasies of childish dependence and servitude have anything to do with woman's true nature, or her true potential. Our present psychology is less than worthless in contributing to a vision that could truly liberate women.

And this failure is not limited to women. The kind of psychology that is concerned with how people act and who they are has failed in general to understand why people act the way they do and what might make them act differently. This kind of psychology divides into two professional areas: academic personality research, and clinical psychology and psychiatry. The basic reason for the failure is the same in both these areas: the central assumption for most psychologists of human personality has been that human behavior rests primarily on an individual and inner dynamic. This assumption is rapidly losing ground, however, as personality psychologists fail again and again to get consistency in the assumed personalities of their subjects, and as the evidence collects that what a person does and who he believes himself to be will be a function of what people around him expect him to be, and what the overall situation in which he is acting implies that he is.

Academic personality psychologists are looking, at least, at the counter evidence and changing their theories; no such corrective is occurring in clinical psychology and psychiatry. Freudians and neo-Freudians, Adlerians and neo-Adlerians, classicists and swingers, clinicians and psychiatrists, simply refuse to look at the evidence against their theory and practice. And they support their theory and their practice with stuff so transparently biased as to have absolutely no standing as empirical evidence.

If we inspect the literature of personality theory that has been written by clinicians and psychiatrists, it is immediately obvious that the major support for theory is "years of intensive clinical experience." Now a person is free to make up theories with any inspiration that works: divine revelation, intensive clinical practice, a random numbers table. He is not free to claim any validity for this theory until it has been tested. But in ordinary clinical practice, theories are treated in no such tentative way.

Consider Freud. What he accepted as evidence violated the most minimal conditions of scientific rigor. In *The Sexual Enlightenment of Children,* the classic document that is supposed to demonstrate the existence of a castration complex and its connection to a phobia, Freud based his analysis on reports from the little boy's father, himself in therapy and a devotee of Freud. Comment on contamination in this kind of evidence is unnecessary.

It is remarkable that only recently has Freud's classic theory on female sexuality—the notion of the double orgasm—been tested physiologically and found just plain wrong. Now those who claim that 50 years of psychoanalytic experience constitute evidence of the essential truth of Freud's theory should ponder the robust health of the double orgasm. Before Masters and Johnson did women believe they were having two different kinds of orgasm? Did their psychiatrists coax them into reporting something that was not true? If so, were other things they reported also not true? Did psychiatrists ever learn anything that conflicted with their theories? If clinical experience means anything, surely we should have been done with the double-orgasm myth long before Masters and Johnson.

But, you may object, intensive clinical experience is the only reliable measure in a discipline that rests its findings on insight, sensitivity and intuition. The problem with insight, sensitivity and intuition is that they tend to confirm our biases. At one time people were convinced of their ability to identify witches. All it required was sensitivity to the workings of the devil.

Clinical experience is not the same thing as empirical evidence. The first thing an experimenter learns is the concept of the double blind. The term comes from medical experiments, in which one group takes a drug that is supposed to change behavior in a certain way, and a control group takes a placebo. If the observers or subjects know which group took which drug, the result invariably confirms the new drug's effectiveness. Only when no one knows which subject took which pill is validity approximated.

When we are judging human behavior, we must test the reliability of our judgments again and again. Will judges, in a blind experiment, agree in their observations? Can they repeat their judgments later? In practice, we find that judges cannot judge reliably *or* consistently.

Evelyn Hooker of U.C.L.A. presented to a group of judges, chosen for their clinical expertise, the results of three widely used clinical projective tests—the Rorschach, the Thematic Apperception Test (TAT) and the Make-A-Picture Story Test (MAPS)—that had been given to homosexuals and a control group of heterosexuals. The ability of these judges to distinguish male heterosexuals from male homosexuals was no better than chance. Any remotely Freudian-like theory assumes that sexuality is of fundamental importance in the deep dynamic of personality. If gross sexual deviance cannot be detected, then what do psychologists mean when they claim that "latent homosexual panic" is at the basis of paranoid psychosis? They can't identify homosexual *anything,* let alone "latent homosexual panic."

More astonishing, the diagnoses of expert clinicians are not consistent. In the Kenneth Little and Edwin S. Shneidman study, on the basis of both tests and interviews, judges described a number of normals as psychotic, assigning them to such categories as "schizophrenic with homosexual tendencies," or "schizoid character with depressive trends." When the same judges were asked to rejudge the same test results several weeks later, their diagnoses of the same subjects differed markedly from their initial judgments. It is obvious that even simple descriptive conventions in clinical psychology cannot be applied consistently. These descriptive conventions, therefore, have no explanatory significance.

I was a member of a Harvard graduate seminar to which two piles of TAT tests were presented. We were asked to identify which pile had been written by males and which pile by females. Although the class had spent one and a half months intensively studying the psychological literature on the differences between the sexes, only four students out of 20 identified the piles correctly. Since this result is far below chance, we may conclude that there is a consistency here. Within the context of psychological teaching, the students judged knowledgeably; the teachings themselves are erroneous.

Some might argue that while clinical theory may be scientifically unsound, it at least cures people. There is no evidence that it does. In 1952, Hans Eysenck of the University of London reported the results of an "outcome-of-therapy" study of neurotics that showed that 44 percent of the patients who received psychoanalysis improved; 64 percent of the patients who received psychotherapy improved; and 72 percent of the patients who received no treatment at all improved. These findings have never been refuted, and later studies have confirmed their negative results, no matter what type of therapy was used. In Arnold Goldstein and Sanford Dean's recent book, *The Investigation of Psychotherapy,* five different outcome-of-therapy studies with negative results are reported.

How, in all good conscience, can clinicians and psychiatrists continue to practice? Largely by ignoring these results and taking care not to do outcome-of-therapy studies.

Since clinical experience and tools are shown to be worse than useless when they are tested for consistency, efficacy and reliability, we can safely conclude that clinical theories about women are also worse than useless.

But even academic personality research that conforms to a rigorous methodology has only limited usefulness. As stated above, most psychologists of human personality have assumed that human behavior rests on an individual and inner dynamic, perhaps fixed in infancy, perhaps fixed by genitalia, perhaps simply arranged in a rigid cognitive network. But they have failed repeatedly to find consistency in the assumed personalities of their subjects. A rigid authoritarian on one test will be unauthoritarian on another. The reason for this inconsistency seems to depend more on the social situation in which a person finds himself than on the person himself.

In a series of experiments, Robert Rosenthal and his co-workers at Harvard showed that if experimenters have one hypothesis about what they expect to find and another group of experimenters has the opposite hypothesis, each group will obtain results that are in accord with its hypothesis. Experimenters who were told that their rats had been bred for brightness found that their rats learned to run mazes better than did the rats of experimenters who believed their animals had been bred for dullness. These results would have happened by chance one out of 100 times.

In a recent study, Robert Rosenthal and Lenore Jacobson extended their analysis to the classroom. They found that when teachers expected randomly selected students to "show great promise," the I.Q.s of these students increased significantly.

Thus, even in carefully controlled experiments, our hypotheses will influence the behavior of both animals and people. These studies are extremely important when we assess psychological studies of women. Since it is fairly safe to say that most of us start with hypotheses as to the nature of men and women, the validity of a number of observations on sex differences is questionable, even when these observations have been made under carefully controlled situations. In important ways, people are what you expect them to be, or at least they behave as you expect them to behave. If, as Bruno Bettelheim has it, women want first and foremost to be good wives and mothers, it is likely that this is what Bettelheim wants them to be.

The obedience experiments of Stanley Milgram point to the inescapable effect of social context. A subject is told that he is administering a learning experiment, and that he is to deal out shocks each time the other "subject" (a confederate of the experimenter) answers incorrectly. The equipment appears to provide graduated shocks ranging from 15 to 450 volts; for each four consecutive voltages there are verbal descriptions such as "mild shock," "danger," "severe shock," and finally, for the 435- and 450-volt switches, simply a red XXX marked over the switches. Each time the stooge answers incorrectly, the subject is supposed to increase the voltage. As the voltage increases, the stooge cries in pain; he demands that the experiment stop; finally, he refuses to answer at all. When he stops responding, the experimenter instructs the subject to continue increasing the voltage; for each shock administered, the stooge shrieks in agony. Under these conditions, about 62.5 percent of the subjects administered shocks that they believed to be lethal.

No tested individual differences predicted which subjects would continue to obey and which would break off the experiment. When 40 psychiatrists predicted how many of a group of 100 subjects would go on to give the lethal shock, their predictions were far below the actual percentage; most expected only one tenth of one percent of the subjects to obey to the end.

Even though psychiatrists have no idea how people will behave in this situation, and even though individual differences do not predict which subjects will obey and which will not, it is easy to predict when subjects will be obedient and when they will be defiant. All the experimenter has to do is change the social situation. In a variant of Milgram's experiment, two stooges were present in addition to the "victim"; these worked with the subject in administering electric shocks. When the stooges refused to go on with the experiment, only 10 percent of the subjects continued to the maximum voltage. This is critical for personality theory. It says that the lawful behavior is the behavior that can be predicted from the social situation, not from the individual history.

Finally, Stanley Schachter and J. E. Singer gave a group injections of adrenalin, which produces a state of physiological arousal almost identical to a state of extreme fear. When they were in a room with a stooge who acted euphoric, they became euphoric; when they were placed in a room with a stooge who acted angry, they became extremely angry.

It is obvious that a study of human behavior requires a study of the social contexts in which people move, the expectations as to how they will behave, and the authority that tells them who they are and what they are supposed to do.

We can now dispose of two biological theories of the nature of women. The first theory argues that females in primate groups are submissive and passive. Until we change the social organization of these groups and watch their subsequent behavior, we must conclude that—since primates are at present too stupid to change their own social conditions—the innateness and fixedness of these sexual differences in behavior are simply not known. Applied to humans, the primate argument becomes patently irrelevant, for the salient feature of human social organization is its variety, and there are a number of cultures in which there is at least a rough equality between men and women.

The second theory argues that since females and males differ in their sex hormones, and since sex hormones enter the brain, there must be innate differences in *psychological nature.* But this argument tells us only that there are differences in *physiological state.* From the adrenalin experiment we know that a particular physiological state can lead to varied emotional states and outward behavior, depending on the social situation.

Our culture and our psychology characterize women as inconsistent, emotionally unstable, lacking in a strong superego, weaker, nurturant rather than productive, intuitive rather than intelligent, and—if they are at all normal—suited to the home and family. In

short, the list adds up to a typical minority-group stereotype—
woman as nigger—if she knows her place (the home), she is really
a quite lovable, loving creature, happy and childlike. In a review of
the intellectual differences between little boys and little girls, Eleanor
Maccoby has shown that no difference exists until high school, or, if
there is a difference, girls are slightly ahead of boys. In high
school, girls begin to do worse on a few intellectual tasks, and
beyond high school the productivity and accomplishment of women
drops off even more rapidly.

In light of the social expectations about women, it is not surprising that women end up where society expects them to; the surprise
is that little girls don't get the message that they are supposed to be
stupid until they get into high school. It is no use to talk about
women being different-but-equal; all the sex-difference tests I can
think of have a "good" outcome and a "bad" outcome. Women
usually end up with the bad outcome.

Except for their genitals, I don't know what immutable differences
exist between men and women. Perhaps there are some other un-
changeable differences; probably there are a number of irrelevant
differences. But it is clear that until social expectation for men
and women are equal, until we provide equal respect for both sexes,
answers to this question will simply reflect our prejudices.

Anne Koedt

THE MYTH OF THE VAGINAL ORGASM

*Anne Koedt, like many other spokeswomen for women's liberation, began
her active participation in the National Organization for Women but found it
too moderate for her tastes. Miss Koedt, a New York artist, then became
involved in a radical women's lib group. In the following essay, she discusses
female sexuality. How have traditional heterosexual relations in our society,
according to Anne Koedt, contributed to male domination? What evidence*

From *Notes from the Second Year: Women's Liberation,* 1970. Reprinted by permission of the author.

*does she present to repudiate the concept of vaginal orgasm? What are the
implications of her argument?*

Whenever female orgasm and frigidity is discussed, a false distinction is made between the vaginal and the clitoral orgasm. Frigidity
has generally been defined by men as the failure of women to have
vaginal orgasms. Actually the vagina is not a highly sensitive area
and is not constructed to achieve orgasm. It is the clitoris which is
the center of sexual sensitivity and which is the female equivalent
of the penis.

I think this explains a great many things: First of all, the fact that
the so-called frigidity rate among women is phenomenally high.
Rather than tracing female frigidity to the false assumptions about
female anatomy, our "experts" have declared frigidity a psychological problem of women. Those women who complained about it
were recommended psychiatrists, so that they might discover their
"problem"—diagnosed generally as a failure to adjust to their role
as women.

The facts of female anatomy and sexual response tell a different
story. There is only one area for sexual climax, although there are
many areas for sexual arousal; that area is the clitoris. All orgasms
are extensions of sensation from this area. Since the clitoris is not
necessarily stimulated sufficiently in the conventional sexual positions, we are left "frigid."

Aside from physical stimulation, which is the common cause of
orgasm for most people, there is also stimulation through primarily
mental processes. Some women, for example, may achieve orgasm
through sexual fantasies, or through fetishes. However, while the
stimulation may be psychological, the orgasm manifests itself physically. Thus, while the cause is psychological, the *effect* is still
physical, and the orgasm necessarily takes place in the sexual organ
equipped for sexual climax—the clitoris. The orgasm experience
may also differ in degree of intensity—some more localized, and
some more diffuse and sensitive. But they are all clitoral orgasms.

All this leads to some interesting questions about conventional
sex and our role in it. Men have orgasms essentially by friction with
the vagina, not the clitoral area, which is external and not able to
cause friction the way penetration does. Women have thus been
defined sexually in terms of what pleases men; our own biology has

not been properly analyzed. Instead, we are fed the myth of the liberated woman and her vaginal orgasm—an orgasm which in fact does not exist.

What we must do is redefine our sexuality. We must discard the "normal" concepts of sex and create new guidelines which take into account mutual sexual enjoyment. While the idea of mutual enjoyment is liberally applauded in marriage manuals, it is not followed to its logical conclusion. We must begin to demand that if certain sexual positions now defined as "standard" are not mutually conducive to orgasm, they no longer be defined as standard. New techniques must be used or devised which transform this particular aspect of our current sexual exploitation.

Freud—A Father of the Vaginal Orgasm

Freud contended that the clitoral orgasm was adolescent, and that upon puberty, when women began having intercourse with men, women should transfer the center of orgasm to the vagina. The vagina, it was assumed, was able to produce a parallel but more mature, orgasm than the clitoris. Much work was done to elaborate on this theory, but little was done to challenge the basic assumptions.

To fully appreciate this incredible invention, perhaps Freud's general attitude about women should first be recalled. Mary Ellman, in *Thinking About Women,* summed it up this way:

> *Everything in Freud's patronizing and fearful attitude toward women follows from their lack of a penis, but it is only in his essay* The Psychology of Women *that Freud makes explicit . . . the deprecations of women which are implicit in his work. He then prescribes for them the abandonment of the life of the mind, which will interfere with their sexual function. When the psychoanalyzed patient is male, the analyst sets himself the task of developing the man's capacities; but with women patients, the job is to resign them to the limits of their sexuality. As Mr. Rieff puts it: For Freud, "Analysis cannot encourage in women new energies for success and achievement, but only teach them the lesson of rational resignation."*

It was Freud's feelings about women's secondary and inferior relationship to men that formed the basis for his theories on female sexuality.

Once having laid down the law about the nature of our sexuality, Freud not so strangely discovered a tremendous problem of frigidity in women. His recommended cure for a woman who was frigid was psychiatric care. She was suffering from failure to mentally adjust to her "natural" role as a woman. Frank S. Caprio, a contemporary follower of these ideas, states:

> . . . whenever a woman is incapable of achieving an orgasm via coitus, provided her husband is an adequate partner, and prefers clitoral stimulation to any other form of sexual activity, she can be regarded as suffering from frigidity and requires psychiatric assistance. (The Sexually Adequate Female, p. 64.)

The explanation given was that women were envious of men—"renunciation of womanhood." Thus it was diagnosed as an anti-male phenomenon.

It is important to emphasize that Freud did not base his theory upon a study of woman's anatomy, but rather upon his assumptions of woman as an inferior appendage to man, and her consequent social and psychological role. In their attempts to deal with the ensuing problem of mass frigidity, Freudians created elaborate mental gymnastics. Marie Bonaparte, in *Female Sexuality,* goes so far as to suggest surgery to help women back on their rightful path. Having discovered a strange connection between the non-frigid woman and the location of the clitoris near the vagina,

> it then occurred to me that where, in certain women, this gap was excessive, and clitoridal fixation obdurate, a clitoridal-vaginal reconciliation might be effected by surgical means, which would then benefit the normal erotic function. Professor Halban, of Vienna, as much a biologist as surgeon, became interested in the problem and worked out a simple operative technique. In this, the suspensory ligament of the clitoris was severed and the clitoris secured to the underlying structures, thus fixing it in a lower position, with eventual reduction of the labia minora. (P. 148.)

But the severest damage was not in the area of surgery, where Freudians ran around absurdly trying to change female anatomy to fit their basic assumptions. The worst damage was done to the mental health of women, who either suffered silently with self-blame, or flocked to the psychiatrists looking desperately for the hidden and terrible repression that kept from them their vaginal destiny.

Lack of Evidence?

One may perhaps at first claim that these are unknown and unexplored areas, but upon closer examination this is certainly not true today, nor was it true even in the past. For example, men have known that women suffered from frigidity often during intercourse. So the problem was there. Also, there is much specific evidence. Men knew that the clitoris was and is the essential organ for masturbation, whether in children or adult women. So obviously women made it clear where *they* thought their sexuality was located. Men also seem suspiciously aware of the clitoral powers during "foreplay," when they want to arouse women and produce the necessary lubrication for penetration. Foreplay is a concept created for male purposes, but works to the disadvantage of many women, since as soon as the woman is aroused the man changes to vaginal stimulation, leaving her both aroused and unsatisfied.

It has also been known that women need no anesthesia inside the vagina during surgery, thus pointing to the fact that the vagina is in fact not a highly sensitive area.

Today, with extensive knowledge of anatomy, with Kinsey, and Masters and Johnson, to mention just a few sources, there is no ignorance on the subject. There are, however, social reasons why this knowledge has not been popularized. We are living in a male society which has not sought change in women's role.

Anatomical Evidence

Rather than starting with what women *ought* to feel, it would seem logical to start out with the anatomical facts regarding the clitoris and vagina.

The Clitoris is a small equivalent of the penis, except for the fact that the urethra does not go through it as in the man's penis. Its erection is similar to the male erection, and the head of the clitoris has the same type of structure and function as the head of the penis. G. Lombard Kelly, in *Sexual Feeling in Married Men and Women,* says:

> The head of the clitoris is also composed of erectile tissue, and it possesses a very sensitive epithelium or surface covering, supplied with special nerve endings called genital corpuscles, which are peculiarly

adapted for sensory stimulation that under proper mental conditions terminates in the sexual orgasm. No other part of the female generative tract has such corpuscles. (Pocketbooks, p. 35.)

The clitoris has no other function than that of sexual pleasure.

The Vagina. Its functions are related to the reproductive function. Principally (1) menstruation, (2) receive penis, (3) hold semen, and (4) birth passage. The interior of the vagina, which according to the defenders of the vaginally caused orgasm is the center and producer of the orgasm, is:

like nearly all other internal body structures, poorly supplied with end organs of touch. The internal entodermal origin of the lining of the vagina makes it similar in this respect to the rectum and other parts of the digestive tract. (Kinsey, Sexual Behavior in the Human Female, *p. 580.)*

The degree of insensitivity inside the vagina is so high that "Among the women who were tested in our gynecologic sample, less than 14 percent were at all conscious that they had been touched." (Kinsey, p. 580.)

Even the importance of the vagina as an *erotic* center (as opposed to an orgasmic center) has been found to be minor.

Other Areas. Labia minora and the vestibule of the vagina. These two sensitive areas may trigger off a clitoral orgasm. Because they can be effectively stimulated during "normal" coitus, though infrequent, this kind of stimulation is incorrectly thought to be vaginal orgasm. However, it is important to distinguish between areas which can stimulate the clitoris, incapable of producing the orgasm themselves, and the clitoris:

Regardless of what means of excitation is used to bring the individual to the state of sexual climax, the sensation is perceived by the genital corpuscles and is localized where they are situated: in the head of the clitoris or penis. (Kelly, p. 49.)

Psychologically stimulated orgasm. Aside from the above mentioned direct and indirect stimulations of the clitoris, there is a third way an orgasm may be triggered. This is through mental (cortical) stimulation, where the imagination stimulates the brain, which in turn stimulates the genital corpuscles of the glans to set off an orgasm.

Women Who Say They Have Vaginal Orgasms

Confusion. Because of the lack of knowledge of their own anatomy, some women accept the idea that an orgasm felt during "normal" intercourse was vaginally caused. This confusion is caused by a combination of two factors. One, failing to locate the center of the orgasm, and two, by a desire to fit her experience to the male-defined idea of sexual normalcy. Considering that women know little about their anatomy, it is easy to be confused.

Deception. The vast majority of women who pretend vaginal orgasm to their men are faking it to, as Ti-Grace Atkinson says, "get the job." In a new best-selling Danish book, *I Accuse* (my own translation), Mette Ejlersen specifically deals with this common problem, which she calls the "sex comedy." This comedy has many causes. First of all, the man brings a great deal of pressure to bear on the woman, because he considers his ability as a lover at stake. So as not to offend his ego, the woman will comply with the prescribed role and go through simulated ectasy. In some of the other Danish women mentioned, women who were left frigid were turned off to sex, and pretended vaginal orgasm to hurry up the sex act. Others admitted that they had faked vaginal orgasm to catch a man. In one case, the woman pretended vaginal orgasm to get him to leave his first wife, who admitted being vaginally frigid. Later she was forced to continue the deception, since obviously she couldn't tell him to stimulate her clitorally.

Many more women were simply afraid to establish their right to equal enjoyment, seeing the sexual act as being primarily for the man's benefit, and any pleasure that the woman got as an added extra.

Other women, with just enough ego to reject the man's idea that they needed psychiatric care, refused to admit their frigidity. They wouldn't accept self-blame, but they didn't know how to solve the problem, not knowing the physiological facts about themselves. So they were left in a peculiar limbo.

Again, perhaps one of the most infuriating and damaging results of this whole charade has been that women who were perfectly healthy sexually were taught that they were not. So in addition to being sexually deprived, these women were told to blame themselves when they deserved no blame. Looking for a cure to a problem that has none can lead a woman on an endless path of self-hatred and insecurity. For she is told by her analyst that not even in her one role allowed in a male society—the role of a woman—is she successful. She is put on the defensive, with phony data as evidence that she better try to be even more feminine, think more feminine, and reject her envy of men. That is, shuffle even harder, baby.

Why Men Maintain the Myth

1. *Sexual penetration is preferred.* The best stimulant for the penis is the woman's vagina. It supplies the necessary friction and lubrication. From a strictly technical point of view this position offers the best physical conditions, even though the man may try other positions for variation.

2. *The invisible woman.* One of the elements of male chauvinism is the refusal or inability to see women as total, separate human beings. Rather, men have chosen to define women only in terms of how they benefited men's lives. Sexually, a woman was not seen as an individual wanting to share equally in the sexual act, any more than she was seen as a person with independent desires when she did anything else in society. Thus, it was easy to make up what was convenient about women; for on top of that, society has been a function of male interests, and women were not organized to form even a vocal opposition to the male experts.

3. *The penis as epitome of masculinity.* Men define their lives greatly in terms of masculinity. It is a *universal,* as opposed to racial, ego boosting, which is localized by the geography of racial mixtures.

The essence of male chauvinism is not the practical, economic services women supply. It is the psychological superiority. This kind of negative definition of self, rather than positive definition based upon one's own achievements and development, has of course chained the victim and the oppressor both. But by far the most brutalized of the two is the victim.

An analogy is racism, where the white racist compensates his feelings of unworthiness by creating an image of the black man (it is primarily a male struggle) as biologically inferior to him. Because of his power in a white male power structure, the white man can socially enforce this mythical division.

To the extent that men try to rationalize and justify male superiority through physical differentiation, masculinity may be symbolized by being the *most* muscular, the most hairy, the deepest voice, and the biggest penis. Women, on the other hand, are approved of (i.e., called feminine) if they are weak, petite, shave their legs, have high soft voices, and no penis.

Since the clitoris is almost identical to the penis, one finds a great deal of evidence of men in various societies trying to either ignore the clitoris and emphasize the vagina (as did Freud), or, as in some places in the Mideast, actually performing clitoridectomy. Freud saw this ancient and still practiced custom as a way of further "feminizing" the female by removing this cardinal vestige of her masculinity. It should be noted also that a big clitoris is considered ugly and masculine. Some cultures engage in the practice of pouring a chemical on the clitoris to make it shrivel up into proper size.

It seems clear to me that men in fact fear the clitoris as a threat to their masculinity.

4. *Sexually expendable male.* Men fear that they will become sexually expendable if the clitoris is substituted for the vagina as the center of pleasure for women. Actually this has a great deal of validity if one considers *only* the anatomy. The position of the penis inside the vagina, while perfect for reproduction, does not necessarily stimulate an orgasm in women because the clitoris is located externally and higher up. Women must rely upon indirect stimulation in the "normal" position.

Lesbian sexuality could make an excellent case, based upon anatomical data, for the extinction of the male organ. Albert Ellis says something to the effect that a man without a penis can make a woman an excellent lover.

Considering that the vagina is very desirable from a man's point of view, purely on physical grounds, one begins to see the dilemma for men. And it forces us as well to discard many "physical" arguments explaining why women go to bed with men. What is left, it seems to me, are primarily psychological reasons why women select men at the exclusion of women as sexual partners.

5. *Control of women.* One reason given to explain the Mideastern practice of clitoridectomy is that it will keep the women from straying. By removing the sexual organ capable of orgasm, it must be assumed that her sexual drive will diminish. Considering how men look upon their women as property, particularly in very backward nations, we should begin to consider a great deal more why it is not in the men's interest to have women totally free sexually. The double standard, as practiced for example in Latin America, is set up to keep the woman as total property of the husband, while he is free to have affairs as he wishes.

6. *Lesbianism and bisexuality.* Aside from the strictly anatomical reasons why women might equally seek other women as lovers, there is a fear on men's part that women will seek the company of other women on a full, human basis. The establishment of clitoral orgasm as fact would threaten the heterosexual *institution.* For it would indicate that sexual pleasure was obtainable from either men *or* women, thus making heterosexuality not an absolute, but an option. It would thus open up the whole question of *human* sexual relationships beyond the confines of the present male-female role system.

Jo Freeman

THE REVOLUTION IS HAPPENING IN OUR MINDS

Jo Freeman, when she wrote the following, was a graduate student at the University of Chicago and an organizer of the women's caucus in political science. In the following article, she traces the growth of feminist awareness and deals extensively with the women's caucus as a new institution. What is the purpose of the caucus? What is "consciousness raising"? What role does the college campus play in women's lib?

From *College and University Business.* Copyright February 1970 by McGraw-Hill, Inc. All rights reserved. Printed in U.S.A.

Slowly, solemnly, the Witches filed around the Federal Building, faces dead white, staring straight ahead, flowing black capes swirling around them. "Our sister justice lies chained and tied," they chanted. "We curse the ground on which she died."

This was Halloween, the annual religious festival of the druidic witches, and a Chicago "coven" of WITCH (Women's International Terrorist Conspiracy from Hell) had chosen the day to announce the beginning of a new, militant phase of the Chicago women's liberation movement.

WITCH is just one branch of the new women's movement that has been building up over the last few years. The guerrilla theater and action group made its initial appearance on Halloween in 1968 when a New York coven (thirteen) whisked down Wall Street to hex the financiers. The Dow-Jones industrial average dropped five points the next day, and WITCH has been expanding its activities ever since. On Halloween 1969 the target was not big money but big government as represented by the conspiracy trial going on in the Federal Building in Chicago. During the same year, other women around the country were doing more than just casting hexes:

—In New York, 400 women filed suit charging that the state abortion laws unconstitutionally deprived women of the right to control their own bodies.

—Students at Grinnell College in conservative Iowa held a "nude-in" when a *Playboy* representative came to speak on his magazine's "philosophy" to protest use of women's bodies as a commodity.

—Berkeley women held hostage an editor of a new underground newspaper, *Dock of the Bay,* until he agreed to stop publication of a special "sextra" issue planned to raise money for the new paper.

—Women from several cities descended on Washington, D.C., in January 1969 to disrupt an inaugural tea given by Mrs. Richard Nixon and again in November to picket HEW.

—The second annual protest of the Miss America contest was held in Atlantic City. The 1969 protest against the use of women as sex objects was milder, with no undergarments thrown into a "Freedom Trash Can" or live sheep crowned "Miss America" as had been done the year before. Participants in the protest were cooled by the police, who segregated them on a small corner of the boardwalk, and by the premature discovery of a women's liberation "plant" among the contestants in the beauty pageant.

—A feminist repertory theater was started in New York, and a private, tax-exempt Human Rights for Women foundation was founded in Washington, D.C., to help fund feminist projects.

—In these and other cities, women were organizing karate classes, agitating for day-care facilities, counseling women on where and how to get abortions, holding numerous women's classes with and without credit, on and off campus, attending more than two dozen regional conferences on women's liberation, with from 60 to 600 participants, and publishing four journals and numerous newsletters.

This fevered activity is only the outward and not always the most significant sign of a new consciousness among women about their "minority" position in society. Only a few years ago most people ridiculed the idea that women had a long way to go. Now women are beginning to recognize and articulate what a West Coast (male) psychologist called the "great reservoir of rage in women— just under the surface." They are beginning to organize themselves into what is called the "women's liberation movement."

The movement actually has two origins, and in many ways there have also been two separate movements that are only now beginning to merge. One, composed primarily of young, white, middle-class, college-educated women, started as a spin-off of the youth and student movements that have been burgeoning over the last 10 years. The other movement has its roots deep within the Establishment and among some of its established critics. Its participants tend to be older, less political, and much more established in career or home. They too are predominantly white, middle-class, and college-educated but less consistently than the other movement's.

Many of the founders of the latter movement come from the network of people built up by the President's Commission on the Status of Women created by President Kennedy in 1961 and the subsequent 50 state commissions. Dissatisfied with the lack of progress being made on the recommendations to come out of these commissions, they met with Betty Friedan, author of *The Feminine Mystique,* and others to form the National Organization for Women (NOW) in 1966.

With the slogan "Full Equality for Women in Truly Equal Partnership with Men," NOW has a top-down structure and an office in New York. It has grown to some 3,000 members, 10 percent of whom are men, and tends to concentrate on eliminating employment discrimination and laws affecting women's rights.

Since its formation, NOW has been joined by such other specifically women's rights organizations as WEAL (Women's Equity Action League), FEW (Federally Employed Women) and several small groups. All these organizations are beginning to join hands with the much older National Women's Party (NWP) to work on the Equal Rights Amendment. The NWP came into existence right after the 19th Amendment was added to the Constitution in 1920. It was the daughter of the radical Congressional Union for Women's Suffrage, which under the leadership of Alice Paul had carried on most of the serious agitation (marching, picketing, fasting) that preceded passage of the amendment. Unlike its more moderate sister, the National American Women's Suffrage Association, which later dissolved into the League for Women Voters, the radicals decided that the battle was not yet won. Ever since 1923, Alice Paul and the NWP have been lobbying for another amendment providing that "equality of rights under law shall not be abridged or denied by reason of sex," and they have twice had it out of committee onto the floor of the U.S. Senate.

In 1967 and 1968, unaware of and unknown to NOW or the state commissions, younger women began forming their own movement. Here too, the groundwork had been laid some years before. The different social action projects of recent years had attracted many women, who were quickly shunted into traditional roles and faced with the self-evident contradiction of working in a "freedom movement" but not being very free. Nor did their male colleagues brook any dissent: They followed the example of Stokeley Carmichael, who cut off all discussion of the issue at a 1964 SNCC conference by saying, "The only position for women in SNCC is prone." In 1967 women in five different cities (Toronto, Detroit, Chicago, Seattle and Gainesville, Fla.) spontaneously, independently, began to meet together. Some came from the New Left groups, some from the southern civil rights movement, and some from the free universities. Unknown even to each other, they began groping for an understanding of why politically aware, affluent, well-educated, white women should feel so downtrodden.

For months they met quietly to analyze their perpetual secondary roles in the radical movement, assimilate lessons learned in study groups, or reflect on their treatment in the civil rights movement. They were constantly ridiculed by the men they worked with and continually told that what they were doing was "counter-revolutionary" because it would further splinter an already badly fragmented movement. In many ways this very ridicule served to feed their growing rage. One immediate result was that all the groups independently banned men from their meetings. In part they borrowed this idea from the then rapidly expanding Black Power movement, which taught the women the importance of running their own show. But their many concurrent bitter experiences also made the ban on men a tactical move, as they learned that female discussions were much more open and honest when there were no men around.

Despite resistance from the men, the women eventually used the infrastructure built up by the civil rights and student movements, the underground press, and the free universities to disseminate women's liberation ideas. In 1968 the groups discovered each other, and at Thanksgiving that year the first, and so far only, national women's liberation convention attracted over 200 women from around the country and Canada on less than a month's notice. Many of them had not been involved in the New Left or other radical activities and were perplexed by the overblown rhetoric used by their more political sisters in the heated debate over whether the women's movement should be a separate one or kept within the radical movement. Nevertheless, they returned to their cities turned on by the idea of women's liberation and since then the movement has expanded at an exponential pace.

This younger women's movement tends to operate as a loose confederation of sister chapters with at best informal ties. However, many cities are now setting up centers to coordinate activities and reach the larger public. As there are no national structures and no membership lists, no one really knows how many women are involved. The best guesses are around 10,000. The number of chapters is also indeterminable. The basic organizational form of the movement, these small groups of 10 to 30 women meet regularly to talk, write or plan actions. They are generally formed on the basis of locality, occupation, marital status, or politics, and some of the more permanent ones have colorful names which add considerably to the political alphabet soup.

Included are: WRAP, Women's Radical Action Project, Chicago; WITCH, everywhere; Redstockings, New York; UWIL, Union for Women's International Liberation, Los Angeles; Women's Majority Union, Seattle, and Cell 16, Boston. Many groups just call themselves Female Liberation, Women's Liberation Front, or Radical Women. It is by these latter terms that the movement as a whole will be referred. The phrase "women's liberation movement" is used for the total new surge of feminism, however, and should not be used to identify just the younger branch which often uses that term to refer to itself.

Nationally the WLF spans a spectrum from an extreme radical feminism that recognizes no other social problems than those of women (these women are often called man-haters, and a few don't object to the term) to women radicals who disdain the word feminism and feel that women's issues should be subsumed under other political concerns. Some areas have become particularly identified with one side or another. Thus, Washington, D.C., and Chicago are highly political, while New York and many of the southern groups are strongly feminist.

Contained in the all-embracing concept of "liberation" is a positive program which gives the WLF an entirely different tone from other student groups. It also makes the radical women seem a good deal quieter than other radicals, because most of their current energy is concentrated on themselves.

When asked what kinds of activities WLF engages in, one West Coast organizer bluntly stated, "We talk to each other about ourselves. That doesn't sound like much, but it turns out to be dynamite. As we exchange experiences, we begin to realize that all these discontents we thought were individual, personal problems have common, social causes. Women have been kept isolated from each other in their individual homes. We've been taught to see each other as enemies, as competitors. Now we're changing that. We're changing our attitude about ourselves, about other women, about society.

The revolution is what is happening in every woman's mind." The intense, often personal discussions which form the core of current WLF activity have not resulted in any detailed programmatic outline. But one thing that has been decided is that sex roles have to go.

To date, all societies have divided labor on the basis of sex, as well as other factors. The sex roles differ with the cultures, but all cultures carefully shape children from birth to fit accepted concepts of masculine and feminine behavior and to believe that these concepts have some eternal validity. In our society, these roles are reflected in our movies, our fiction, our advertising and our opinions; they stereotype women, and men, as rigidly as any ethnic minority.

The new feminists feel that these roles are degrading, confining and anachronistic. While they might have been necessary in the primitive society in which they were developed, they have no place in the complex technology of the 20th Century. Now it is individual ability that is important in performing most socioeconomic functions, not muscular strength nor the possession of a uterus. For the first time in human history, we have the potential to liberate all people to be creative self-fulfilling human beings.

The women's liberation movement feels that one of the greatest barriers to this potential for liberation is the way our society automatically assumes that all people have, or ought to have, particular abilities or interests determined by their sex and treats them accordingly. While men are also adversely affected by this stereotyping (and therefore men cannot be liberated until women are), it is particularly bad for women because the basic values are male, and the basic structures are set up to benefit men. One example often given is the fact that if a man is drafted, his job must be held for him by law, and his scholarship or place in school usually is. When he returns he is given the honors of a veteran and other more tangible benefits such as those available under the G.I. Bill. But if a woman gets pregnant, she is likely to lose her job or be forced to drop out of school, and often she cannot return for several years because the major responsibility of caring for the child is hers. This is the only industrialized nation in the world that does not provide state child-care facilities, and those women who seek other means of caring for their young children are made to feel guilty because they are "neglecting" them. These discrepancies in the treatment of men and women have rarely been pointed out until the last few years.

One of the primary goals of the movement is to break down discriminatory structures and sexual stereotypes. The new feminists feel that men and women should share the privileges and responsibilities of work, home and children. Each person should be free to choose the extent of his or her participation in both domestic and economic spheres. To do this requires changes in the social structure and changes in people's ideas about what women can and should do.

In their discussion groups, women are learning a whole new concept of themselves and how to stand up and fight for what they want. Their purpose is to change people's heads, and enough heads have been changed so that the ideas of women's liberation are taken much more seriously by many more people than they were when the groups were first formed two and a half years ago. "Even those who felt themselves the most enlightened laughed at us at first," declared Joreen, a founder of the first group and one of those who prefers not to use a last name because it is inherited from her father. "But they aren't laughing anymore. Most people don't understand women's liberation, so they try to ignore it. But they can't. It's silent, subtle and subversive. It is spreading everywhere, because it is an idea whose time has come. Discussions may be the main thing now, but this verbalization of the rage within women is only the first step. Eventually it will erupt into action and no one will know quite how it happened."

So far, the most frequent eruptions have been the sporadic WITCH actions. The intent of this WLF offshoot is to use theatrical means to "blow people's minds." Apart from the hexes, most public actions by the radical women tend to be symbolic, like the Miss America protests. Because so much of women's "oppression" involves individual attitudes, there is a good deal of individual confrontations.

Although women's liberation is not primarily a student phenomenon, perhaps the most disruptive action to date has taken place on a campus. When the University of Chicago erupted in January 1969 with massive protests and a two-week sit-in over the firing of radical feminist professor Marlene Dixon, women's issues were not lost in the shuffle. It was largely due to the efforts of Mrs. Dixon, now teaching at McGill University, and the primarily undergraduate WRAP that women's liberation issues were publicly aired in Chicago for the first time. Protesting the general attitude of the university toward women, WRAP demanded more women faculty and more courses on women, objected to advisers who recommend marriage instead of a continued academic career and teachers who disparage women as a group in class or who see them primarily as sex objects.

Women in the professional schools began to form caucuses in their departments to analyze their problems as professionals.

Women in one caucus even formed their own separate organization—the Association of Women Psychologists. The need for this is perhaps indicated by the closed-mind response of a council member of the American Psychological Association to a request that accreditation be withheld from the department that cannot show non-discrimination. With a shocked expression on his face he declared: "You can't make that demand. We haven't even conceded that to the blacks yet." This statement at last September's Washington conference prompted one surprised woman to comment: "This just shows that women are even a second-class minority group. We can only ask for what blacks have already got."

Organization of women professionals and graduate students has just begun, and indications are that it will be one of the most potent forces to hit the academic world since SDS. Concerted efforts are being made to organize women horizontally through their professional organizations, and vertically on their campuses by departments, into what has the potential for becoming a tightly-knit national structure. Although it is not yet clear what specific institutional changes the caucuses will demand of higher education—beyond those already expressed at the ASA APA and APSA conventions, their mere existence serves to strengthen the position of women in the departments.

According to Sociologist Alice Rossi, long-time radical feminist,

The caucuses make it easier for women to do things for themselves—they don't have to wait until the institutions deign to do something. Just organizing provides a support group which helps women get through graduate school, confront the usual put-downs by male professors and

*colleagues, understand that many of the problems they face are struc-
tural, not personal, and open up new fields of inquiry by pointing out the
flaws in sex role conceptions. The solidarity function of the caucuses is
as important as the institutional changes demanded.*

The caucuses are interested not only in the condition of women in
the university, but also in what the university teaches about women.
Their conclusion is that it teaches them nothing good. "There is an
anti-woman bias inherent in the social sciences we are being taught,"
declared a graduate student in sociology. "Women are rarely
studied by the predominantly male social scientists, and when they
are the data are always interpreted to justify their inferior position."
She went on to point out that new studies are just being done

*which show that women are taught the same kind of self-hate and group-
hate that blacks and other minority groups have suffered from. Children
respond to the expectations others have about them, particularly parents
and teachers, and girls learn early that they are not supposed to amount
to much of anything. We live in a society which rewards high achievement—outside the home—yet a recent University of Michigan study
shows that even college women have learned to fear success as something which is 'unfeminine.' As students we can't even look to our
professors for examples of how to act as women professionals because
all but a handful of them are male.*

These conclusions are resulting in a concerted effort to include
more courses on women and more material on women in regular
courses. This demand has often mystified most professors because
they don't see anything particularly lacking or wrong with what is
already being taught. Some of this confusion is cleared up by social
psychologist Judith Long Laws, one of the few researchers on
women respected by the new feminists:

*Most of the work on women in the social sciences is derived from
three myths. They are (1) anatomy is destiny, in the tradition of Freud;
(2) women aren't serious about work, therefore working women shouldn't
be taken seriously, and (3) the individualistic fallacy, which says "excel-
lence will out" despite prejudice, and then points to the lack of great
achievements by women.*

Dr. Laws went on to say that the field of "women studies" is just
beginning to open up as these assumptions are being questioned

and that this development is being accelerated by the growing women's liberation movement. She predicted that within a few years forward-looking universities will be hunting for people to make their reputations in this field. But "in the short run, they will have to hire women to research and define these problems, because it will take men a long time to get the sensitizations necessary to do so, and the women aren't going to wait." Several foundations have already indicated their interest in financing relevant studies, so "women studies" may soon rival "black studies" as the newest interdisciplinary area.

While graduate students and faculty are becoming concerned with their situation as professionals without necessarily feeling they are part of the women's liberation movement—the movement has been spreading to the undergraduates from off campus. For a long time it was of no interest to undergraduate women, who, living in the most egalitarian situation they will ever know, were simply not familiar with the problems. However, now that women's liberation has become "in" many are discovering that it does in fact have much to say to them.

One Iowa woman student said, "How many times have we been told 'You'd better get a teaching certificate, just in case' rather than encouraged to go on to, say, science." At Cornell College, the women complain they are tired of the "shame of graduating without a 'Mrs.,' " or "the feeling you're going to die if you don't get a date on Saturday night." A recent Florida graduate talked of "the split personality you develop. You have to be competent in school and then act like a helpless little girl on dates to keep the male ego bolstered."

Although the women's movement did not start on the college campus, higher education has a good deal to do with its cause. The number of women, and men, going to college has risen steadily until today more than half of all college-age youth are in college. There is always a direct correlation between revolt and education. In the case of women, it is proving impossible to "keep them barefoot and pregnant," when they have B.A.s and Ph.D.s. Like their male counterparts women want to use what they have learned, and very little of their higher education has anything to do with housekeeping and child care. It is no more surprising that college-educated women are in the forefront of the women's liberation movement than it is that a higher percentage of women with degrees work full time than do those of lesser education.

The campus is also providing a testing area for new interpersonal relationships which are having a strong effect on the traditional family structure. Women no longer go from the house of their father to that of their husband. They go to college first. There the experience of college roommates provides a model of living with someone else in an egalitarian relationship which is transferred by both men and women into marriage. The developing practice of living with someone of the opposite sex as a test of compatibility before marriage is still another transitional stage. This new "gradualism" of family formation, which incorporates at least some egalitarian experiences, is providing the time necessary to work out new living arrangements which was not possible under the rigid, traditional system.

The campus is not a major source of women's discontent, but it may turn out to be a major focal point of their anger. It manages at one and the same time to incorporate an egalitarian philosophy with an authoritarian structure. While women students are, theoretically at least, told they are the intellectual equals of men, they have only to look around them to see the lack of women among their teachers and their disproportionate staff positions.

For the young female activists of today, the university is a ready-made example of hypocrisy they find so deplorable. If higher education doesn't listen to some of its own advice and change some of its own policies to further equalize the position of women in its own departments, it may find that it has educated its women students to make the changes themselves.

Martha Weinman Lear
THE SECOND FEMINIST WAVE

In the last few years, newspapers and magazines have published numerous stories about the women's liberation movement. Martha Weinman Lear, a free-lance writer, wrote one of the most comprehensive summaries. What do her biographies of leading feminists reveal? What are the full implications of Ti-Grace Atkinson's views, for example, those regarding communal living? How feasible or desirable, do you think, would be the abolition of the nuclear family in our society? In what ways do Betty Friedan and Ti-Grace Atkinson agree and disagree?

It was billed as a black comedy, nothing elaborate. Twelve comely feminists, dressed for cocktails, would crash the hearings of the Equal Employment Opportunities Commission on sex discrimination in employment. They would make some noise, possibly get arrested, certainly get thrown out, meet the press, and all the while give prominent display to large, home-lettered signs, of which my favorite read: "A Chicken in Every Pot, A Whore in Every Home."

The feminists were members of the New York chapter of NOW (a multilayered acronym: The National Organization for Women, which wants "full equality for all women in America, in truly equal partnership with men," *now*). To the press, they would explain that they were protesting all those prejudices and laws of the land which keep women at home and in the bottom of the job market, but exclude them from jobs that utilize intelligence in any significant way.

This makes it clear, they would say, that women are valued not for their intelligence but only for their sexuality—i.e., as wives and mothers—which, stripping the matter of its traditional sacred cows, reduces the Woman's Role to a sort of socially acceptable whoredom.

The point was delicate and not necessarily crystal clear, and certain NOW officials foresaw a disastrous misunderstanding. As one of them pointed out, how might the banner headlines look: "Prostitutes Picket E.E.O.C."?

By compromise, 12 "whores" metamorphosed into two secretaries who picketed the E.E.O.C. several weeks back, literally chained to

From *The New York Times Magazine,* March 10, 1968, pp. 24–25; 50–60. © 1968 by The New York Times Company. Reprinted by permission.

their typewriters. This made a precise point in an eminently respectable way, and the press coverage was good.

Shortly before that, NOW members had picketed The New York Times in protest against the "Help Wanted—Male" and "Help Wanted—Female" column headings in classified advertising. They maintained these designations violate Title VII of the Civil Rights Act of 1964, which prohibits sex discrimination in employment. The E.E.O.C. permits such column headings, by a logic which seems capricious to feminists and complex to almost everyone. NOW representatives met with officials of The Times ("We told them," one feminist said, "that those column headings perpetuate the employment ghetto." "We told them," said Monroe Green, then The Times vice president in charge of advertising, "that if we discontinued the column headings there might be fewer jobs for women because men would be applying for them. After all, men can be just as militant as women.") Nothing swayed, the NOW people recently announced that they are bringing suit against the E.E.O.C. to get a ruling on the matter.

They also are helping two stewardesses' unions fight for the right of an airline hostess to stay on the job after she dodders past her 32d birthday. In New York, they are pushing for the repeal of all state abortion laws. In Washington, they are lobbying for passage of a civil-rights amendment for women, which has been getting tossed out of every Congress since 1923. In various states they have pending court cases which will test the validity of so-called "protective laws" (i.e., women may work only so many hours; women may lift only so many pounds). NOW says these laws are obsolescent and keep women from earning more money and getting better jobs.

What NOW wants, by way of immediate implementation of its goals, is total enforcement of Title VII; a nationwide network of child-care centers, operating as optional community facilities; revision of the tax laws to permit full deduction of housekeeping and child-care expenses for working parents; maternity benefits which would allow some period of paid maternity leave and guarantee a woman's right to return to her job after childbirth; revision of divorce and alimony laws ("so that unsuccessful marriages may be terminated without hypocrisy, and new ones contracted without undue financial hardship to either man or woman"), and a constitutional amendment withholding Federal funds from any agency, institution or organization discriminating against women.

In short, feminism, which one might have supposed as dead as the Polish Question, is again an issue. Proponents call it the Second Feminist Wave, the first having ebbed after the glorious victory of suffrage and disappeared, finally, into the great sandbar of Togetherness. When I prepared to do an article on this new tide, I prepared also to be entertained; it is the feminist burden that theirs is the only civil-rights movement in history which has been put down, consistently, by the cruelest weapon of them all—ridicule.

"We must not be afraid of ridicule," they say to one another. And, indeed, when pink refrigerators abound, when women (51 percent of the population) hold unparalleled consumer power, when women control most of the corporate stocks, when women have ready access to higher education and to the professions, when millions of women are gainfully employed, when all the nation is telling American women, all the time, that they are the most privileged female population on earth, the insistence on a civil-rights movement for women does seem a trifle stubborn. "Oh, come off it; why ruin it for the rest of us?" a New York matron recently commented to a NOW member, and she wasn't half kidding.

But the feminists, in answer, pose a question: Ruin *what?* In the anti-feminist view, the status quo is plenty good enough. In the feminist view, it is a sellout: American women have traded their rights for their comfort, and now are too comfortable to care.

Economic power is a fraud, the feminists say, when it devolves ultimately upon the power to decide which breakfast food to buy; that is not what *men* mean when they speak of power. The corporate power is a myth. "What it means generally," says NOW's president, Betty Friedan, whose book, *The Feminine Mystique,* provided a powerful undercurrent to this second wave, "is that wives and widows own the stocks and men vote them."

Equal opportunity in education is seen as similarly mythical. "By the time a girl is ready for medical school, she doesn't want to go anymore," says Kate Millet of NOW's New York chapter, an artist and English instructor at Barnard. "She never really had a choice. She's been conditioned to her role ever since she got the doll to play with, and her brother got the gun." Seven percent of the nation's doctors are women, 3 percent of its lawyers, 1 percent of its engineers. Nor does this represent progress; the figures have been moving downward quite steadily since World War II, when that first feminist wave receded entirely.

As to the job market: 28 million women are in it and three-quarters of them are in the rock-bottom of it. Ninety percent earn less than $5,000 a year. John F. Kennedy's Commission on the Status of Women reported in 1963 that women earn up to 40 percent less than men, on the same jobs. It further noted:

> *The subtle limitations imposed by custom are, upon occasion, reinforced by specific barriers. . . . Some of these discriminatory provisions are contained in the common law. Some are written into statute. Some are upheld by court decisions. Others take the form of practices of industrial, labor, professional or governmental organizations that discriminate against women in apprenticeship, training, hiring, wages and promotion.*

In a paper called "Jane Crow and the Law," written by New York lawyer Pauli Murray and Mary O. Eastwood, a lawyer with the Justice Department, the pivotal point was made that the doctrine of legislative classification by sex, which generally has been upheld in the courts, "totally defeats the meaning of equal protection of the law for women."

It's all there, but most women seem not to consider it a burning issue of the day. What, then, makes the feminist? One kind of answer is provided by Jean Faust of New York's NOW: 37, married, attractive, a research assistant to Congressman William F. Ryan. Of her marriage, she says:

> *I do not agree with the concept of marriage; but I must live in our society, and this is still the most convenient way for a man and a woman to remain together.*
>
> *I grew up in North Carolina, a sharecropper's daughter. In a farm surrounding, muscle counts. I had eight brothers and sisters, and it was constantly drummed into me that the men rule, that they are smarter and more important and may live a freer life.*
>
> *In school, I was always way ahead of the boys. So I began to ask myself: "How can they say boys are smarter?" As I grew older, I realized more and more that girls had no real part in forming the lives they would lead, or their roles or aspirations. The boys could go as far as their talents would allow, but the girls had it all planned out for them.*

I managed to get to college. I would try to express my ideas, and the men would laugh. They'd say, "That's funny; you don't look like a feminist." You know—if you're a feminist, you're not feminine.

When I got married, it was worse. I had worked myself into an executive position with a cosmetics firm, and there were two men working for me who made more money than I did. When I asked for a raise, my employer said: "You're a married woman. You don't need a raise. Your husband will support you." So I quit.

I joined NOW as soon as I heard of it, and I believe we will be historic. Men all along have determined what part we should take in society. And for the first time, we are saying: "NO!"

In point of fact, it has been getting said for centuries, and men have said it. Socrates said that the state shortchanged itself and its women by confining them to the domestic role. Auguste Comte spoke of "the feminine revolution" that "must now complete the proletarian revolution. . . ." John Stuart Mill wrote that "the legal subordination of one sex to the other . . . ought to be replaced by a principle of perfect equality." In our own decades, Gunnar Myrdal has written: "As the Negro was awarded his 'place' in society, so there was a 'woman's place'. . . . The myth of the 'contented woman,' who did not want to have suffrage or other civil rights and equal opportunities, had the same social function as the myth of the 'contented Negro.' "

NOW often makes this analogy between the Negro and the woman in society, calling itself, in fact, a sort of N.A.A.C.P. for women. (Not that there is unanimity on this point; predictably, there are feminist evolutionaries and feminist revolutionaries, and the revolutionaries prefer an analogy to the early CORE.)

The women who formed NOW, in 1966, had no need individually of a civil rights organization. They wanted, they say, to reach those masses of women who stand outside the mainstream of society, and help them swim. Among the charter members were Dr. Kathryn Clarenbach, a Wisconsin educator; Alice Rossi, a Chicago sociologist; Aileen Hernandez, a California lawyer and former member of the E.E.O.C.; Caroline Davis, a Detroit U.A.W. executive, and Betty Friedan.

For years feminism has been an apology [says Mrs. Friedan]. All those ladies' auxiliaries like the League of Women Voters, saying, "Don't

*get us wrong: we're not feminists." What self-denigration! I call them
Aunt Toms. Aunt Toms think there are three kinds of people—men,
women and themselves.*

*Once I was interviewed on television and said something about getting
more satisfaction out of having a byline than out of washing dishes. And
the hostess, a big, tough battle-axe who has worked ruthlessly for her
success, smiled tenderly at the studio audience and said, "Oh, girls . . .
what does a byline mean? Don't we all know that being home washing
the dishes and caring for her loved ones is the most satisfying work a
woman can do?" That's a real Aunt Tom.*

*A group of us met in Washington with the head of the E.E.O.C. We
said one of our complaints was that women were employed only in the
most menial jobs in his department. He said, "I'm interviewing girls right
now for important jobs." I said, "Mr. Chairman, I would hope you're interviewing women." It's like calling a 50-year-old Negro "boy." He got the
point.*

Today NOW has 1,200 members, with a heavy concentration of
lawyers, sociologists and educators. Among these 1,200 are some
hundred men, many of them also lawyers. For all of them the central
issue is civil rights, as purely defined as in the Negro civil-rights
movement.

"There are striking parallels," says New York attorney Florynce
Henderson, an ebullient revolutionary spirit who represents H. Rap
Brown. "In court, you often get a more patronizing attitude to blacks
and women than to white men: 'Your Honor, I've known this boy
since he was a child, his mother worked for my family. . . .' 'Your
Honor, she is just a woman, she has three small children. . . .' And
I think white male society often takes the same attitude toward both:
'If we want to *give* power to you, O.K. But don't act as if you're
entitled to it.' That's too manly, too . . . white."

Not all of the new feminist activity is centered within NOW. To its
left is a small group called Radical Women—young, bright-eyed,
cheerfully militant—which recently splintered off from Students for
a Democratic Society. "One of our main problems in the liberal left,"
says Anne Koedt, a New York commercial artist, "was that we were
considered a sort of sex pool. The so-called 'emancipated male'
wants women to be free because he thinks that means free love. It's
the Playboy image, the same old adolescent sex hang-up. We want
to get *away* from relating to men merely as sex objects. We believe
in a total change in the social structure to achieve total equality of

the sexes, so that men and women will be free to come together in more humane, meaningful relationships." So go the Radical Women. Some of them recently joined—infiltrated?—NOW, whose conservative faction ponders the alliance with a certain ambivalence.

There is also the Quid Pro Quo in New Orleans. It is a one-member civil-rights organization for women, and the member is a man: Richard N. Matthews, an attorney, who currently represents 16 women in a suit to challenge the state protective laws. "Some of these women support their families and have to moonlight," Mr. Matthews says. "They can't work more than eight hours for one employer, but they can work eight hours each for two employers. Women always have gotten the short end of the industrial stick. It's archaic. It's absurd. If women stopped working, they could shut down the country."

The evolutionaries attack concrete issues, tied primarily to employment. They are NOW's pragmaticians, and its overwhelming majority. The militants are its theoreticians—atypical, but they are interesting, because they are the movement's intellectual hip, the female version of Black Power.

Mostly they are young, incipiently successful, unmarried. (Married feminists tend to retain their maiden names, as with Suzanne Schad-Somers, a sociologist named Schad married to a sociologist named Somers, who says: "My husband urged me to join NOW. Neither of us believes you can have a good marriage on the basis of a traditional division of labor.) Philosophically they are by Comte out of Simone de Beauvoir, whose book *The Second Sex* shattered the serenity of a postwar generation of sociology majors raised on *Kirche, Küche und Kinder*. Their thesis is that true equality for women can come only with profound social revolution. Their *haute* thinker, and thus the key to their spirit and style, is Ti-Grace Atkinson (in the *patois* of Louisiana, where she was born, "Ti" designates a namesake), president of the New York chapter.

Miss Atkinson is 29, unmarried, good-looking (in *The Times,* she has been described as "softly sexy," which is not *necessarily* a compliment to a feminist). She is an analytic philosopher, working for her doctorate at Columbia.

I saw her at a recent American Philosophical Association convention in Boston, standing toe-to-toe with a social philosopher, his nose pointed belligerently up at her chin, as he insisted angrily upon the biological superiority of men. He was perhaps 5 foot 5, and Miss Atkinson is 5 foot 9, and it really wasn't fair. Later, she sparred lightly with another philosopher, noting: "We seem to have a chary attitude toward one another." And he, sparring less lightly, replied, "Yes, but mine is much charier than yours." To a third, she said, "You mean, you don't believe women should have equal rights?" And he answered: "I don't believe they exist, so how can they have rights?" Philosophers.

Later, she said:

> *He wasn't kidding. Why should men think women are equal, when so many women don't?*
>
> *Most women don't really see themselves as human beings with potential. They live through their husbands and children. They see themselves vicariously as the men they're married to. They achieve their status through "the other"* [a de Beauvoir concept].
>
> *The institution of marriage has the same effect the institution of slavery had. It separates people in the same category, disperses them, keeps them from identifying, as a class. The masses of slaves didn't recognize their condition, either. To say that a woman is really "happy" with her home and kids is as irrelevant as saying that the blacks were "happy" being taken care of by Ol' Massa. She is defined by her maintenance role. Her husband is defined by his productive role. We're saying that all human beings should have a productive role in society.*
>
> *We've always been so defensive. "Oh, no, we're not feminists, but can we just have a little more, huh? Please? Huh?" I think it's time for us to go on the offensive. I think we ought to say, "Listen, you, you dumb broad, you look funny. You stay home, you're kind of empty, you're bored, you take your frustrations out on your husband, you dominate your kids, and when you get older you disintegrate. You fill the doctor's offices with headaches and backaches and depression, you tell the psychiatrists you don't feel 'fulfilled,' you get menopausal breakdown. . . . What good are you? Who are you? Get with it."*

Miss Atkinson herself was a late starter, as feminists go. She was married at 17, with the blessing of social and conservative parents who felt that marriage would soothe their daughter's rebellious (not feminist, simply rebellious) spirit. For a time, she lived with her student husband in a campus community where, as she recalls "I went to little tea parties given by faculty wives and sat there feeling that life was over. At 17."

When her husband went into the service, she enrolled at the University of Pennsylvania, got a fine arts degree, later got a divorce, and spent several years commuting between New York, where she was writing criticism for *Art News,* and Philadelphia, where she helped found the Institute of Contemporary Art. She was its first director, in 1963.

"I felt I was budding, growing, but I had no clear idea of my direction. I still knew nothing of feminist concepts." Then friends recommended that she read de Beauvoir's *The Second Sex.* Whammo. "It changed everything for me. It changed my life." She enrolled at Columbia as a graduate student in philosophy and embarked upon a correspondence with de Beauvoir, who suggested that Miss Atkinson put herself in touch with some women's civil-rights group in the United States. Thus she came to the infant NOW, and was put to work as a national fund raiser; her social connections were good, and it may have occurred to some NOW officials that her appearance might help dissipate the traditional image of the feminist as a castrating crow in bloomers.

"I think, in the beginning, they thought that with my kind of genteel Republican background I might be too conservative for them," says Miss Atkinson. "Ho, ho."

She was elected president of the New York chapter last summer, and promptly drafted the position paper on abortion, which claims as a civil right a woman's control of her own reproductive process up to the time of birth.

I'm a little bored with the abortion issue now [she says]. "I'd rather talk about the demise of marriage.

I'm afraid the women's movement in this country is still pretty low-class, intellectually. Practically all we talk about is equal rights in employment. That's not opportunity; it's opportunism. Who the hell can say that getting a woman's job changed from a stewardess to a typist is a breakthrough? [She is referring to the case of Pauline Dziob, a ship's stewardess who recently fought for the traditionally male rating of yeoman. Miss Dziob was upheld by the New York State Human Rights Commission.] The breakthrough can come only with a change in the social institutions.

We're afraid of the truth. To say that you can be both a career woman and a wife and mother, and that the institutions won't change and won't be threatened—that's a cop-out. De Beauvoir says that some men may *be limited by marriage, but few women fail to be annihilated by it. Any real change in the status of women would be a fundamental assault on marriage and the family. People would be tied together by love, not legal contraptions. Children would be raised communally; it's just not honest to talk about freedom for women unless you get the child-rearing off their backs. We may not be ready for any of this yet, but if we're going to be honest, we've got to talk about it. Face it, raise the questions.*

The trouble is, hardly anybody wants to. Even feminists who take a most cavalier attitude toward marriage turn cautious when the question of children arises. Miss Atkinson's own view is that the concept of the nuclear family must be abolished entirely, giving way to a society in which the bonds between generations would be maintained communally instead of by the one-to-one parent-child relationship—a society, she says, in which "all children would be loved by all adults. They would form close relationships within their own age groups, rather than needing to get approval and value from authority figures. Of course, close human contact is essential, but there is no reason to believe that it must come from a mother. Children can get it from one another, as adults do."

In Miss Atkinson's view, the early communal experiments in Russia and Israel, and those which pertain in many Communist countries today, are bound to fail because they don't go far enough —in other words, parents still identify with individual children. "The continuance of the inheritance idea—the idea of living on through things, property, children—subverts any possibility of the communal society succeeding. For people to live communally instead of competitively, the bonds of inheritance must be completely broken." The question then arises: Why bother to have children at all? And Miss Atkinson answers: "Because of a rational decision to continue the human race."

Well, this is where the shouting starts. As regards communal child-raising experiments in our time (none of which, by the way, has gone nearly so far as Miss Atkinson proposes, nor is likely to), no one can call them a failure, and no one can call them a roaring success, either. Sociologist Schad-Somers, who teaches at Rutgers, says: "My own conclusion, based on the empirical evidence, is that children raised collectively are more independent, more cooperative, with fewer psycho-sexual problems than kids raised in the United

States." Mrs. Schad-Somers would not for a moment, however, advocate a complete break of the family ties. "We would be giving up something precious, needlessly," she says. "I surely want children, and I would hope to raise them in a good day-care center. The day-care supervisors and the natural parents would provide alternate models and love objects for the child, which probably would be much better for him than the exclusive and highly interdependent relationship with his mother."

On the other hand, Dr. Selma Fraiberg, director of the Child Development Project at the University of Michigan's Child Psychiatric Hospital, says some research on the early kibbutz children suggests that they turned out to be "a bunch of cool cookies who wouldn't give one the feeling of knowing them awfully well. Certainly, they seem in no way superior to children raised in our family system."

And a third view comes from the director of a leading child-research clinic in New York, who says that, on the basis of current evidence, no one can say much about communally raised children except that, like all children, they have problems. Besides, he says, this is not the point. "The point is that we are moving in this direction, inevitably. In the next few years, the interrelationship between family and communal care of children will be a major topic on the American scene. We are not talking, of course, about *destroying* the parent-child relationship, but *supplementing* it, and the findings from other countries give us no reason to feel apprehensive."

Dr. Fraiberg takes the most conservative position. In her view, even a day-care system would have its hazards.

"It is almost impossible in such a system to maintain true intimacy, continuity, a continuous dialogue," she says. "Whatever problems may emerge from the intimacy between mother and child, the things we value most also emerge from just this intimacy. It needn't be a crushing intimacy. Sometimes it is. But because human ties sometimes produce neurosis doesn't mean we should throw out the ties." And as to Miss Atkinson's vision, she says: "It is at least comforting to know that such women are not going to reproduce their own kind."

Within NOW, there is an altogether understandable reluctance to pursue the matter. Here are the radicals, wanting to be heard. Out there are the mothers' clubbers, waiting to be alienated. The feminists are not anxious to alienate anyone, and even mild threats to the abiding institutions do tend to frighten most women to death.

I remember the extraordinary response to an article Marya Mannes once wrote for *The Times Magazine,* in which she espoused child day-care centers, hardly a revolutionary idea. What impressed me about the flood of readers' letters was not their disapproval, but their rage. One woman called Miss Mannes a prostitute, and another wrote that she was dirty-minded and un-American and ought to go back to wherever she had come from, which happened to be New York.

> *I do think we have to raise these questions* [says Betty Friedan, with caution]. *As an individual, not as a member of NOW, I can't help but raise them. Marriage, for example: It may be that we are asking too much of it, and that almost inevitably it will become a straitjacket for both sexes. The inefficacy of all this tinkering, the assumption of "Can this marriage be saved?" makes you want to vomit.*
>
> *We work with the realities of American life, and in reality our job now is to make it possible for women to integrate their roles at home and in society. But as to whether we will finally have to challenge the institutions, the concepts of marriage and the nuclear family—I don't know. I just don't know.*
>
> *What I do know is this: If you agree that women are human beings who should be realizing their potential, then no girl child born today should responsibly be brought up to be a housewife. Too much has been made of defining human personality and destiny in terms of the sex organs. After all, we share the human brain.*

Strategies of the New Feminism

NOW, the National Organization for Women, was organized in October 1966 by Betty Friedan. The purpose of the organization was to secure equal human rights for women within the framework of our society. The following news report describing NOW's formation as well as the 1970 editorial from the new president, Aileen Hernandez, provide some insight into the goals and methods of NOW. How does this organization differ from the Feminist Alliance of the 1910's? How does it compare with the philosophy and the groups of the radical feminists of the 1960's?

Lisa Hammel

NOW ORGANIZED

Although no one in the dim ruby and sapphire Victorian parlor actually got up and cried: "Women of the world, unite! You have nothing to lose but your chains," that was the prevailing sentiment yesterday morning at the crowded press conference held by the newly formed National Organization for Women.

NOW, which is the organization's urgent acronym, was formed three weeks ago in Washington to press for "true equality for all women in America . . . as part of the world-wide revolution of human rights now taking place."

The organization has been informally styled by several of its directors the "N.A.A.C.P. of women's rights."

The board of directors asked President Johnson, in the text of a letter released yesterday, to give "top priority among legislative proposals for the next Congress to legislation which would give effective enforcement powers to the Equal Employment Opportunity

Commission," which, the letter stated, "is hampered . . . by a reluctance among some of its male members to combat sex discrimination as vigorously as they seek to combat racial discrimination."

Separate letters were also sent to Acting Attorney General Ramsey Clark and the three current commissioners of the Equal Employment Opportunity Commission.

"As part of the Great Society program," the letter to the President read, "your administration is currently engaged in a massive effort to bring underprivileged groups—victims of discrimination because of poverty, race or lack of education—into the mainstream of American life. However, no comprehensive effort has yet been made to include women in your Great Society program for the underprivileged and excluded."

The press conference was held amid the dark Victorian curlicues and oriental carpeting in the apartment of the organization's president, Betty Freidan.

Mrs. Friedan who became a household word when she gave "the problem that has no name" the name of "The Feminine Mystique" in a best-seller published three years ago, explained in her book to disgruntled housewives across the country that they had been sold a bill of goods by society.

Creative dishwashing and a life unremittingly devoted to the care and feeding of a husband and children is not the alpha and omega of a woman's existence, Mrs. Friedan maintained, nor is a woman likely to find complete fulfillment as an adult human being either among the diapers and soapsuds or in the boudoir.

"Our culture," Mrs. Friedan wrote, "does not permit women to accept or gratify their basic need to grow and fulfill their potentialities as human beings, a need which is not solely defined by their sexual role."

Mrs. Friedan said last week in an interview in her apartment that NOW had "just begun to think about methods" to implement its goals of enabling women to "enjoy the equality of opportunity and freedom of choice which is their right . . . in truly equal partnership with men."

Speaking in a gravelly alto from the depths of the large fur collar that trimmed her neat black suit, the ebullient author suggested that women today were "in relatively little position to influence or control major decisions."

"But," she added, leaning forward in the lilac velvet Victorian chair and punching the air as if it were something palpable, "what women do have is the vote.

"We will take strong steps in the next election," Mrs. Friedan continued, "to see that candidates who do not take seriously the question of equal rights for women are defeated."

The position paper issued by NOW at its formation on Oct. 29 stated that: "We shall strive to ensure that no party, candidate, president, senator, governor, congressman, or any public official who betrays or ignores the principle of full equality between the sexes is elected or appointed to office" and that to this end the organization would "mobilize the votes of men and women who believe in our cause."

"Politics?" the Rev. Dean Lewis repeated yesterday in answer to a question. "What do you have for women in that field? Women's political auxiliaries. They are put aside in nice separate structures without policy-making powers."

Reason for Joining

Mr. Lewis, a slender man with a neat pointed beard, is the secretary of the Office of Social Education and Evangelism of the United Presbyterian Church in the United States.

"Why did I join NOW?" he said. "It's like asking somebody why they joined the N.A.A.C.P. I'm interested in equal rights for anybody who desires them. The structure of both law and custom in our society deprives women of their rights."

Mr. Lewis is one of the 5 men on NOW's 28-member board of directors. The vice president of the organization is Richard Graham, director of the National Teacher Corps and a former Equal Employment Opportunity Commissioner.

NOW states in its position paper that it is concerned with discrimination where it exists against men as well as against women.

Mrs. Friedan explained that the organization believed that most alimony laws were discriminatory against men and that NOW intended to reexamine current laws.

The 500 members of NOW have been drawn from many fields,

including education, labor, government, the social sciences, mass communications and religion. Two Roman Catholic nuns are members of the board of directors.

"There is religious discrimination in the church, but that is not my main reason for joining the organization," said Sister Mary Joel Read, chairman of the department of history at Alverno College, a Roman Catholic college for women in Milwaukee.

"This is not a feminist movement," the nun continued. "It is not a question of getting male privileges. In the past the possibility of realizing one's humanity was limited to an elite group at the top. Women are not equal in our society. This movement centers around the possibility of being human."

Aileen Hernandez

EDITORIAL FROM NOW'S PRESIDENT

In the Chinese calendar, this is the Year of the Dog. And in the NOW calendar, this is the Year of Dogged Determination—determination to implement our program for full liberation. This year we set goals, organize our troops, and devise strategies to meet those goals.

It's a "do-your-own-thing, but-do-it-effectively" year. It's the year NOW members and supporters across the country turn on and turn out to *work* at the things we believe in. It's the year we put our money where our mouth is and finance our movement; it's the year we get off the soapbox and into the battle.

NOW has been fantastically effective in the brief few years since October of 1966 in Washington, D.C., when 300 men and women pledged an all-out war on sex discrimination. We have eighty chapters or chapters in formation in twenty-four states (and by the time I get that written a new chapter has come into existence and another state has been added to the list.) *We are growing.* And we're reaching people who haven't been tuned in to the women's move-

From the July 1970 newsletter of NOW. Reprinted by permission of the author.

ment before. Radio wants our voices; TV wants our faces; newspapers and magazines want our "profiles." In short—we're fast becoming the "in" thing. And there's danger in that—the danger of becoming infatuated with our voices, faces and profiles—and forgetting that the guts of the movement is *not* in what we say, but in what we do.

There are things to do this year and in the years to come. We have *programs* to implement, and to turn away from Virginia Slims and on to Robert Frost: "[we] have promises to keep, and miles to go before [we] sleep."

Promise #1: Passage of the equal rights amendment Introduced into Congress every session since 1923, the amendment presently languishes in the Senate Judiciary Committee, has a vague commitment from the House Judiciary Committee for "late summer hearings," and has still not been endorsed by sufficient members of the House of Representatives to ensure passage. How do your Senators and Representatives stand? Write them immediately urging them to support the amendment this year. If you need "talking points," contact NOW.

Promise #2: Child-care centers A must item if we are going to free women to improve their educational level, hold jobs, or just get a respite from the narrow confines of the home. NOW is committed to developing child-care centers throughout the United States —open to all, regardless of need. The commitment must now be translated into action. As a goal—realizable this year—each NOW chapter should actually establish a child-care center or substantially aid other groups in establishing a center.

Promise #3: Control of reproductive processes NOW can take a lot of credit for the significant changes in the abortion laws in many states, but we have not completed the job. Abortion—despite the legal changes—is still outside the financial possibility of most women. NOW can help to define the new approaches to abortion— use of para medical people, abortion clinics, etc. Write to U.S. Senator Robert Packwood of Oregon commending him for introducing a bill to remove abortion from the criminal statutes, but urging that the bill be further amended to eliminate the present requirement that all abortions be performed in hospitals. Demand a voice on environment control committees, many of which are on the right cause, but with the wrong emphasis—women are still being manipulated—this time *not* to have babies. Women want the right to make these determinations themselves.

Promise #4: Inclusion of "sex" in all titles of Civil Rights Act Support H.R. 16098, introduced by Congresswoman Edith Green of Oregon. The bill, now pending in Congress, prohibits discrimination based on sex by any program receiving federal assistance, eliminates the exemption of teachers from application of Title 7 of the Civil Rights Act, adds sex discrimination to the jurisdiction of the U.S. Civil Rights Commission, and removes the exemption of executive, administrative and professional employes from the provision in the Fair Labor Standards Act requiring equal pay for equal work. However, H.R. 16098 does not prohibit discrimination based on sex in public accommodations (such as restaurants, bars, etc.). Write your Congressman and Rep. Green supporting the bill, but urging inclusion of public accommodations.

NOW has other promises to keep this year—a change in the media image of women, changes in the educational system to assist women in opening up new career opportunities, radical change in the political system to admit women into political decision-making, elimination of discrimination in religious groups and many more. We can be kept busy on any one of a hundred programs. If any of these has particular interest for you, *Do your thing.*

But, also let us do things together. We have designated *August 26* (the day on which Tennessee became the last state necessary to ratify the 19th Amendment for women's suffrage) as *National NOW Day.* Women are being asked to define their own exploitation and to take action on that day to begin their liberation. Make *August 26* the *beginning* of an ongoing program to achieve our goals. Be imaginative; be constructive; and be successful.

1970 is our year—*You'd better believe it.*

Roxanne Dunbar

FEMALE LIBERATION AS THE BASIS FOR SOCIAL REVOLUTION

Roxanne Dunbar is viewed as a leading theoretician of modern feminism. Her articles in No More Fun and Games, *a Boston women's lib magazine, have been popularly received. How does Miss Dunbar use the concept of caste to explain women's position in our society? In what ways does she rely on the Marx-Engels analysis of society and in what ways does she revise their judgments? According to Miss Dunbar, why are females particularly suited for leading the needed social revolution? What methods should they employ to create the desired changes? What will society look like if female liberation succeeds? How desirable is her model in your vision of American society?*

The present female liberation movement must be viewed within the context of international social revolution and within the context of the long struggle by women for nominal legal rights. The knowledge that is now available, gained in past struggles, makes the current women's movement more scientific and potent. Black people in America and Vietnamese people have exposed the basic weakness of the system of white, Western dominance which we live under. They have also developed means of fighting which continually strengthen themselves and weaken the enemy. The dialectics of liberation have revealed that the weak and oppressed can struggle against and defeat a larger enemy. Revolutionary dialectics teach that nothing is immutable. Our enemy today may not be our enemy next year, or the same enemy might be fighting us in a different way tomorrow. Our tactics must be fitted to the immediate situation and open to change; our strategy must be formed in relation to our overall revolutionary goals. Black Americans and the Vietnamese have taught most importantly, that there is a distinction between the consciousness of the oppressor and the consciousness of the oppressed.

Reprinted by permission of the author.

I

Women have not just recently begun to struggle against their suppression and exploitation. Women have fought in a million ways in their daily, private lives to survive and to overcome existing conditions. Many times those "personal" struggles have taken a self-destructive form. Almost always women have had to use sex as a tool, and have thereby sunk further in oppression. Many women still believe in the efficacy of fighting a lone battle. But more and more women are realizing that only collective strength and action will allow us to be free to fight for the kind of society that meets basic human needs. Collective activity has already had an enormous effect on our thinking and on our lives. We are learning not to dissipate our strength by using traditional methods of exerting power—tears, manipulation, appeals to guilt and benevolence. But we do not ignore what seem to be the "petty" forms of female oppression, such as total identification with housework and sexuality as well as physical helplessness. Rather we understand that our oppression and suppression are institutionalized; that all women suffer the "petty" forms of oppression. Therefore they are not petty or personal, but rather constitute a widespread, deeply rooted social disease. They are the things that keep us tied down day to day, and do not allow us to act. Further, we understand that all men are our policemen, and no organized police force is necessary at this time to keep us in our places. All men enjoy male supremacy and take advantage of it to a greater or lesser degree depending on their position in the masculine hierarchy of power.

It is not enough that we take collective action. We must know where we have come from historically and personally, and how we can most effectively break the bonds. We have identified a system of oppression—*Sexism*. To understand how sexism has developed and the variety of its forms of suppression and mutations, female liberation must, as Betsy Warrior puts it, "reexamine the foundations of civilization."

What we find in reexamining history is that women have had a separate historical development from men. Within each society, women experience the particular culture, but on a larger scale of human history, women have developed separately as a caste. The original division of labor in all societies was by sex. The female capacity for reproduction led to this division. The division of labor by sex has not put a lighter physical burden on women, as we might believe, if we look only at the mythology of chivalry in Western ruling class history. Quite the contrary. What was restricted for women was not physical labor, but mobility.

Because woman's reproductive capacity led to her being forced into sedentary (immobile, not inactive) life, the female developed community life. Adult males were alien to the female community. Their job was to roam, to do the hunting and war-making, entering the community only to leave again. Their entrances and exits probably disrupted normal community life. What hunters experienced of the community were feasts and holidays, not day-to-day life. At some point, when women had developed food production and animal domestication to the point of subsistence, hunters began settling down. However, they brought to the community a very different set of values and behavioral patterns which upset the primitive communism of the community.

In a very real sense, the hunter was less civilized than the female. He had little political (governing) experience. The experience of the hunter had led him to value dominance; he had become unsuited for living as equals in the community, because he knew only how to overpower and conquer the prey. Other masculine values, formed in the transient existence as hunters, included competition (with the prey) and violence (killing the prey). Hunters developed a taste for adventure and mobility. They developed technical skills and a sense of timing and accuracy and endurance. Though hunters worked together and developed a sense of brotherhood, their brotherhood developed outside community life.

Gradually in some cases, but often through violent upheaval, former hunters took over female communities, suppressing the female through domination and even enslavement. The political base for the taking of power often came from the secret male societies formed by men in reaction to female control of community institutions.

As societies became more affluent and complex, life was rationalized and ordered by introducing territoriality, or private property, and inheritance. Patrilineal descent required the control of a female or a number of females to identify the father. The offspring served as labor as well as fulfilling the function of transcendence for the father (the son taking over), and females were used for barter, as were cattle. This then led to the dominance of the male over a wife or wives and her (his) offspring. The female, like the land, became private property under masculine dominance. Man, in conquering nature, conquered the female, who had worked with nature, not against it, to produce food and to reproduce the human race.

II

In competing among themselves for dominance over females (and thereby the offspring) and for land, a few males came to dominate the rest of the male population, as well as the entire female population. A peasant laboring class developed. Within that laboring class, males exploited females, though the male peasant had no property rights over females (or land). The landlord could take any young girl or woman he wanted for whatever purpose, and the peasant was not allowed to "protect" "his" woman.

The pattern of masculine dominance exists almost universally now, since those cultures where the pattern developed have come to dominate (colonize) pre-literate societies, and have introduced patterns of private property and nationalism. The Western nation-states, which have perfected colonialism, were developed as an extension of male dominance over females and the land. Other races and cultures were bought and sold, possessed, dominated through "contract" and ultimately through physical violence and the threat of destruction, of the world if necessary. We live under an international caste system, at the top of which is the Western white male ruling class, and at the very bottom of which is the female of the non-white colonized world. There is no simple order of "oppressions" within this caste system. Within each culture, the female is exploited to some degree by the male. She is classed with the very old and very young of both sexes ("the women, children, and old men"). White dominates black and brown. The caste system, in all its various forms, is always based on identifiable physical characteristics—sex, color, age.

Why is it important to say that females constitute a lower *caste*? Many people would say that the term "caste" can only properly be used in reference to India or Hindu culture. If we think that caste can only be applied to Hindu society, we will then have to find some other term for the kind of social category to which one is assigned at birth and from which one cannot escape by any action of one's own; also we must distinguish such social categories from economic classes or ranked groups as well as understand their relationship.

A caste system establishes a definite place into which certain members of a society have no choice but to fit (because of their color or sex or other easily identifiable physical characteristics such as being aged, crippled, or blind). A caste system, however, need not at all be based on a prohibition of physical contact between different castes. It only means that physical contact will be severely regulated, or will take place outside the bounds deemed acceptable by the society; it means that the mobility of the lower castes will be limited. It means that whatever traits associated with the lower caste will be devalued in the society or will be mystified in some way.

Under the caste system in the Southern states, physical contact between black and white is extensive (particularly through white male sexual exploitation of black women). In the South under slavery, there was frequent contact between black "mammy" and white child, between black and white pre-adolescent children, and between white master and black slave women.

Between male and female, thousands of taboos control their contact in every society. Within each, there is a "woman's world" and a "man's world." In most, men initiate contact with women, usually for the purpose of exploitation. Women have little freedom to initiate contact with adult males. The same is true for black and white in America.

The clearest historical analogy of the caste status of females is African slavery in English-speaking America. When slaves were freed during the Civil War, the female slaves were included, but when the right to citizenship was in question, female blacks were excluded. To many, comparing the female's situation in general with that of a slave in particular seems far-fetched. Actually, the reason the analogy is indicated has to do with the caste status of the African in America, not with slavery as such.

Slave status in the past did not necessarily imply caste status by birth. The restriction of slavery to Africans (black people) in the English colonies rested on the caste principle that it was a status rightly belonging to Africans as innately (racially) inferior beings. (Of course, this was a rationalization on the part of the English, but it became a ruling ideology and was connected with the past.) If a person was black, he was presumed to be a slave unless he could prove otherwise. Caste was inclusive of the slave and free status, just as the caste status of females is inclusive of all economic classes, age, and marital status, though some are more "privileged" and some are more exploited, depending on the female's relationship with a male, or whether she has one or not.

Caste, then, is not analogous to slavery. In Rome, where slaves were not conceived of as innately inferior, and did not differ racially from the enslaving group, slaves did not form a separate caste when they were freed. While they were slaves, however, they had no rights to property nor any legal rights. The master had the power of life and death over his slaves, just as in the slave South. As far as the legal category of the slave as property went, Rome and America had the same social form. It was caste which produced the contrast between the effects of the two systems of slavery. It was the system of caste which gave African slavery in America its peculiarly oppressive character. That caste oppression is analogous to the situation of females both legally and traditionally. (When jurists were seeking a legal category for the position of African slaves in Virginia, they settled on the code of laws which governed wives and children under the power of the patriarch, the head of the family.)

In order to understand the power relations of white and black in America society, of white imperialist America and the third-world, and of male and female in all human societies, we must comprehend the caste system which structures power, and within which caste roles we are conditioned to remain.

Often, in trying to describe the way a white person oppresses or exploits a black person, or a man oppresses or exploits a woman, we say that the oppressor treats the other person as a "thing" or as an "object." Men treat women as "sex objects," we say; slavery reduced black human beings to "mere property," no different from horses or cattle. This interpretation of caste oppression overlooks the crucial importance of the fact that it is human beings, not objects, which the person in the higher caste has the power to dominate and exploit. Imagine a society becoming as dependent upon cattle as Southern plantation society was upon black people, or as men are upon women. The value of slaves as property lay precisely in their being persons, rather than just another piece of property. The value of a woman for a man is much greater than the value of a machine or animal to satisfy his sexual urges and fantasies, to do his housework, breed and tend his offspring. Under slavery, the slave did what no animal could do—planting and harvest, as well as every other kind of backbreaking labor for which no machines existed. But the slave served a much larger purpose in terms of power. It is convenient and "fun" for a man to have satisfactions from "his woman," but his relation to her *as a person,* his position of being of a higher caste, is the central aspect of his power and dominance over her and his need for her.

(A further example of the importance to the higher castes of dominating human beings, not mere objects, is the way men view their sexual exploitation of women. It is not just the satisfaction of a man's private, individual, sexual urge which he fantasizes he will get from a woman he sees. In addition, and more central to his view of women, he visualizes himself taking her, dominating her through the sexual act; he sees her as the *human* evidence of his own power and prowess. Prostitution, however exploitative for the woman, can never serve this same purpose, just as wage labor, however exploitative to the wage slave, could not have served the same purpose in Southern society that black slaves served.)

Black people fell under two patterns of dominance and subservience which emerged under slavery, and which are analogous to patterns of male-female relations in industrial societies. One pattern is the paternalistic one (houseservants, livery men, entertainers, etc.). The second pattern is the exploitative pattern of the fieldhands. Among females today, housewives and women on welfare are subject to the paternalistic pattern. The exploitative pattern rules the lives of more than a third of the population of females (those who work for wages, including paid domestic work) in the United States. But it is important to remember that females form a caste within the labor force; that their exploitation is not simply double or multiple, but is *qualitatively* different from the exploitation of workers of the upper caste (white male).

Though the paternalistic pattern may seem less oppressive or exploitative for females, it is actually only more insidious. The house-wife remains tied by emotional bonds to a man and children, cut off from the more public world of work; she is able to experience the outside world only through the man or her children. If she were working in public industry, however exploitative, she could poten-tially do something about her situation through collective effort with other workers.

However, even for women who hold jobs outside the home, their caste conditioning and demands usually prevail, preventing them from knowing even that they have the *right* to work, much less to ask for something more. Also, the jobs women are allowed to have are most often "service" and domestic ones, demanding constant con-tact with men and children. Females and blacks, even under the alienating capitalist system, are subject to the paternalistic pattern of caste domination every minute of their lives. White men, however exploited as laborers, rarely experience this paternalism, which in-fantilizes and debilitates its victims.

A caste system provides rewards that are not entirely economic in the narrow sense. Caste is a way of making human relations "work," a way of freezing relationships, so that conflicts are mini-mal. A caste system is a *social system,* which is economically based. It is not a set of attitudes or just some mistaken ideas which must be understood and dispensed with because they are not really in the interest of the higher caste. No mere change in ideas will alter the caste system under which we live. The caste system does not exist just in the mind. Caste is deeply rooted in human history, dates to the division of labor by sex, and is the very basis of the present social system in the United States.

III

The present female liberation movement, like the movements for black liberation and national liberation, has begun to identify strongly with Marxist class analysis. And like other movements, we have taken the basic tools of Marxist analysis (dialectical and historical ma-terialism) and expanded the understanding of the process of change. Our analysis of women as an exploited caste is not new. Marx and Engels as well as other nineteenth-century socialist and communist theorists analyzed the position of the female sex in just such a way.

Engels identified the family as the basic unit of capitalist society, and of female oppression. "The modern individual family is founded on the open or concealed domestic slavery of the wife, and modern society is a mass composed of these individual families as its molecules." And "within the family, he [the man] is the bourgeois and the wife represents the proletariat." (Frederick Engels, *Origin of the Family, Private Property, and the State*).

Marx and Engels thought that the large-scale entrance of women into the work force (women and children were the first factory workers) would destroy the family unit, and that women would fight as workers, with men, for the overthrow of capitalism. That did not happen, nor were women freed in the socialist revolutions that succeeded. In the West (Europe and the U.S.) where proletarian revolutions have not succeeded, the family ideology has gained a whole new lease on life, and the lower caste position of women has continued to be enforced. Even now when 40 percent of the adult female population is in the work force, woman is still defined completely within the family, and the man is seen as "protector" and "breadwinner."

In reality, the family has fallen apart. Nearly half of all marriages end in divorce, and the family unit is a decadent, energy-absorbing, destructive, wasteful institution for everyone except the ruling class, the class for which the institution was created. The powers that be, through government action and their propaganda force, the news media, are desperately trying to hold the family together. Sensitivity, encounter, key clubs, group sex, income tax benefits, and many other devices are being used to promote the family as a desirable institution. Daniel Moynihan and other government sociologists have correctly surmised that the absence of the patriarchal family among blacks has been instrumental in the development of "anti-social" (revolutionary) black consciousness. Actually, in the absence of the patriarchal family, which this society has systematically denied black people, a sense of community life and collective effort has developed. Among whites, individualism and competitiveness prevail in social relations, chiefly because of the propagation of the ideology of the patriarchal family. The new sense of collective action among women is fast destroying the decadent family ideology along with its ugly individualism and competitiveness and complacency. Our demand for collective public child care is throwing into question the private family (or individual) ownership of children.

Yet, under this competitive system, without the family unit and without the tie with a male, the female falls from whatever middle-class status she had gained from the family situation. She quickly falls into the work force or has to go on welfare. Such was the case for black slaves when a master voluntarily freed them, and when slavery was ended as an institution. In both cases, the "helplessness" is used as the rationale for continued domination. Lower caste status almost always means lower class status as well. For women who are supported by and gain the status of their husbands, working-class status is always a potential threat, if they do not perform their wifely duties properly. However, many of these supported women have chosen to enter the work force in the vast pool of female clerical workers, in order to gain the economic independence that is necessary to maintain self-respect and sanity. On these jobs, women are still subjected to patterns of masculine dominance. But often on the less personal ground of workplace, a woman can begin throwing off the bonds of servitude.

IV

How will the family unit be destroyed? After all, women must take care of the children, and there will continue to be children. Our demand for full-time child care in the public schools will be met to some degree all over, and perhaps fully in places. The alleviation of the duty of full-time child care in private situations will free many women to make decisions they could not before. But more than that, the demand alone will throw the whole ideology of the family into question, so that women can begin establishing a community of work with each other and we can fight collectively. Women will feel freer to leave their husbands and become economically independent, either through a job or welfare.

Where will this leave white men and "their" families? The patriarchal family is economically and historically tied to private property, and under Western capitalism with the development of the national state. The masculine ideology most strongly asserts home and country as primary values, with wealth and power an individual's greatest goal. The same upper class of men who created private property and founded nation-states also created the family. It is an expensive institution, and only the upper classes have been able to maintain it properly. However, American "democracy" has spread the ideology to the working class. The greatest pride of a working man is that he can support "his" wife and children and maintain a home (even though this is an impossibility for many and means misery for most). The very definition of a bum or derelict is that he does not maintain a wife, children, and home. Consequently, he is an outcast. It is absurd to consider the possibility of women sharing with men the "privilege" of owning a family. Even though 5.2 million families are headed by females in this country, they gain no prestige from doing so. In fact, the family without a male head or support is considered an inferior family. A woman supporting her family actually degrades the family in terms of social status.

At this point in history, white working-class men will fight for nothing except those values associated with the masculine ideology, the ideology of the ruling class—family, home, property, country, male supremacy, and white supremacy. This force, the organized or organizable working class, has been vital in other social revolutions. However, because of the caste system which reigns here, the American democracy of white males, and the power of the nation in the world with which white workers identify, white male workers are not now a revolutionary group in America. Among the most oppressed part of the white working-class males—Irish, Italian, French Canadian (in the U.S.), Polish immigrants—the patriarchal Catholic church buttresses the masculine ideology with its emphasis on family. Even among lower caste (color) groups, Puerto Ricans and Mexican-Americans, the church reinforces masculine domination.

However, the women who "belong" to these men are going to revolt along with the women who belong to middle-class men, and women on welfare and women not yet in the cycle of marriage and family. Black women will probably continue to fight as blacks alongside black men with a reversal of the trend toward taking second place to the black man in order for him to gain his "due" masculine status according to the prevailing masculine ideology. When the white working-class man is confronted with the revolt of women against the family and the society, he will no longer have the escape valve of supremacy over those beneath him in the caste system.

V

Feminism is opposed to the masculine ideology. I do not suggest that all women are feminists, though many are; certainly some men are, though very few. Some women embrace the masculine ideology, particularly women with a college education. But most women have been programmed from early childhood for a role, maternity, which develops a certain consciousness of care for others, self-reliance, flexibility, non-competitiveness, cooperation, and materialism. In addition, women have inherited and continue to suffer exploitation which forces us to use our wits to survive, to know our enemy, to play dumb when necessary. So we have developed the consciousness of the oppressed, not the oppressor, even though some women have the right to oppress others, and all have the right to oppress children. If these "maternal" traits, conditioned into women, are desirable traits, they are desirable for everyone, not just women. By destroying the present society, and building a society on feminist principles, men will be forced to live in the human community on terms very different from the present. For that to happen, feminism must be asserted, by women, as the basis of revolutionary social change. Women and other oppressed people must lead and structure the revolutionary movement and the new society to assure the dominance of feminist principles. Our present female liberation movement is preparing us for that task, as is the black liberation movement preparing black people for their revolutionary leadership role.

The female liberation movement is developing in the context of international social revolution, but it is also heir to a 120-year struggle by women for legal rights. The nineteenth-century feminist movement as well as its child, the women's suffrage movement, were comparatively modest in their demands. They fought from a basis of no rights, no power at all. In the first movement, women began fighting for the right of females to speak publicly for abolition of slavery. The cause of female rights and the abolition of slavery were inexorably linked. The early feminists did not see the family as a decadent institution. They wanted to find a way to force men to share responsibility in the institution they created by supporting their families. They saw alcohol as an enemy of family solidarity.

With the end of slavery, only black males received citizenship.

Black women and white women remained unenfranchised. Women then began the long struggle for the vote. They felt they could make the large-scale and basic changes in society which they saw as necessary by their influence in politics. They believed that woman's political involvement would bring her out of privacy. Many of them questioned the very foundations of civilization, but their strategy and tactics for gaining the desired upheaval of their society revolved around political influence within the system.

In the process of their struggle, the feminists and suffragists opened the door for our present female liberation movement. They won not only the right to vote, but other legal rights as well including the custodial rights to their children. More than that, women began to fight their oppression and lift up their heads. At the same time, working women were fighting their wage slavery. Women began to emerge from privacy and to know that they did in fact have rights for which they must fight. They gained confidence in the struggle, and asserted a new independence, which we all inherited.

We also inherited an understanding of the weakness of single-issue tactics, and of "organizing" women around issues rather than teaching a complete analysis of female oppression. We learned that there is no key to liberation. We must fight on many fronts at once. Thanks to gains made by our feminist predecessors, though, we have the confidence to assert feminism as a positive force, rather than asking for equality in the man's world. We can demand that men change. We can consider leading a social revolution, not just working in supportive positions, and hope for the justness, benevolence, and change of heart of men. We can assert the necessity of industrializing all housework, and for right now to have school cafeterias open to adults as well as children. We can demand the extension of public education facilities and funds to include infant and child care. We can demand the development of maternal skills and consciousness in men. We can insist on the necessity for revolution to be based on the needs and consciousness of the most oppressed of women. We can revoke any privileges we have which divide us from other women.

We are developing necessary skills—self-defense and physical strength, the ability to work collectively and politically, rather than privately and personally, and the ability to teach our ideas to many other women in such a way that they then can become teachers as well. From these new relations and skills will be built the values of the new society. Right now they are our tools of struggle. Though we may work in isolated and difficult and dangerous situations, we can know our larger strategy and goals, and know that we are a part of a worldwide struggle for human liberation.

Margaret Benston

THE POLITICAL ECONOMY OF WOMEN'S LIBERATION

Margaret Benston, when she wrote the following article, was a member of the chemistry department faculty at Simon Fraser University in Vancouver, British Columbia. She provides us with an essay that systematically views feminism within a Marxist frame of reference. In what ways does her analysis compare to Charlotte Perkins Gilman's? to Roxanne Dunbar's? Why, according to Miss Benston, are women systematically kept in the home? If women leave the home in large numbers, the ultimate revolution will be hastened. Why? Do you agree with Miss Benston's critique of and cure for American society?

> *The position of women rests, as everything in our complex society, on an economic base.* —*Eleanor Marx and Edward Aveling*

The "woman question" is generally ignored in analyses of the class structure of society. This is so because, on the one hand, classes are generally defined by their relation to the means of production and, on the other hand, women are not supposed to have any unique relation to the means of production. The category seems instead to cut across all classes; one speaks of working-class women, middle-class women, etc. The status of women is clearly inferior to that of men, but analysis of this condition usually falls into discussing socialization, psychology, interpersonal relations, or the role of

From *Monthly Review,* Vol. 21, No. 4 (September 1969), pp. 13–25; notes to the original have been omitted. Reprinted by permission of Monthly Review Inc. Copyright © 1969 by Monthly Review Inc.

marriage as a social institution. Are these, however, the primary factors? In arguing that the roots of the secondary status of women are in fact economic, it can be shown that women as a group do indeed have a definite relation to the means of production and that this is different from that of men. The personal and psychological factors then follow from this special relation to production, and a change in the latter will be a necessary (but not sufficient) condition for changing the former. If this special relation of women to production is accepted, the analysis of the situation of women fits naturally into a class analysis of society.

The starting point for discussion of classes in a capitalist society is the distinction between those who own the means of production and those who sell their labor power for a wage. As Ernest Mandel says:

> The proletarian condition is, in a nutshell, the lack of access to the means of production or means of subsistence which, in a society of generalized commodity production, forces the proletarian to sell his labor power. In exchange for this labor power he receives a wage which then enables him to acquire the means of consumption necessary for satisfying his own needs and those of his family.
>
> This is the structural definition of wage earner, the proletarian. From it necessarily flows a certain relationship to his work, to the products of his work, and to his overall situation in society, which can be summarized by the catchword alienation. But there does not follow from this structural definition any necessary conclusions as to the level of his consumption . . . the extent of his needs, or the degree to which he can satisfy them.

We lack a corresponding structural definition of women. What is needed first is not a complete examination of the symptoms of the secondary status of women, but instead a statement of the material conditions in capitalist (and other) societies which define the group "women." Upon these conditions are built the specific superstructures which we know. An interesting passage from Mandel points the way to such a definition:

> The commodity . . . is a product created to be exchanged on the market, as opposed to one which has been made for direct consumption. Every commodity must have both a use-value and an exchange-value.
> It must have a use-value or else nobody would buy it. . . . A com-

modity without a use-value to anyone would consequently be unsalable, would constitute useless production, would have no exchange-value precisely because it had no use-value.

On the other hand, every product which has use-value does not necessarily have exchange-value. It has an exchange-value only to the extent that the society itself, in which the commodity is produced, is founded on exchange, is a society where exchange is a common practice. . . .

In capitalist society commodity production, the production of exchange-values, has reached its greatest development. It is the first society in human history where the major part of production consists of commodities. It is not true, however, that all production under capitalism is commodity production. Two classes of products still remain simple use-value.

The first group consists of all things produced by the peasantry for its own consumption, everything directly consumed on the farms where it is produced. . . .

The second group of products in capitalist society which are not commodities but remain simple use-value consists of all things produced in the home. Despite the fact that considerable human labor goes into this type of household production, it still remains a production of use-values and not of commodities. Every time a soup is made or a button sewn on a garment, it constitutes production, but it is not production for the market.

The appearance of commodity production and its subsequent regularization and generalization have radically transformed the way men labor and how they organize society.

What Mandel may not have noticed is that his last paragraph is precisely correct. The appearance of commodity production has indeed transformed the way that *men* labor. As he points out, most household labor in capitalist society (and in the existing socialist societies, for that matter) remains in the pre-market stage. This is the work which is reserved for women and it is in this fact that we can find the basis for a definition of women.

In sheer quantity, household labor, including child care, constitutes a huge amount of socially necessary production. Nevertheless, in a society based on commodity production, it is not usually considered "real work" since it is outside of trade and the market place. It is pre-capitalist in a very real sense. This assignment of household work as the function of a special category "women" means that this group *does* stand in a different relation to production than the group "men." We will tentatively define women, then, as that group of people who are responsible for the production of simple use-values in those activities associated with the home and family.

Since men carry no responsibility for such production, the difference between the two groups lies here. Notice that women are not excluded from commodity production. Their participation in wage labor occurs but, as a group, they have no structural responsibility in this area and such participation is ordinarily regarded as transient. Men, on the other hand, are responsible for commodity production; they are not, in principle, given any role in household labor. For example, when they do participate in household production, it is regarded as more than simply exceptional; it is demoralizing, emasculating, even harmful to health. (A story on the front page of the *Vancouver Sun* in January 1969 reported that men in Britain were having their health endangered because they had to do too much housework!)

The material basis for the inferior status of women is to be found in just this definition of women. In a society in which money determines value, women are a group who work outside the money economy. Their work is not worth money, is therefore valueless, is therefore not even real work. And women themselves, who do this valueless work, can hardly be expected to be worth as much as men, who work for money. In structural terms, the closest thing to the condition of women is the condition of others who are or were also outside of commodity production, i.e., serfs and peasants.

In her recent paper on women, Juliet Mitchell introduces the subject as follows:

> *In advanced industrial society, women's work is only marginal to the total economy. Yet it is through work that man changes natural conditions and thereby produces society. Until there is a revolution in production, the labor situation will prescribe women's situation within the world of men.*

The statement of the marginality of women's work is an unanalyzed recognition that the work women do is *different* from the work that men do. Such work is not marginal, however; it is just not wage labor and so is not counted. She even says later in the same article, "Domestic labor, even today, is enormous if quantified in terms of productive labor." She gives some figures to illustrate: In Sweden,

2,340 million hours a year are spent by women in housework compared with 1,290 million hours spent by women in industry. And the Chase Manhattan Bank estimates a woman's overall work week at 99.6 hours.

However, Mitchell gives little emphasis to the basic economic factors (in fact she condemns most Marxists for being "overly economist") and moves on hastily to superstructural factors, because she notices that "the advent of industrialization has not so far freed women." What she fails to see is that no society has thus far industrialized housework. Engels points out that the "first premise for the emancipation of women is the reintroduction of the entire female sex into public industry. . . . And this has become possible not only as a result of modern large-scale industry, which not only permits the participation of women in production in large numbers, but actually calls for it and, moreover, strives to convert private domestic work also into a public industry." And later in the same passage: "Here we see already that the emancipation of women and their equality with men are impossible and must remain so as long as women are excluded from socially productive work and restricted to housework, which is private." What Mitchell has not taken into account is that the problem is not simply one of getting women into *existing* industrial production but the more complex one of converting private production of household work into public production.

For most North Americans, domestic work as "public production" brings immediate images of Brave New World or of a vast institution —a cross between a home for orphans and an army barracks— where we would all be forced to live. For this reason, it is probably just as well to outline here, schematically and simplistically, the nature of industrialization.

A pre-industrial production unit is one in which production is small-scale and reduplicative; i.e., there are a great number of little units, each complete and just like all the others. Ordinarily such production units are in some way kin-based and they are multi-purpose, fulfilling religious, recreational, educational, and sexual functions along with the economic function. In such a situation, desirable attributes of an individual, those which give prestige, are judged by more than purely economic criteria: for example, among approved character traits are proper behavior to kin or readiness to fulfill obligations.

Such production is originally not for exchange. But if exchange of commodities becomes important enough, then increased efficiency of production becomes necessary. Such efficiency is provided by the transition to industrialized production which involves the elimination of the kin-based production unit. A large-scale, non-reduplicative production unit is substituted which has only one function, the economic one, and where prestige or status is attained by economic skills. Production is rationalized, made vastly more efficient, and becomes more and more public—part of an integrated social network. An enormous expansion of man's productive potential takes place. Under capitalism such social productive forces are utilized almost exclusively for private profit. These can be thought of as *capitalized* forms of production.

If we apply the above to housework and child rearing, it is evident that each family, each household, constitutes an individual production unit, a pre-industrial entity, in the same way that peasant farmers or cottage weavers constitute pre-industrial production units. The main features are clear, with the reduplicative, kin-based, private nature of the work being the most important. (It is interesting to notice the other features: the multi-purpose functions of the family, the fact that desirable attributes for women do not center on economic prowess, etc.) The rationalization of production effected by a transition to large-scale production has not taken place in this area.

Industrialization is, in itself, a great force for human good; exploitation and dehumanization go with capitalism and not necessarily with industrialization. To advocate the conversion of private domestic labor into a public industry under capitalism is quite a different thing from advocating such conversion in a socialist society. In the latter case the forces of production would operate for human welfare, not private profit, and the result should be liberation, not dehumanization. In this case we can speak of *socialized* forms of production.

These definitions are not meant to be technical but rather to differentiate between two important aspects of industrialization. Thus the fear of the barracks-like result of introducing housekeeping into the public economy is most realistic under capitalism. With socialized production and the removal of the profit motive and its attendant alienated labor, there is no reason why, *in an industrialized society,* industrialization of housework should not result in better production, i.e., better food, more comfortable surroundings, more intelligent and loving child care, etc., than in the present nuclear family.

The argument is often advanced that, under neocapitalism, the work in the home has been much reduced. Even if this is true, it is not structurally relevant. Except for the very rich, who can hire someone to do it, there is for most women, an irreducible minimum of necessary labor involved in caring for home, husband, and children. For a married woman without children this irreducible minimum of work probably takes fifteen to twenty hours a week; for a woman with small children the minimum is probably seventy or eighty hours a week. (There is some resistance to regarding child-rearing as a job. That labor is involved, i.e., the production of use-value, can be clearly seen when exchange-value is also involved —when the work is done by baby-sitters, nurses, child-care centers, or teachers. An economist has already pointed out the paradox that if a man marries his housekeeper, he reduces the national income, since the money he gives her is no longer counted as wages.) The reduction of housework to the minimums given is also expensive; for low-income families more labor is required. In any case, household work remains structurally the same—a matter of private production.

One function of the family, the one taught to us in school, and the one which is popularly accepted, is the satisfaction of emotional needs: the needs for closeness, community, and warm secure relationships. This society provides few other ways of satisfying such needs; for example, work relationships or friendships are not expected to be nearly as important as a man-woman-with-children relationship. Even other ties of kinship are increasingly secondary. This function of the family is important in stabilizing it so that it can fulfill the second, purely economic, function discussed above. The wage-earner, the husband-father, whose earnings support himself, also "pays for" the labor done by the mother-wife and supports the children. The wages of a man buy the labor of two people. The crucial importance of this second function of the family can be seen when the family unit breaks down in divorce. The continuation of the economic function is the major concern where children are involved; the man must continue to pay for the labor of the woman. His wage is very often insufficient to enable him to support a second family. In this case his emotional needs are sacrificed to the necessity to support his ex-wife and children. That is, when there is a conflict the economic function of the family very often takes precedence over the emotional one. And this in a society which teaches that the major function of the family is the satisfaction of emotional needs.

As an economic unit, the nuclear family is a valuable stabilizing force in capitalist society. Since the production which is done in the home is paid for by the husband-father's earnings, his ability to withhold his labor from the market is much reduced. Even his flexibility in changing jobs is limited. The woman, denied an active place in the market, has little control over the conditions that govern her life. Her economic dependence is reflected in emotional dependence, passivity, and other "typical" female personality traits. She is conservative, fearful, supportive of the status quo.

Furthermore, the structure of this family is such that it is an ideal consumption unit. But this fact, which is widely noted in Women's Liberation literature, should not be taken to mean that this is its primary function. If the above analysis is correct, the family should be seen primarily as a production unit for housework and child-rearing. *Everyone* in capitalist society is a consumer; the structure of the family simply means that it is particularly well suited to encourage consumption. Women in particular *are* good consumers; this follows naturally from their responsibility for matters in the home. Also, the inferior status of women, their general lack of a strong sense of worth and identity, make them more exploitable than men and hence better consumers.

The history of women in the industrialized sector of the economy has depended simply on the labor needs of that sector. Women function as a massive reserve army of labor. When labor is scarce (early industrialization, the two world wars, etc.) then women form an important part of the labor force. When there is less demand for labor (as now under neocapitalism) women become a surplus labor force—but one for which their husbands and not society are economically responsible. The "cult of the home" makes its reappearance during times of labor surplus and is used to channel women out of the market economy. This is relatively easy since the pervading ideology ensures that no one, man or woman, takes women's participation in the labor force very seriously. Women's real work, we are taught, is in the home; this holds whether or not they are married, single, or the heads of households.

At all times household work is the responsibility of women. When they are working outside the home they must somehow manage to get both outside job and housework done (or they supervise a substitute for the housework). Women, particularly married women with children, who work outside the home simply do two jobs; their participation in the labor force is only allowed if they continue to fulfill their first responsibility in the home. This is particularly evident in countries like Russia and those in Eastern Europe where expanded opportunities for women in the labor force have not brought about a corresponding expansion in their liberty. Equal access to jobs outside the home, while one of the preconditions for women's liberation, will not in itself be sufficient to give equality for women; as long as work in the home remains a matter of private production and is the responsibility of women, they will simply carry a double work-load.

A second prerequisite for women's liberation which follows from the above analysis is the conversion of the work now done in the home as private production into work to be done in the public economy. To be more specific, this means that child-rearing should no longer be the responsibility solely of the parents. Society must begin to take responsibility for children; the economic dependence of women and children on the husband-father must be ended. The other work that goes on in the home must also be changed—communal eating places and laundries for example. When such work is moved into the public sector, then the material basis for discrimination against women will be gone.

These are only preconditions. The idea of the inferior status of women is deeply rooted in the society and will take a great deal of effort to eradicate. But once the structures which produce and support that idea are changed then, and only then, can we hope to make progress. It is possible, for example, that a change to communal eating places would simply mean that women are moved from a home kitchen to a communal one. This *would* be an advance, to be sure, particularly in a socialist society where work would not have the inherently exploitative nature it does now. Once women are freed from private production in the home, it will probably be very difficult to maintain for any long period of time a rigid definition of jobs by sex. This illustrates the interrelation between the two preconditions given above: true equality in job opportunity is probably impossible without freedom from housework, and the industrialization of housework is unlikely unless women are leaving the home for jobs.

The changes in production necessary to get women out of the home might seem to be, in theory, possible under capitalism. One of the sources of women's liberation movements may be the fact that alternative capitalized forms of home production now exist. Day care is available, even if inadequate and perhaps expensive; convenience foods, home delivery of meals, and take-out meals are widespread; laundries and cleaners offer bulk rates. However, cost usually prohibits a complete dependence on such facilities, and they are not available everywhere, even in North America. These should probably then be regarded as embryonic forms rather than completed structures. However, they clearly stand as alternatives to the present system of getting such work done. Particularly in North America, where the growth of "service industries" is important in maintaining the growth of the economy, the contradictions between these alternatives and the need to keep women in the home will grow.

The need to keep women in the home arises from two major aspects of the present system. First, the amount of unpaid labor performed by women is very large and very profitable to those who own the means of production. To pay women for their work, even at minimum wage scales, would imply a massive redistribution of wealth. At present, the support of a family is a hidden tax on the wage earner—his wage buys the labor power of two people. And second, there is the problem of whether the economy can expand enough to put all women to work as a part of the normally employed labor force. The war economy has been adequate to draw women partially into the economy but not adequate to establish a need for all or most of them. If it is argued that the jobs created by the industrialization of housework will create this need, then one can counter by pointing to (1) the strong economic forces operating for the status quo and against capitalization discussed above, and (2) the fact that the present service industries, which somewhat counter these forces, have not been able to keep up with the growth of the labor force as presently constituted. The present trends in the service industries simply create "underemployment" in the home; they do not create new jobs for women. So long as this situation exists, women remain a very convenient and elastic part of the industrial reserve army. Their incorporation into the labor force on terms of equality—which would create pressure for capitalization of housework—is possible only with an economic expansion so far achieved by neocapitalism only under conditions of full-scale war mobilization.

In addition, such structural changes imply the complete breakdown of the present nuclear family. The stabilizing consuming functions of the family, plus the ability of the cult of the home to keep women out of the labor market, serve neocapitalism too well to be easily dispensed with. And, on a less fundamental level, even if these necessary changes in the nature of household production were achieved under capitalism it would have the unpleasant consequence of including *all* human relations in the cash nexus. The atomization and isolation of people in Western society is already sufficiently advanced to make it doubtful if such complete psychic isolation could be tolerated. It is likely in fact that one of the major negative emotional responses to women's liberation movements may be exactly such a fear. If this is the case, then possible alternatives—cooperatives, the kibbutz, etc.—can be cited to show that psychic needs for community and warmth can in fact be better satisfied if other structures are substituted for the nuclear family.

At best the change to capitalization of housework would only give women the same limited freedom given most men in capitalist society. This does not mean, however, that women should wait to demand freedom from discrimination. There *is* a material basis for women's status; we are not merely discriminated against, we are exploited. At present, our unpaid labor in the home is necessary if the entire system is to function. Pressure created by women who challenge their role will reduce the effectiveness of this exploitation. In addition, such challenges will impede the functioning of the family and may make the channeling of women out of the labor force less effective. All of these will hopefully make quicker the transition to a society in which the necessary structural changes in production can actually be made. That such a transition will require a revolution I have no doubt; our task is to make sure that revolutionary changes in the society do in fact end women's oppression.

Alice S. Rossi

VISIONS FOR THE FUTURE

The final selection, taken from Alice Rossi's essay (portions of which appear earlier) gives us her picture of what an emancipated woman would be like after society has made the necessary alterations. Will violent revolution be necessary to accomplish Mrs. Rossi's goals? How can these changes be effected? How do her suggestions differ from the previous two feminists' views? Which vision of American society most appeals to you? Whose methods would you support? What concrete feminist proposals for change would you recommend implementing right away? How do the current generation of feminists compare to their ancestors in terms of vision, feasibility, reception?

She will be reared, as her brother will be reared, with a combination of loving warmth, firm discipline, household responsibility and encouragement of independence and self-reliance. She will not be pampered and indulged, subtly taught to achieve her ends through coquetry and tears, as so many girls are taught today. She will view domestic skills as useful tools to acquire, some of which, like fine cooking or needlework, having their own intrinsic pleasures but most of which are necessary repetitive work best gotten done as quickly and efficiently as possible. She will be able to handle minor mechanical breakdowns in the home as well as her brother can, and he will be able to tend a child, press, sew, and cook with the same easy skills and comfortable feeling his sister has.

From "Equality Between the Sexes: An Immodest Proposal," in *The Woman in America,* edited by Robert Jay Lifton, *Daedalus,* Vol. 93 (Spring 1964). Reprinted by permission of *Daedalus,* Journal of the American Academy of Arts and Sciences, Boston, Massachusetts.

During their school years, both sister and brother will increasingly assume responsibility for their own decisions, freely experiment with numerous possible fields of study, gradually narrowing to a choice that best suits their interests and abilities rather than what is considered appropriate or prestigeful work for men and women. They will be encouraged by parents and teachers alike to think ahead to a whole life span, viewing marriage and parenthood as one strand among many which will constitute their lives. The girl will not feel the pressure to belittle her accomplishments, lower her aspirations, learn to be a receptive listener in her relations with boys, but will be as true to her growing sense of self as her brother and male friends are. She will not marry before her adolescence and schooling are completed, but will be willing and able to view the college years as a "moratorium" from deeply intense cross-sex commitments, a period of life during which her identity can be "at large and open and various." Her intellectual aggressiveness as well as her brother's tender sentiments will be welcomed and accepted as *human* characteristics, without the self-questioning doubt of latent homosexuality that troubles many college-age men and women in our era when these qualities are sex-linked. She will not cling to her parents, nor they to her, but will establish an increasingly larger sphere of her own independent world in which she moves and works, loves and thinks, as a maturing young person. She will learn to take pleasure in her own body and a man's body and to view sex as a good and wonderful experience, but not as an exclusive basis for an ultimate commitment to another person, and not as a test of her competence as a female or her partner's competence as a male. Because she will have a many-faceted conception of her self and its worth, she will be free to merge and lose herself in the sex act with a lover or a husband.

Marriage for our hypothetical woman will not mark a withdrawal from the life and work pattern that she has established, just as there will be no sharp discontinuity between her early childhood and youthful adult years. Marriage will be an enlargement of her life experiences, the addition of a new dimension to an already established pattern, rather than an abrupt withdrawal to the home and a turning in upon the marital relationship. Marriage will be a "looking outward in the same direction" for both the woman and her husband. She will marry and bear children only if she deeply desires a mate and children, and will not be judged a failure as a person if she decides against either. She will have few children if she does have them, and will view her pregnancies, childbirth and early months of motherhood as one among many equally important highlights in her life, experienced intensely and with joy but not as the exclusive basis for a sense of self-fulfillment and purpose in life. With planning and foresight, her early years of child bearing and rearing can fit a long-range view of all sides of herself. If her children are not to suffer from "paternal deprivation," her husband will also anticipate that the assumption of parenthood will involve a weeding out of nonessential activities either in work, civic or social participation. Both the woman and the man will feel that unless a man can make room in his life for parenthood, he should not become a father. The woman will make sure, even if she remains at home during her child's infancy, that he has ample experience of being with and cared for by other adults besides herself, so that her return to a full-time position in her field will not constitute a drastic change in the life of the child, but a gradual pattern of increasing supplementation by others of the mother. The children will have a less intense involvement with their mother, and she with them, and they will all be the better for it. When they are grown and establish adult lives of their own, our woman will face no retirement twenty years before her husband, for her own independent activities will continue and expand. She will be neither an embittered wife, an interfering mother-in-law nor an idle parasite, but together with her husband she will be able to live an independent, purposeful and satisfying third act in life.

Suggestions for Additional Reading

A general narrative of the history of women in America has not been done adequately, but one attempt in that direction is Andrew Sinclair's *The Emancipation of the American Woman* (New York, paperback edition, 1965). A book of readings entitled *Up From the Pedestal,* edited by Aileen Kraditor (Chicago, 1969), provides the reader with selections from major feminist writers throughout American history. The single most comprehensive survey of the original source material on the woman's suffrage movement is the multi-volumed *History of Woman's Suffrage,* by Susan B. Anthony and Ida H. Harper, 1883–1900 (Indianapolis, 1902). Two more recent interpretive studies of suffrage are Eleanor Flexner's *Century of Struggle: The Woman's Rights Movement in the United States* (Cambridge, 1959) and Aileen Kraditor's *The Ideas of the Woman's Suffrage Movement, 1890–1920* (New York, 1965). There are a number of biographies of the early suffragettes. For example, Alma Lutz's *Susan B. Anthony: Rebel, Crusader, Humanitarian* (Boston, 1959) gives the reader some insight into the world of this energetic suffrage leader. Alice Paul's *Woman's Party* deserves further study. Inez Haynes Irwin, a colleague of Miss Paul's in the struggle for the vote, wrote *The Story of the Woman's Party* (New York, 1921), and it still stands as an important first-hand account of the subject.

For further information on feminism in the 1910's, a few general studies as well as the memoirs of some of the participants are particularly helpful. For a general look at the intellectual interest in feminism as well as other current radical ideologies during that decade, see Henry May's *The End of American Innocence* (New York, 1959). Allen Churchill's *The Improper Bohemians* (New York, 1959) and Albert Parry's *Garrets and Pretenders: A History of Bohemianism in America* (New York, rev. ed., 1960) give the reader a view of Greenwich Village life during the 1910's—the major place where feminist ideas were discussed and accepted. Max Eastman's *Enjoyment of Living* (New York, 1948) and *Love and Revolution* (New York, 1964) describe his reasons for being a male feminist as well as his sister Crystal's ideas and activities. Floyd Dell's writings also are enlightening reading on this subject. His *Homecoming* (New York, 1933), *Love in Greenwich Village,* a book of short stories on life in the Village (New York, 1926), and *Women as World Builders: Studies in Modern Feminism* (Chicago, 1913) are all good sources for an understanding and description of feminism during the early years of this century.

Neither Crystal Eastman nor Henrietta Rodman published a complete account of their beliefs and achievements; but their views were often reported in *The New York Times* of the day. Also, magazines such as *Survey,* the social worker's journal, the *New Republic,* as well as the radical magazines *The Masses* and *The Liberator* reported their activities. Thus, a reading of the contemporary periodical and newspaper literature makes for exciting and interesting reading. Much of the fiction of the decade of the 1910's contains discussions of the role of the modern woman. Little-remembered women writers such as Neith Boyce Hapgood, Susan Glaspell, and Mary Heaton Vorse contributed a great deal of fiction to the popular magazines such as *Harper's Magazine, Good Housekeeping,* and *Woman's Home Companion.* Mrs. Vorse's stories such as "A Modern Love Story," *Good Housekeeping,* LVI (June 1913), "How I Kept My Husband," GH, LVII (November 1913), and "Is the American Man a Failure?" *Woman's Home Companion,* XXXIX (January 1912) are worth reading. The plays and novels of Susan Glaspell are also noteworthy, especially her novel *Fidelity* (Boston, 1915), and in the same vein, Floyd Dell's *Janet March* (New York, 1923). Through a study of the fictional literature of a period, one often gains valuable insights into the attitudes and problems of a period.

Charlotte Perkins Gilman wrote both in-depth studies and magazine articles on the subject of feminism. By consulting the Readers' Guide to Periodical Literature, one can find numerous articles authored by Mrs. Gilman during the 1910's. Margaret Sanger's ideas and activities were well publicized also. Her crusade for birth control was a highly controversial topic during the decade. Newspapers reported her infamous behavior and her frequent clashes with the authorities. Popular discussions on this never before discussed subject were forced into the open because of Mrs. Sanger's insistent actions. The controversy lingered into the 1920's and many magazine articles on the subject continued to appear.

When we turn to the 1960's we find some interesting general studies on the status of women, or more frequently, descriptions of the position of professional, educated women in America. Note especially Jessie Bernard's *Academic Women* (University Park, 1964) and Sophonisba P. Breckenridge, *Women in the Twentieth Century: A Study of Their Political and Economic Activities* (New York, 1952). *The Annals of the American Academy of Political and Social Science* has devoted issues to the subject of women, most recently the January 1968 volume. A more general collection of papers on American women, viewed from many different perspectives, is the Spring 1964 issue of *Daedalus,* which has been edited by Robert J. Lifton and published as *The Woman in America* (Boston, 1965), now in paperback. In addition to the Alice Rossi selection, which is reprinted in this volume, Erik Erikson's discussion of the psychology of women is another of the many valuable pieces in that collection.

Betty Friedan's *The Feminine Mystique* (New York, 1963) is a well-known popular study as is Caroline Bird's *Born Female* (New York, 1969). A more erudite and sophisticated study of how women have been treated in literature is Mary Ellmann's *Thinking About Women* (New York, 1969). Kate Millet's *Sexual Politics* (New York, 1970) is another, more polemical, discussion of the subject. Women's liberation literature, which began emerging around 1967, was originally published in pamphlet form for the local membership of a particular women's lib group. The first "public" printing of women's lib material was *Notes from the Second Year: Major Writings of the Radical Feminists* (Boston, 1970). The *Notes from the First Year,* published in 1968, was essentially an underground publication with no serious desire to publicize or mass distribute the material.

The popular magazines, including the women's magazines, have run numerous feature stories on the new feminism of the 1960's. Samples of them have been reprinted in this volume; a review of the Readers' Guide would supply the reader with numerous other illustrations of popular material on the subject. One recent scholarly effort has been made to view feminism in this century: William L. O'Neill's *Everyone Was Brave: The Rise and Fall of Feminism in America* (Chicago, 1969). Because of the current interest in the history of feminism, many popular as well as scholarly books on the subject will be emerging in the near future. There is still much to be done in terms of specialized as well as comprehensive treatments of the history of the woman in this country. Hopefully, the 1970's will witness new and exciting contributions to this field.